Photoshop® Album For Dummies®

D1306774

Daily Activities

Set general preferences	Ctrl+K
Get Photoshop Album help	F1
Access Quick Guide	Shift+F1
Access catalog	Ctrl+Shift+C
Delete selected item from catalog	Delete key
Copy	Ctrl+C
Select All	Ctrl+A
Select None	Ctrl+Shift+A
Rotate photo to the right	Ctrl+R
Rotate photo to the left	Ctrl+Shift+R
Print	Ctrl+P
Access Page Setup	Ctrl+Shift+P
Export selected items	Ctrl+E
OK	Enter
Undo last operation	Ctrl+Z
Redo last operation	Ctrl+Y
Cancel	Esc
Quit Photoshop Album	Ctrl+Q

Navigating in Photoshop Album

Scroll up or down through Photo Well	PgUp and PgDn
Move selection in Photo Well up/down/left/right	Up Arrow; Down Arrow; Left Arrow; Right Arrow
Select first item in Photo Well	Home
Select last item in Photo Well	End
Add to selection in Photo Well	Shift+Up Arrow; Shift+Down Arrow; Shift+Left Arrow; Shift+Right Arrow
Access Single Photo view	Double-click a selected photo or press Enter
Move through buttons and commands in Shortcuts bar, Options bar, and Properties pane	Tab

For Dummies: Bestselling Book Series for Beginners

Photoshop® Album For Dummies®

Fixing photos in the Fix Photo dialog box

Zoom In	Ctrl+(Ctrl and the Plus sign)
Zoom Out	Ctrl+— (Ctrl and the Minus sign)
View at 100%	Ctrl+Alt+0
Fit on Screen	Ctrl+0
Move selection area 1 pixel up, down, left, or right	Up Arrow; Down Arrow; Left Arrow; Right Arrow
Move selection area 10 pixels up, down, left, or right	Shift+Up Arrow; Shift+Down Arrow; Shift+Left Arrow; Shift+Right Arrow

Tagging

Display Tags pane	Ctrl+T
New tag	Ctrl+N
Find Items with tags	Ctrl+F
Show Dates and tags	Ctrl+D

Miscellaneous Goodies

Show image full screen	F11
Refresh Photo Well	F5
Instant slideshow of selected items	Ctrl+space
Display timeline	Ctrl+L
Display Properties pane	Alt+Enter
Display Workspace	Ctrl+W
Display Calendar	Ctrl+Alt+C

For Dummies: Bestselling Book Series for Beginners

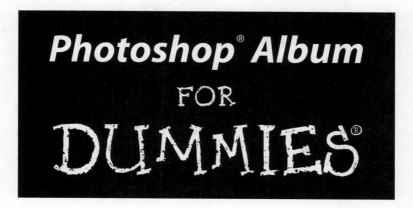

Photoshop® Album
FOR
DUMMIES®

by Barbara Obermeier
Author of *Photoshop 7 All-in-One Desk Reference For Dummies*

WILEY

Wiley Publishing, Inc.

Photoshop® Album For Dummies®

Published by
Wiley Publishing, Inc.
111 River Street
Hoboken, NJ 07030
www.wiley.com

Copyright © 2003 by Wiley Publishing, Inc., Indianapolis, Indiana

Published by Wiley Publishing, Inc., Indianapolis, Indiana

Published simultaneously in Canada

For general information on our other products and services or to obtain technical support, please contact our Customer Care Department within the U.S. at 800-762-2974, outside the U.S. at 317-572-3993, or fax 317-572-4002.

Wiley also publishes its books in a variety of electronic formats. Some content that appears in print may not be available in electronic books.

Library of Congress Control Number: 2003105673

ISBN: 0-7645-4212-5

Manufactured in the United States of America

10 9 8 7 6 5 4 3 2 1

WILEY is a trademark of Wiley Publishing, Inc.

About the Author

Barbara Obermeier is principal of Obermeier Design, a graphic design studio in Ventura, California. She is the author of the *Photoshop 7 All-in-One Desk Reference For Dummies* and coauthor of *Photoshop 7 For Dummies, Illustrator 10 For Dummies* and *Adobe Master Class: Illustrator Illuminated*. She has contributed as coauthor, technical editor, or layout designer for 18 books. Barb also teaches computer graphics at the University of California, Santa Barbara, and at Ventura College.

Dedication

To Gary, Kylie, and Lucky.

Author's Acknowledgments

I would like to thank my phenom project manager, Nicole Haims, who, as always, demonstrated her unparalleled expertise at getting a book on the shelf; Bob Woerner, who always manages to get great titles for me; Andy Cummings, who makes the For Dummies series a nice place to work; David Herman, the best technical editor this planet has seen; Kim Darosett, who can magically massage text to make it sound so much better; and the dedicated production crew at Wiley. Special thanks to my friend and fellow author, Ted Padova, who is always there to cheerlead, commiserate, and remind to buy lottery tickets.

Publisher's Acknowledgments

We're proud of this book; please send us your comments through our online registration form located at www.dummies.com/register/.

Some of the people who helped bring this book to market include the following:

Acquisitions, Editorial, and Media Development

Project Manager: Nicole Haims

Development Editor: Kim Darosett

Acquisitions Editor: Bob Woerner

Copy Editor: Nicole Haims

Technical Editor: David Herman

Editorial Manager: Carol Sheehan, Leah Cameron

Permissions Editor: Carmen Krikorian

Media Development Manager: Laura VanWinkle

Media Development Supervisor: Richard Graves

Editorial Assistant: Amanda Foxworth

Cartoons: Rich Tennant www.the5thwave.com

Production

Project Coordinator: Regina Snyder

Layout and Graphics: Seth Conley, Stephanie Jumper, Tiffany Muth

Proofreaders: TECHBOOKS Production Services, Kathy Simpson, Brian H. Walls

Indexer: TECHBOOKS Production Services

Publishing and Editorial for Technology Dummies

    Richard Swadley, Vice President and Executive Group Publisher

    Andy Cummings, Vice President and Publisher

    Mary C. Corder, Editorial Director

Publishing for Consumer Dummies

    Diane Graves Steele, Vice President and Publisher

    Joyce Pepple, Acquisitions Director

Composition Services

    Gerry Fahey, Vice President of Production Services

    Debbie Stailey, Director of Composition Services

Contents at a Glance

Table of Contents

Introduction

If I had a dime for every time I wrote "Organize Photos" on my to-do list, only to leave it undone, I'd have enough cash to retire to some tropical hideaway and do nothing but photograph coconuts all day. Unfortunately, no dimes came my way, and I find myself here. The good news, however, is that Adobe has given me, and you, Photoshop Album. Within this inexpensive piece of software lies all of the tools you need in order to import, organize, and manage your collection of photos. And it doesn't stop there. Album is also capable of handling video and audio clips and, as an added bonus, lets you flex your creative muscles with the capability to create fun and interesting projects — all with simplicity and ease.

Because of Album I finally crossed "Organize Photos" off my to-do list for good.

About This Book

For some people, me included, launching a new program for the first time is like driving in a strange city with no road map. Sure, you could drive around and probably find where you need to go — eventually. But you would waste a lot of time going down the wrong streets, stopping and asking for directions, and pulling over to call people for help. You get the picture. Armed with a map, on the other hand, you're a virtual road warrior.

That's how it is with Album. Even though it's a user-friendly program, it's not without its quirk or two. Sure, you could figure it out — eventually. Consider this book your handy road map to Album. Armed with it, you don't have to worry about driving in circles.

What's in This Book and How to Use It

This book is divided into several parts that correlate to the feature you'll find in Album. If you're brand new to Album, you may want to start at the beginning and continue forward somewhat linearly. If you've already got your images into Album and are wondering what to do next, feel free to check out the chapters on organizing, managing, and creations. If you've been working in Album awhile and have a specific topic or a problem you want help with, flip to the index to find what you need, read up, get out, and move on with your business. Here's a brief overview of what you'll find within the spine.

Part I: Getting Started with Photoshop Album

In these first chapters, I introduce Album and its features. This part is the place to start if you have just installed the program and haven't a clue as to what Album can do for you. I cover the basics, like the Album interface, setting your preferences, and getting help if you find yourself lost. The most important chapter in this part is Chapter 3. Here's where you'll find the lowdown on working with resolution, color modes, and file formats. These topics pop up throughout the book because understanding resolution and formats is key to working with digital images. If those topics are new to you, don't skip this chapter.

Part II: Importing, Organizing, and Managing Photos

Before you can really reap the benefits Album has to offer, you need to import and organize your files. These chapters show you how to import your files from a variety of sources, such as your digital camera and your Photo CDs. The info in this part also shows you how to create and use tags, captions, and notes for optimum identification and organization. Finally, I show you how to work with different versions of your photos and how to create new and backup copies of catalogs — the database backbone of your collection of files.

Part III: Finding, Viewing, and Editing Photos

The chapters in this part deal with locating and looking. Album has numerous ways to find your images and clips quickly and efficiently, so you don't waste time scrolling thorough endless numbers of thumbnails. Find out how to change your viewing options — from various thumbnail sizes to creating instant slide shows. Discover how to sort your images, by date, folder, media type, and more, depending on what's most meaningful and efficient for your purpose at the time.

In this part I also give you details on repairing and enhancing your images. I offer some advice on setting up your editing environment, and I show you how adjusting contrast, eliminating red eye, and fixing color casts are just a mouse-click away. And I give you some tips in how to seamlessly integrate an outside image editor, like Photoshop Elements, into your imaging repertoire so that you can take care of digital fixes that Album can't handle.

Part IV: Sharing and Printing Photos

Part IV describes all the ways you can spread the love with your photos, clips, and creations. Album makes it quick and easy to e-mail attachments, print, and even post images online. In fact, sharing images in a variety of ways with Album is so fool-proof that you'll end up recommending the program to even the most computer-challenged of your family and friends.

Part V: Creating Larger Projects with Photos

After importing, organizing, and editing your inventory of files, you'll want to check out these chapters. Here you can find how to make all of the great *creations* Album is capable of — slideshows, photo books, calendars, eCards, and much more. Before you know it, you'll be a creations addict and will have made enough personalized gifts to last until the year 2010.

Part VI: The Part of Tens

These three chapters are chock-full o' tips. If you find that people are nodding off when you show them your vacation slideshow, maybe a few tips in composing better images will help remedy the situation. And, if you're looking to add to your repertoire of digital camera goodies, take a gander at Chapter 20. Here you'll find a brief description of some practical and fun camera accessories. Finally, if you encounter the occasional snafu, look at Chapter 21. You may find that the cure to your problem lies in these few pages.

Conventions Used in This Book

If you've worked on a computer even a short time, you've probably discovered that sometimes commands require using the mouse along with the keyboard. Working in Album sometimes involves that keyboard/mouse combo. For example, "To select more than one item, press the Ctrl key and click on additional items."

When you see a command arrow (⇨) in the text, it means that you should select a command from the menu bar. For example, "Choose Edit⇨Preferences" means to click on the Edit menu and choose Preferences from the list of commands.

Icons Used in This Book

The icons you see in this book aren't here just because they're cute. Their purpose is to alert you that something noteworthy is coming your way.

 You know it's a law in most states that you can't have a computer book without a sprinkling of computer-geek tech talk. Even though Album is more user friendly than most computer programs, a few explanations required the presence of this nerdy icon.

 Whenever you see a target, look for a tidbit that hits the spot, making your time spent in Album a little easier.

 This icon is a gentle reminder of things I've already mentioned and want to make sure you haven't already tossed out of your memory banks.

 Don't skip the information that appears next to the Warning icon. The information here is stronger than a gentle reminder — ignore what I'm saying and the consequences could be permanent, like lost files.

Feedback, Please

If you want to praise, complain, or query, you can contact the publisher or authors of the *For Dummies* books by visiting www.dummies.com, sending an e-mail to info@wiley.com, or sending snail mail to Wiley Publishing, Inc., 10475 Crosspoint Boulevard, Indianapolis, IN 46256.

Part I

Getting Started with Photoshop Album

The 5th Wave   By Rich Tennant

"THAT'S A LOVELY SCANNED IMAGE OF YOUR SISTER'S PORTRAIT. NOW TAKE IT OFF THE BODY OF THAT PIT VIPER BEFORE SHE COMES IN THE ROOM."

In this part. . .

If you just recently tore the shrink wrap on your Album package, this is a good place to start. I guarantee that Part I will prevent you from staring blankly at the screen or timidly poking about at unknown buttons. The chapters in the first part introduce you to Album and get you over the new software jitters. I cover the basics in Chapters 1 and 2 — what Album does and how it works. You'll find useful information about the user interface and about setting your preferences. And very importantly, you'll find out where and how to find other sources of help, should you find yourself either lost or pulling out your hair. Chapter 3 is an important chapter that helps you work with resolution, file formats, and color modes. By the time you're done with the chapters in Part I, you and Album will have gone beyond the awkward introduction and should be nicely acquainted.

Chapter 1

Introducing Album

• •

In This Chapter

▶ The growth of digital photography

▶ What Album does and why you need it

• •

*O*wning and using Photoshop Album is like having the world's best personal assistant — organized, efficient, always at your beck and call, saves you time, money, and frustration and just makes your life easier. I admit it. Before Album came into my life, I was a closet photo "shoeboxer." Well, actually, more like a "33-gallon storage toter." Maybe you're the same way.

Album and Organization

I bet that you love photos — taking them, looking at them, and sharing them. I bet that you love knowing that you've captured and preserved the memory of special events, milestones and moments of your life and those of your family and friends.

And maybe you're like me because the thing you don't love is the time-consuming task of organizing, labeling, and placing the photos into albums. That task always seemed to stay permanently affixed to my to-do list.

When I switched to a digital camera, things improved some. I didn't need any more storage totes or garage space. But, digital images bring on a whole new set of problems. Does this scenario sound familiar? Do you have a clutter of inconsistently named folders and unintelligible alpha-numerically named files scattered all over your hard drives or burned haphazardly onto CDs?

Enter Album — your photo organizing personal assistant phenom. Album quickly (and with a miniscule learning curve), enables you to import, organize, find, manage, fix, and share your photo collections.

Sure, there's an initial time investment. And Album doesn't turn lazy people into efficient organizers (I still have to scan my analog prints). But because of its ease of use, you might find yourself (like me) full of renewed enthusiasm for the task of organizing your images. The proof, as they say, is in the pudding, or in this case, in the albums. I have seen how efficient Album is at transforming unorganized clutter into an ordered, streamlined system. I have seen the best organizational system since the Dewey Decimal system at work. I have seen the light!

And the bonus is that after you've gotten your images organized and manageable, you can relax and use those images in some creative and expressive ways. And Album is there to help you with that as well, allowing you to make wonderful creations. So Album not only makes your life easier, it makes it more fun, too. It's the best 50 bucks I ever spent.

What Album Does and Why You Need It

The bottom line is that when you save time you save money. And the program that's going to save you both time and money is downright dirt cheap. I mean, for the cost of a cheap dinner and a couple of movie tickets, you probably just purchased a program that can make you more organized, more productive, and even get some creative juices flowing.

You may have thought when you first bought your camera that the software that came bundled with the camera was all you needed. Now you may see that the features of those programs are limited and really intended to just facilitate the importing of images onto your computer.

Album allows you to import, identify, organize, export, manage, edit, and share your photos, as shown in Figure 1-1. About the only thing it can't do is make you a latte while you enjoy all the free time you gain from Album doing all the work. Here's a quick glance at Album's multiple features:

- **Import:** After you take photos, you can move (or *import*) them into Album. It only takes a few minutes, and your camera and memory card are ready for the next outing or event. In addition to a digital camera or card reader, you can import images directly from your scanner, hard drive, or CDs. After they're imported, your images are stored in what Album calls a *catalog*. If you're short on hard drive space, you can even store your images offline, while retaining a *proxy* (low-resolution copy) in your catalog. You also can import video and audio clips.

For the two readers who don't already have a digital camera

Not too long ago if you had a digital camera, you were considered to be on the technological cutting edge. Now it is just as common to see a digital camera as it is a film camera. Some estimates predict that, worldwide, consumers will buy 10 million digital cameras in 2003.

The digital trend has steadily escalated for many reasons. Anytime a product offers convenience, immediate satisfaction, and a time and cost savings, it is bound to be embraced by the masses. If you haven't jumped on the digital bandwagon yet, here are a few reasons why you may want to make the switch:

✔ **Immediacy:** There's nothing like being able to correct your mistakes immediately after you make them, instead of regretting it later. Shooting digitally allows you to take a photo, view it in the LCD (Liquid Crystal Display), monitor attached to your digital camera, and, if you like what you see, great. On the other hand, if the exposure, lighting, or composition is a little off, delete the photo, make your adjustments and reshoot right then and there. And, as an added bonus, because you can make instant adjustments, you can improve your photographic skills more quickly.

You can try different angles and compositions. If they don't work, you just delete them from the memory card. You also can really test your camera's features and get to know how it ticks by taking shots using different settings. Hey, and no more streaked or fogged film from airport x-ray machines!

✔ **Convenience and time savings:** Here are four nice words for you: *No more photo*

processing. No more driving to the photo lab, filling out the order, waiting for the development, and picking up the order. You also find that the time you spend scanning steadily declines. Going digital means simply cabling up the camera or card reader to your computer, making a couple of mouse clicks and the photos are on your hard drive, ready for action.

✔ **Less expense:** Just like time isn't wasted with photo processing, neither is money wasted paying for processing. Just print (and pay for) only the photos you really want. Invest the savings from paying for film and processing toward accessories for your digital camera (see Chapter 20).

Some people argue that a high-quality digital camera is more expensive than a comparable film camera. This may be a true statement now, but is becoming less so. Because the technology is still evolving, quality cameras are becoming less expensive and will continue to do so.

✔ **Less clutter, and less retouching:** Going digital means not having to store negatives, slides, or prints. Storing all that output not only consumes precious storage space, but keeping track of it all is tedious. And because there is no film or prints involved, you'll spend less time retouching dust, dirt, or scratches.

✔ **Flexibility:** Digital images allow you to share your images in different ways. Print them, e-mail them as attachments, burn them onto CDs, or post them online.

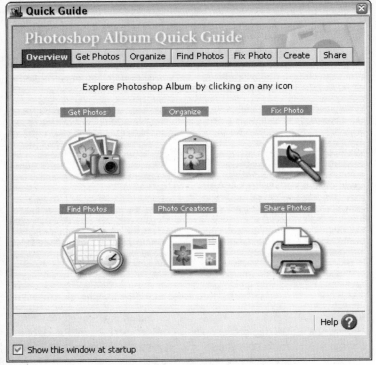

Figure 1-1:
Photoshop Album has multiple features to make the photographic part of your life easier.

✔ **Identify, view, and export:** After your images are imported into your catalog, you can view them in one location — any time, all the time, as shown in Figure 1-2.

Album provides you with a tagging system that enables you to attach keywords or phrases to your images to make sorting and locating them a breeze. You can locate and view your images by tags, dates, folders, and other criteria. It doesn't matter where the images reside, whether on your computer or on other external media. Album also keeps a history of each image, details such as if you e-mailed or printed the photo. And you can even export images in a variety of file formats for use in other applications.

✔ **Edit:** If you didn't quite get your images perfect during the shooting process, Album lets you edit your images using cropping, red-eye removal, and color and contrast tools, all of which require only a mouse click or two. Album also provides seamless integration with many external image editors, such as Photoshop Elements, for those images that require extra-strength editing.

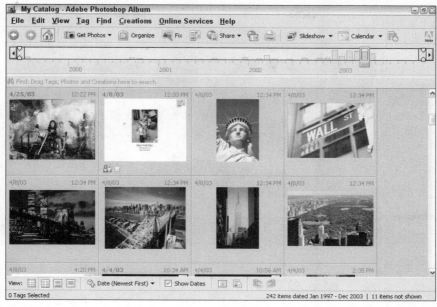

Figure 1-2:
Album
allows you
to see all of
your images
in one
organized
location.

✔ **Create:** Keep it simple and just e-mail or print your images. Or be a little more innovative and make projects, called *creations,* such as albums, slide shows, cards, calendars, photo books (shown in Figure 1-3), and more in just five easy steps.

✔ **Share:** After your images have been cleaned up and enhanced, Album makes sharing your files a snap. You can e-mail images and creations as attachments, post them online via a photo sharing Web site like Shutterfly. com, or view them as a Web gallery.

You can print the images, or burn them to CD or DVD. Album can save your files as PDFs (Portable Document Format), which means that anyone, anywhere with just a computer and free Acrobat reader can view your images and creations.

✔ **Preserve:** Album makes it quick and easy to back up your catalog or archive your images to CD or DVD. Store the media in a safety deposit box or other offsite location to ensure your memories are safe from disaster — natural or man-made.

Figure 1-3:
Create
wonderful
projects in
Album, such
as hard-
bound photo
books.

Chapter 2

Performing Basic Tasks

After you've successfully installed Album, you're ready to get started using it. Often, even with the most user-friendly programs, launching it for the first time can be a little overwhelming. You sit staring at the screen, not quite knowing where to start first. To get over that awkward hump, this chapter introduces the main elements of the interface to give you a feel for how Album works. You discover how to set your preferences so the program works the way you want it to. You also find out where to go for assistance, both within Album and outside of it. After going through this chapter, you'll be ready to dive in and start wrangling your files into Album.

Using the Quick Guide

When you first launch Album, the Quick Guide window appears, as shown in Figure 2-1. The Quick Guide is an easy place for you to get started if you're new to Album. Think of it as the "Getting Started Wizard." Using the Quick Guide, you can execute just about task. Here are your options:

- ✔ Get photos
- ✔ Organize
- ✔ Fix photos
- ✔ Find photos

✔ Make photo creations

✔ Share photos

You also can use the menus, palettes, and bars to execute all of these tasks, as discussed later in this chapter.

The Quick Guide appears by default when you first launch Album. You also can access it at anytime by any of these methods:

✔ Choose Help⇨Quick Guide.

✔ Press Shift+F1.

✔ Click the Quick Guide button in the Shortcuts bar (it's the icon that looks like a book and a stopwatch). For more on the Shortcuts bar, stay tuned.

Icons   Close Help

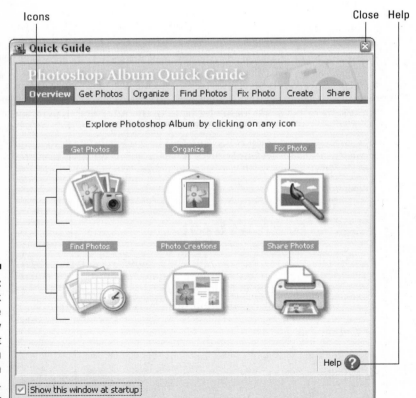

Figure 2-1:
The Quick
Guide
appears by
default
when you
launch
Album.

Here's how to use the Quick Guide:

1. **From the Quick Guide Overview window, click the icon or the tab for the task you want to execute.**

   Most likely, if you're new to Album, the first thing you'll be doing is getting, or importing, photos.

2. **Depending on which icon or tab you selected, click the task you want to execute.**

   For example, if you click the Get Photos icon, you're presented with all the ways to import photos, as shown in Figure 2-2. For intricate details on how to import files, see Chapter 4.

If you need more information about a particular task, click the Help button in the bottom, right corner of the Quick Guide window. For more on using Help, see the section, "Using Help," later in this chapter.

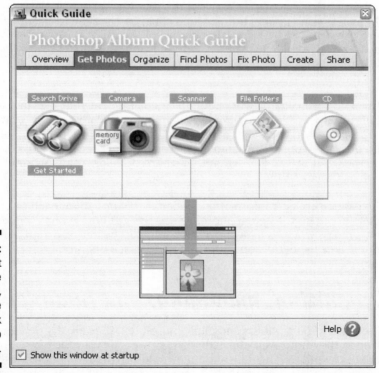

Figure 2-2: In the next Quick Guide window, select the next task you want to execute.

After you become comfortable using Album, you may not want the Quick Guide to appear when you launch Album. If so, uncheck the Show This Window at Startup button in the bottom, left corner of the Quick Guide window.

What You Can Do in Album

Album enables you to do a variety of tasks, as discussed in the next few sections. In order to perform most of the tasks, however, you first have to get your photos into Album. Once you've imported your files, you can then organize them, edit them and share them with others in a variety of fun and creative ways.

Getting photos

Album lets you import photos, video clips, and audio clips from your hard drive, camera, card reader, scanner, CDs or DVDs, and external media such as Zip disks. When you import items into Album, it creates *links* to your files so it knows where the photo is located, what the file format is, and other information.

Here's how this linking works. Album keeps track of your files in a database of information called the *catalog*. Album automatically creates a catalog (appropriately named My Catalog.psa) when you first launch the program and brings in your photos and clips. The catalog keeps track of your files, whether they are on your computer's hard drive or reside on other media such as CDs or DVDs.

The catalog collects information (called *metadata*) about each photo, but it doesn't contain the actual photos themselves. Album retains the metadata and a *proxy,* which is a low-resolution copy of the image, a kind of file body double. For full details on importing photos, see Chapter 4.

Organizing, managing, and finding photos

When you import photos and clips into Album, they are, by default, organized in the Photo Well, the main display area for your files, by the date and time of the photo. The date and time could be when the photo was taken by your digital camera or when the image was scanned. You also can arrange your photos by folder location, import batch, color similarity, media type, or tags.

Tags are keywords that you attach to your images to further identify and
locate them. They could be based on people's names, certain events, or specific locations, as shown in Figure 2-3. Tags give you much more control when
it comes to identifying, organizing, and locating your photos. You can further
identify your images with written captions, audio captions, and notes.

Album allows you to use a variety of tools and criteria to find your images.
For example, you can use the timeline (described later in this chapter) to
specify a date range. Or you can search for specific images based on a
common history, such as which photos have been printed. For lots of info
on organizing, managing, and finding images, see Chapters 5, 6, 7, and 8.

Viewing photos

All of your files — photos, video clips, audio clips, and creations — appear
in the Photo Well arranged in a grid of *thumbnails,* small display versions of
your images. You can select from various size thumbnails, or you can choose
to see your selected file in a single photo view.

Figure 2-3:
Attaching
tags to your
images is a
great way to
organize
and locate
them.

The buttons in the Options bar help you organize and sort your files in the Photo Well. And you're not restricted to viewing your images as static photos in the Photo Well. You also can select images and view them in an instant slide show, which provides a more enriching viewing experience. For details on viewing photos, see Chapter 9.

Editing photos

Album provides you with a slew of easy-to-use editing tools to clean up and enhance your images. You can rotate, crop, get rid of red eye, and adjust color, contrast and lighting — all from the Fix Photo dialog box, shown in Figure 2-4.

Album divides these editing tools into two categories — Single Click fixes and manual adjustments.

Album saves your edited file as a copy, thereby preserving the original. That way, you can revert to the original later if you desire.

For hard-core editing that goes beyond Album's capability, the program provides seamless integration with many external image editors, such as Photoshop Elements and Photoshop. For more on editing images, see Chapters 10, 11, and 12.

Sharing and printing photos

If you like taking photos, you probably like sharing them, too. You're in luck. Album makes it easy to share your photos in a variety of ways:

- ✔ **E-mail:** You can e-mail your photos as image attachments. Or you can e-mail your photos after you've incorporated them into creations, such as albums, slide shows or eCards.

- ✔ **Online:** Album allows you to share your images online in a couple ways. You can create galleries that you can then upload onto the Web. Or you can post your photos on a photo sharing Web site such as Shutterfly.com.

- ✔ **Print:** If you or your recipients want hard copies, you also can print your photos at home. Album gives you choices between printing individual images, contact sheets, and picture packages. Of course you also can print several types of creations, such as greeting cards and calendars. Or if you want a professional print job, you can order photo lab-quality prints and hard-bound photo books from online service providers using the Online Wizard in Album.

If you need to export your images to a certain file format, Album can handle that as well. Check out Chapters 13, 14, and 15 for details on e-mailing, printing, and using online services.

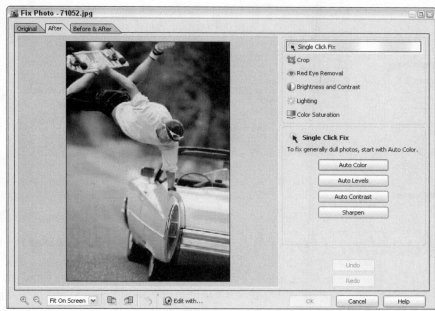

Figure 2-4: The Fix Photo dialog box gives you access to Single Click fixes and manual adjustments.

Creating with photos

Another great feature of Album is its Creations feature. In a mere five steps, Album's Creation Wizard lets you create a variety of great creations: albums, slide shows, greeting cards (see Figure 2-5), eCards, calendars, photo books, Video CDs, a Web gallery, and an Adobe Atmosphere 3D gallery. You'll also discover that you can use your photos and your digital camera in a variety of ways, besides just in Album's creations. See Chapters 16, 17, and 18 for all you need to know about making creations and more.

Happy Birthday Bobby!

Figure 2-5:
Album's
creations
are easy
and fun, and
only take
five steps
to make.

Checking Out the Album Interface

The Album work area is chock full of bars, panes and areas to work in. I make
a lot of references to these features in the book, so it would good to get an idea
of where they reside and what they do. Here is a brief synopsis of each component of Album's work area. To get the details on each, see the referenced
chapter.

Working with the Photo Well

All of your files — photos, video clips, audio clips, and creations — are
imported and displayed in the *Photo Well,* organized in a grid of thumbnails,
shown in Figure 2-6. The size of the thumbnails depends on your selected
viewing option, which you can change at any time. You also can view your
images as single photos. How your photos are organized depends on how
you've sorted your files. By default, files are sorted by date, newest files being
first. But you also can sort by folder location, import batch, color similarity

or media type. The easiest way to change the viewing options, both in size and sorting criteria, is to click the icons in the Options bar, located below the Photo Well. Video clips are displayed by the first frame of the clip. Audio clips are displayed with a generic audio icon. Depending on the size of your thumbnails, date, time and tags will also appear on or around your thumbnails. When you search for images, the Photo Well displays all search results. For more on working with Photo Well, see Chapters 4 and 5.

Using the Workspace

The *Workspace* is a separate window, shown in Figure 2-7, which you use primarily when you select items to use in a *creation* (a special project such as a slide show or greeting card). To access the Workspace, you select your desired items in the Photo Well and then click the Create button on the Shortcuts bar (described later in this chapter). The items are copied to the Workspace window, where you can rearrange their order, if necessary. If no items are selected, an empty Workspace appears. You can then drag and drop items from the Photo Well into the Workspace. In the Workspace, you can edit and remove items, as well.

Photo Well

Figure 2-6:
The Photo Well displays a grid of thumbnails of your files.

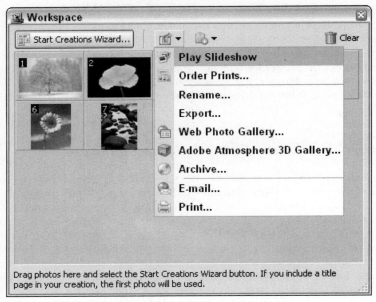

Figure 2-7:
The
Workspace
lets you
gather your
files for
making
creations or
performing
other
tasks, like
e-mailing,
archiving, or
printing.

You also can use the Workspace to attach tags, play a slide show, export, archive, e-mail, print, or create a Web photo or Adobe Atmosphere 3D Gallery. To access the Workspace for these tasks, choose View⇨Workspace and drag your desired files into the window. For more on the using the Workspace, see Chapter 16.

Using the Menu bar

The Menu bar, shown in Figure 2-8, contains commands for executing most tasks. The menus are organized according to the kind of task you perform. For example, the View menu contains commands for viewing slide shows, for choosing the size and arrangement or your Photo Well thumbnails and for accessing panes and other Album components. The Create menu contains commands for making all sorts of projects with your images.

Saving time with the Shortcuts bar

The Shortcuts bar, located just below the Menu bar, displays buttons for commonly used commands (refer to Figure 2-8). Those buttons with black down-pointing triangles next to their names have drop-down sub-menus that contain additional commands. With just a couple clicks with the mouse, you can execute commands such as printing, creating slide shows or sharing your photos with others. Because the Shortcuts bar is so multifaceted, details on using it are sprinkled throughout the book.

Instead of using the Menu bar, save yourself a few seconds and click these buttons. If you're not sure what a button does, hover your mouse over the button. The handy tool tip appears, describing what the button does.

Working with the Options bar

The Options bar is located below the Photo Well. The buttons in the Options bar allow you to change your viewing and sorting options of your files in the Photo Well. It also has buttons to that enable you to quickly show and hide the Properties pane and Workspace. And finally, you can rotate your images clockwise and counter-clockwise with one click of the rotate buttons, located on the far-right side of the Options bar. For more on the Options bar, see Chapter 9.

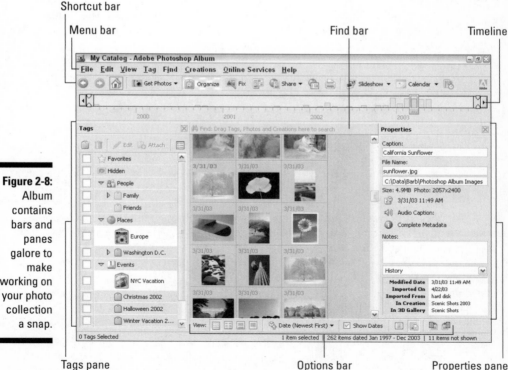

Figure 2-8: Album contains bars and panes galore to make working on your photo collection a snap.

Using the Find bar

The Find bar comes into play when you are searching for images based on various criteria. If you drag one or more tags onto the bar, for example, Album gathers up all images containing those tags and displays them in the Photo Well. To start a new search, just click the Clear button.

When you're not searching, the Find bar takes a break and is represented by the small, horizontal blue bar above the Photo Well (refer to Figure 2-8). When you're searching for files, the Find bar expands, and the Search Criteria field opens within the Find bar so you can see the tags you've chosen for the search, shown in Figure 2-9. For details on the Find bar, see Chapter 8.

Getting to know the timeline

The timeline, located just below the Menu bar, allows you find photos by the date, folder location, or import batch, depending on the option you chose in the Options bar.

The timeline shows how items are distributed, and bars in the timeline represent the images. The height of each bar is proportional to the number of images.

Figure 2-9:
The Find bar allows you to perform quick searches of specifically tagged images.

Using the timeline to find images by date is probably the most common usage for this tool. You designate a range of time or select a specific date in the timeline, and all files that were created or saved with applicable date(s) display in the Photo Well.

The timeline is divided into years and months. Hover your mouse pointer over a bar in the timeline, and the name of the month appears. For more information on using the timeline, see Chapter 8.

Viewing info in the Properties pane

The Properties pane, shown in Figure 2-10, contains oodles of information about your files. To display the Properties pane, choose View⇨Properties or click the Show or Hide Properties button in the Options bar. Select a file to view the following information:

- ✔ The filename
- ✔ Any captions or notes you've added to the image
- ✔ The date you imported or modified the file
- ✔ Any creations it's been used in
- ✔ Any tags
- ✔ Metadata (like digital camera details)
- ✔ The file's location on your computer

You also can record or listen to audio annotations attached to photos by clicking on the Audio icon in the Properties pane.

The Properties pane allows you rename a file, add a caption or notes, and adjust the date and time of the photo file. For details on using the Properties pane, see Chapter 6.

Working with the Tags pane

Tags offer you an excellent way to identify, organize, and quickly find your photos. You can create, edit, attach, and remove tags by using the Tags pane. To display the Tags pane (see Figure 2-11), choose View⇨Tags or click the Organize button in the Shortcuts bar. For everything you need to know about tags, see Chapter 5.

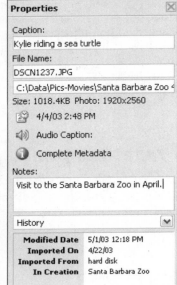

Figure 2-10:
The
Properties
pane is
information
central for
all of your
photos.

Figure 2-11:
Create,
attach, and
remove tags
using the
Tags pane.

Because your list of tags can get extensive, you can expand or collapse the list of tags by clicking the gray triangles in the pane. To quickly find and view specifically tagged images, simply click in the square in the first column. The Find icon (which looks like a pair of binoculars) appears in the square, and your tagged images appear in the Photo Well. You can't get any more efficient than that.

Setting Your Preferences

Most computer applications enable you to set preferences to establish the way your application works in various circumstances. Album's no different. When you first install Album, it comes equipped with default preferences. The defaults remain intact until you change them. Choose Edit➪Preferences to bring up the huge Preferences dialog box. Album has a few different areas where you can set your preferences.

Setting general preferences

These preferences, shown in Figure 2-12, allow you customize Album to suit your needs. Here are the specifics on each:

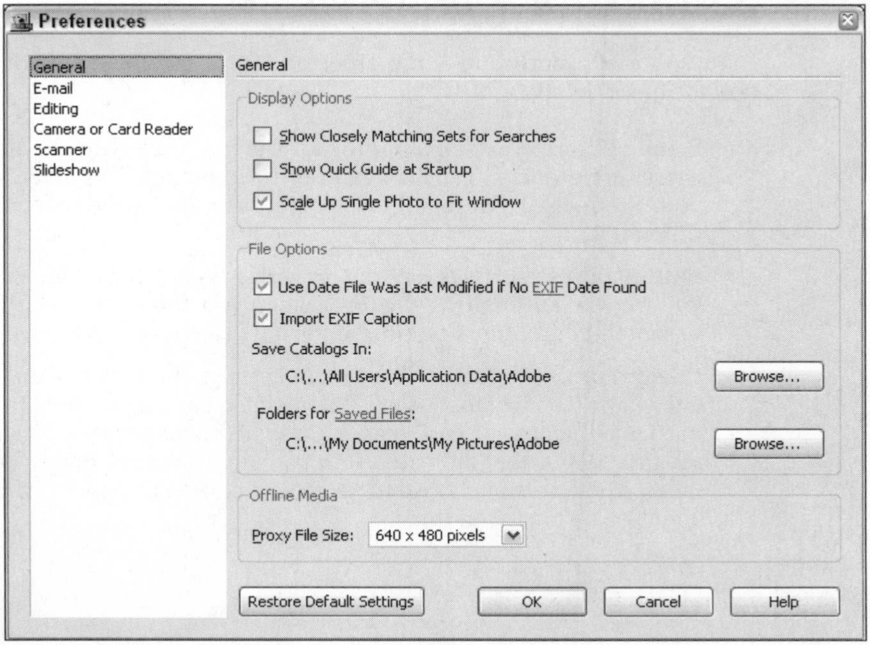

Figure 2-12:
Customize
Album by
setting your
preferences.

Preferences dialog box:

| General |
| E-mail |
| Editing |
| Camera or Card Reader |
| Scanner |
| Slideshow |

General

Display Options
- ☐ Show Closely Matching Sets for Searches
- ☐ Show Quick Guide at Startup
- ☑ Scale Up Single Photo to Fit Window

File Options
- ☑ Use Date File Was Last Modified if No EXIF Date Found
- ☑ Import EXIF Caption

Save Catalogs In:
C:\...\All Users\Application Data\Adobe   [Browse...]

Folders for Saved Files:
C:\...\My Documents\My Pictures\Adobe   [Browse...]

Offline Media
Proxy File Size: 640 x 480 pixels ▾

[Restore Default Settings]   [OK]   [Cancel]   [Help]

✔ **Display Options:** Here are your options:

- **Show Closely Matching Sets for Searches:** Select this option to have Album find not only exact matches, but any photos that are close matches. Photos that are tagged with one or more, but not all, of the search criteria tags are considered close matches.

- **Show Quick Guide at Startup:** Select this option to have Album show or hide the Quick Guide when you launch Album.

- **Scale Up Single Photo to Fit Window:** Select this option to maximize the size of the photos that appear in the Photo Well.

✔ **File Options:** You can choose locations on your hard drive for saving your catalogs and saved files. If you don't want to use the default paths, click the Browse button to choose a new file location.

EXIF (Exchangeable, Image File) data is extra information that is saved with digital photos. Info such as shutter speed, exposure, flash settings, ISO number and the date and time the image was taken are included in the EXIF data. You can choose to import EXIF captions or use the modification date of a file if lacks EXIF data.

✔ **Offline Media:** You can choose a proxy file size for files that will be stored on offline media, such as CDs and DVDs. For more on storing images offline, see Chapter 7.

Setting other preferences

Here is a brief description of the other preferences. Check out specific chapters for more details:

✔ **E-mail:** Before you e-mail photos for the first time, you should set your e-mail preferences. You also can set these preferences when you send your first e-mail. For full details on setting e-mail preferences, see Chapter 13.

✔ **Editing:** These settings have to do with which external image editor you want to automatically launch when you choose Edit⇨Edit with . . . Command in Album. For more on using external editors, see Chapter 12.

✔ **Camera or card reader:** The default settings for cameras and card readers will be fine for most users. But you also can adjust them to fit your particular camera or card reader. Choose the name of your camera, or the drive letter that indicates your camera, from the Camera pop-up menu. You also can choose to delete the photos from your camera after you've imported them.

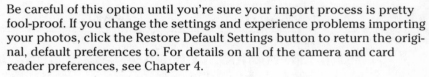

Be careful of this option until you're sure your import process is pretty fool-proof. If you change the settings and experience problems importing your photos, click the Restore Default Settings button to return the original, default preferences to. For details on all of the camera and card reader preferences, see Chapter 4.

✔ **Scanner:** Choose your scanner from the pop-up menu. Choose a file format from the Save As pop-up menu.

JPEG is the default format, but I recommend choosing TIFF instead. For more information about the difference between TIFF files and JPEGs, see Chapter 3. You will have larger file sizes, but better quality images. Choose the folder where you want your scanned photos to be stored. For more on scanning preferences, see Chapter 4.

✔ **Slide show:** Establish your settings for viewing instant slide shows. These are the quickie slide shows that are designed to be viewed within Album. You can select background music, transitions, page durations, and other options. For intricate details on these preferences, see Chapter 9.

When your preferences have been set, click OK to close the Preferences dialog box.

Getting a Helping Hand

Album, being the benevolent, user-friendly program that it is, provides you with a host of ways to get help while you're working. You can access the built-in Help menu, use context-sensitive menus and tool tips, and perform tasks using the Quick Guide. You also can find some Portable Document Format (PDF) files on the Album Install CD, which include late-breaking news, undocumented features, and other useful information. You can read these PDFs using the free Adobe Acrobat Reader, which is included on the CD and also downloadable from www.adobe.com.

Using Help

Album includes a user guide via a built-in, HTML-based Help system. This system contains information and illustrations on using Album commands, features, and tools. When you launch Help, the Help page is displayed in your Web browser.

Your best friends: The Undo/Redo commands

One of the best friends you can have in the world of software programs is Ctrl+Z. That just happens to be the keyboard shortcut for the Undo command. This command does what you think it does. Make a mistake, and choose Edit Undo, or press Ctrl+Z, and your operation is undone. If you didn't mean to choose Undo, you also can then choose Edit Redo, or press Ctrl+Y, which reapplies the last operation.

You also can use Undo and Redo from the Fix Photo dialog box. So if you don't like the color or contrast adjustment you applied, or you cropped someone's head off, choose Undo.

You need to have either Netscape Communicator (4.75 or higher) or Microsoft Internet Explorer (5.0 or higher) installed, and you need to be connected to the Internet in order to use the HTML-based Help system. The Help system uses frames and JavaScript, so be sure that your browser supports both. You must also set your browser to always accept cookies.

The Help window, shown in Figure 2-13, is divided into two frames: the Navigation frame on the left and the Topic frame on the right. To resize the frames, just drag the border between them.

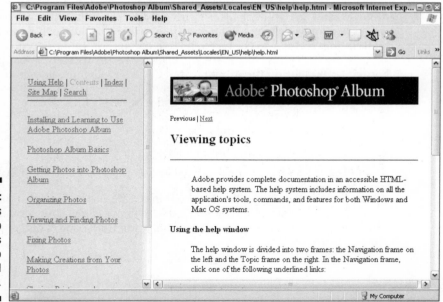

Figure 2-13: Album's built-in Help system is easy to access and navigate.

There are three ways to launch Help:

- ✔ Choose Help➪Adobe Photoshop Album Help.
- ✔ Click the Help button in the lower-right corner of the Quick Guide window.
- ✔ Press the F1 key.

There are several ways you can use the Help system. Here they are:

- ✔ **Index:** The index contains keywords followed by links to the online locations where the topics are discussed. Click Index at the top of the Navigation frame. Then click a letter in the alphabet that corresponds with the Help topic you're looking for information about. For example, if you want to find out about cropping, click C.

  Select the entry you're interested in and click one of the numbered links after the entry to see more information.

  If you're using Internet Explorer 5 or Netscape 6, you can display the title of a link's target by just hovering your mouse over a numbered link.

- ✔ **Site Map:** The Site Map contains links to all topics in Help and all entries in the Index. Click Site Map at the top of the Navigation frame. Scroll through the Site Map until you spot your desired topic or index entry. Click the title or the numbered link at the after the index entry.

- ✔ **Contents:** The Contents contains links to chapter titles in Help. Click Contents at the top of the Navigation frame. Then click a title. The topic appears in the Topic frame, equipped with links to all related subtopics. Click a subtopic link.

- ✔ **Search:** Click Search to look for topics containing a keyword.

Here are a few tips to help navigate around the Topic frame:

- ✔ Click Previous to display the previous topic.
- ✔ Click Next to display the next topic.
- ✔ Click Top to go to the top of a topic.
- ✔ Click the cross-references to other topics to go to that referenced topic.
- ✔ Click the parent topic links at the top and bottom of the topic to move back in the structure of Help topics.
- ✔ Click the related subtopics, if there are any at the end of the topic.

Checking out the Adobe Web site

I am assuming you have an Internet connection. But if you don't, you really should consider getting one. It will allow you to share your photos via e-mail or on the Web. It will also allow you to access resources for working in Album. Visit Adobe's Web site, shown in Figure 2-14, by using one of the following methods:

✓ Click the Go to Adobe.com button in the top-right corner of the Album window. Click the Go to the Adobe Web site (`www.adobe.com`) button near the top-right corner of the application window.

✓ Choose Help➪Adobe Online.

✓ Go to `www.adobe.com` in your Web browser.

At the site, you'll find the goodies, such as

✓ Album software updates (called *patches*)

✓ Tutorials

✓ User-to-user forum

✓ Support Knowledgebase database of commonly reported problems and issues

Figure 2-14: Visit `www.adobe.com` often to get useful information and download software updates.

✔ Adobe Support Marketplace where you can ask technical questions online

✔ Tech Support contact information

Choose Help➪Support to go right to the Customer Support page of www.adobe.com.

Using Context-Sensitive Menus and Tool Tips

Album makes use of context-sensitive menus that can save you time by allowing you to quickly execute commands with a single mouse click. These context-sensitive menus display different commands and options and dynamically change according to what you've already selected or where you are within Album. To display a context-sensitive menu, position your mouse pointer over an image or item in a pane (mini-window) in Album. Right-click your mouse. If a context-sensitive menu doesn't appear, no menu is available for that tool, pane, or item.

You may have noticed while taking a breather and resting your mouse that if you position your mouse pointer and pause over almost any item on the screen — a tool, a button, or an icon — that a name, keyboard shortcut or explanation appears. That name or explanation is known as a tool tip and is a handy feature, especially when you're first learning the ropes of Photoshop Album.

You can access the helpful Quick Guide window if you need some visual guidance in executing a task in Album. See the earlier section, "Using the Quick Guide."

Color Plate 11-1:

Applying the Auto Color Single Click Fix can do wonders in removing nasty blue color cast.

Color Plate 11-2:

Although this wasn't a great image to begin with, its clarity is vastly improved by applying the Auto Contrast Single Click Fix, which removed the haze created by photographing through glass.

Color Plate 11-3:

Adjusting the Fill Flash lighter brings out details in shadowy areas; cropping the image eliminates distracting background elements.

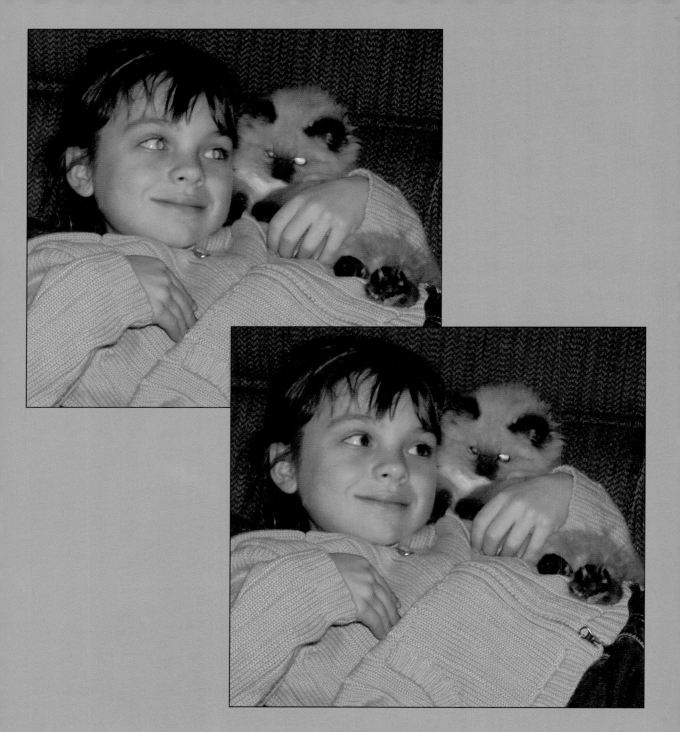

Color Plate 11-4:

A photo flawed by red eye is easily fixed using Album's Red Eye Removal feature.

Color Plate 12-5:

Using an external image editing program like Photoshop Elements helps you take your creativity to another level. You can combine multiple photos, add stylized text, and apply filters for artistic edges.

Season's Greetings

Season's Greetings

Wishing you a happy holiday season

Color Plate 18-6:

Album makes it easy to quickly create personalized greeting cards.

 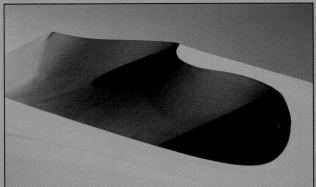

Color Plate 19-8:

Following a few compositional rules, such as using optimum lighting for the subject matter, following the Rule of Thirds, and using leading lines can give everyday snapshots more impact.

Color Plate 19-9:

Light is rarely white. The light at sunset bathes everything in a reddish-orange glow, while the blue hue of a snowy winter light makes everything feel colder.

Chapter 3

Working with Resolution, Color Modes, and File Formats

In This Chapter

▶ Understanding resolution

▶ Getting familiar with color modes

▶ Working with different file formats

Digital images come in two flavors: pixel based and vector based. *Pixel-based images,* also called raster or bitmap images, usually are photographic in nature, although they also can be comprised of artwork, objects, or even miscellaneous parts of the body that have been scanned on a scanner.

Vector-based images, also called object-oriented images, are mathematically defined by lines, curves, and points. The vector format is perfect for illustrations such as logos and line art. Adobe Illustrator, CorelDRAW, and Macromedia Freehand are examples of popular vector drawing programs. Because you will be dealing primarily with raster images in Photoshop Album, this chapter focuses on the characteristics of that type of digital image.

Before delving into the heart and soul of Photoshop Album, I think it's useful to cover some of the more general and technical aspects of the digital imaging world. Don't worry. I'll try not to get too eggheady. It's just that to properly size images (both in dimension and file size), display or print images at their optimum quality, and choose the appropriate image format for their intended usage, you should have a basic understanding of resolution, color, and format. Although the information may not make for the most exciting leisure reading, it will be beneficial in the long run. Think of the information in this chapter as a dose of preventive medicine.

Getting a Handle on Resolution

Resolution can take on many meanings depending on what you're referring to. For example, when people discuss resolution, they may be referring to image resolution, which describes the number of pixels per linear inch (a line 1 inch long). Or they may be discussing the resolution of certain devices such as printers, cameras, scanners, and monitors. All are entwined and interrelated, and comprehending the differences can be somewhat confusing.

Introducing pixels

Raster images, such as digitized photographs, are made up of a grid of squares called *pixels* (short for *PICture Element*). Each pixel lives in a specific location on that grid and contains a single color. When you edit a raster image, you're editing one or more of those pixels.

Think of a grid of pixels as a mosaic. When viewed from afar, the mosaic looks like a painting. But up close, you see the individual square tiles that comprise the image.

Although it doesn't seem like it when you're viewing an image that fits nicely inside your monitor window, your entire image can be broken down into a grid of square pixels — which becomes very evident when you try to zoom *waaay* in on the image. Suddenly, that photo leaves the realm of reality and looks like stacks of colored building blocks. Even round, curvy shapes have to fit within this grid of squares.

Raster images try to fake a curve by mimicking the overall shape with square pixels, as shown in Figure 3-1. Amazingly, this con job is virtually impercepti-ble at high resolutions viewed at full size (100 percent). But when you zoom in at high magnifications, those square pixels are plain as day.

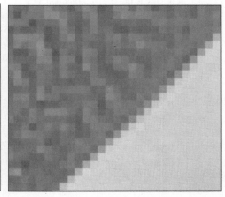

Figure 3-1: This ball quickly loses its roundness when you zoom in on the pixels.

Resolution in a nutshell

If you're to the point where you're going to tear this book into smithereens if you read the word *resolution* one more time, the information here may help to lower your blood pressure a bit. Keep it simple by following these few points:

✔ **If you want to make images available on the Web for the general public, keep your camera's setting at 640 x 480.** Use 800 x 600 if your audience is middle of the road in sophistication. Reserve 1024 x 768 only for the snobby techno-lusters. Remember, the smaller the size of your graphics, the quicker they download on-screen, especially for those who are using older computers and/or dialup Internet connections.

✔ **If your images are destined for print, be sure and capture enough pixels with your** camera or scanner so that your output resolution is around 300 ppi. Check with your printer documentation for any specific recommendations. Not sure? Go with the highest. At least you won't be stuck with poor image quality as a result of not having enough pixels. Just be sure and have lots of memory available on your computer's hard drive and in your camera's flash card or memory stick.

✔ **Don't have a clue what you want to do with your photos?** Again, err on the side of high resolution. Use Album to resize your images smaller if your creations and Web galleries require smaller images. In the long run, it's a lot less damaging to have too many pixels than not enough.

Understanding the pixel-resolution connection

Image resolution refers to the number of pixels along the total width and height of the image, known also as *pixel dimensions*. For example, if the pixel dimensions of a photo are 640 x 480, the image contains 640 pixels in its width and 480 pixels in its height.

The pixel dimensions, in turn, correspond to the image's file size. The larger the pixel dimensions, the more data (and therefore the larger the file size). Every image has a set number of pixels. How does it get these pixels in the first place? You establish the number by the capture setting on your digital camera or the resolution setting on your scanner (see the sections "Working with Camera Resolution" and Working with scanner resolution" later in this chapter).

To see the pixel dimensions and file size of an image in Photoshop Album, choose View⇨Size⇨Single Photo. The file size and pixel dimensions appear below the photo and also in the Properties pane, as shown in Figure 3-2. If your Properties pane isn't visible, choose View⇨Properties.

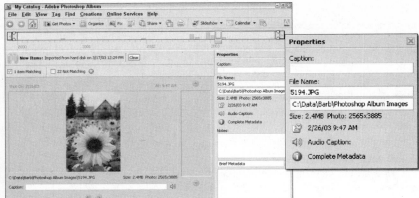

Size takes on two roles in digital imaging:

- **File size:** A result of the pixel dimensions just mentioned
- **Print or image size:** The width and height of an image when printed on paper (described in the section "Working with output and printer resolution," later in this chapter)

The file sizes of raster images can be very large, in comparison to slim and petite file sizes of vector images. You may have discovered this fact on your own while working with your digital camera or scanner. It seems that in no time flat, that CompactFlash card, memory stick, or hard drive space is eaten up. Another disadvantage of raster images is that because they contain a fixed number of pixels, when they're enlarged the quality can go downhill fast.

Changing the resolution by enlarging the pixels

Album allows you to resize your images in certain instances. You should be careful in choosing a new size that is a significant increase from the original. What happens is that the original number of pixels is spread across a larger area resulting in pixelated mush, as shown in Figure 3-3. Here are a few scenarios in which you want to avoid increasing the size of images with small pixel dimensions:

- **Web Photo Gallery:** I took a small photo of a dog, which had dimensions of 66 x 100 pixels. When I created my Web Photo Gallery, I chose X-Large in the Resize Photos option and set the quality to Medium. The result from enlarging a photo with such a small number of pixels to full-screen view was an indefinable, grainy animal (refer to Figure 3-3). I then took a new photo of the dog with pixel dimensions of 2048 x 3072 and used the same settings. The result was a happy dog — sharp and recognizable.

Figure 3-3:
Be careful of increasing the size of images with small pixel dimensions or you may get junk.

▶ **Slide Show:** Similarly, if you take a photo with small pixel dimensions and use it in Slide Show creation, Album responds with a warning that your image is `low resolution and will not display well at this size`.

▶ **Greeting Card:** When you take low-resolution images and try and use them in creations such as greeting cards, which are intended to be printed and require images with higher resolution, Album warns you that the images you chose are `below optimum resolution for printing`.

All the preceding scenarios involve taking the set number of pixels in an image and spreading them across a larger area, whether on-screen or on paper. The result is larger-sized pixels and therefore a chunkier, pixelated-looking image. Enlarging pixels isn't recommended. The best thing to do is to start with images that contain enough pixels for their intended end-usage size.

Working with output and printer resolution

When you print an image from Photoshop or Photoshop Elements, you can enter the desired output resolution. The output resolution is measured in pixels per linear inch (a line that is 1 inch long), or *ppi,* and can be calculated by dividing the number of pixels wide or high by the printed size in width or height. For example, if an image is 800 pixels wide and you print it so that it's 4 inches wide, the output resolution is 200 ppi. The higher the ppi, the higher the quality, as shown in Figure 3-4.

Changing the resolution by resampling

In programs such as Photoshop and Photoshop Elements, you can manually change the image size (height and width) and resolution. But rather than increasing the size of the individual pixels to fill the space, Photoshop, Photoshop Elements, and other image-editing programs perform a kind of voodoo called *resampling*. (Photoshop Album doesn't allow you to resample images.)

Resampling enables you to add or delete pixels to increase the pixel dimensions of an image. Many graphics programs perform a process called *interpolation*. Interpolation is as fancy and technical as it sounds. The process involves performing an algorithm that manufactures pixels by averaging the color of original pixels and adding them to the existing ones.

When you *downsample* (resample down), you eliminate pixels and therefore delete information and detail from your image. Downsampling is done pretty frequently because high-resolution images must be downsampled for posting on the Web. And in actuality, you may not notice much degradation in the image quality because the images are just being viewed on-screen — unless, of course, you take it to the extreme.

Upsampling, on the other hand, is almost always a visual disaster. When you upsample (resample up), you add pixels. The result is that your image tends to lose sharpness and get blurry, soft, and mushy. The more you upsample, the worse the image looks.

After an image is printed onto paper, the resolution is measured in *dots per inch,* or *dpi.* Generally, the greater the number of dots, the better the print quality. Although Photoshop Album doesn't allow you to manually manipulate the output resolution, it warns you if you've chosen a print size that will cause the photo to print poorly — at a dpi setting of less than 150 dpi.

Figure 3-4:
An image at 300 ppi (left) looks much sharper than one at 72 ppi (right).

Here are a few tips for working with printer resolution:

- ✔ **Read the documentation that shipped with your printer.** The documentation will give you the various resolution settings it can print at, as well as tips on the recommended image resolution of your photos.

- ✔ **Be sure that your image has an adequate resolution.** Raster images are *resolution dependent*. Because raster images contain a fixed number of pixels, generally, your printer's resolution doesn't much influence the quality of these images. For example, an image of only 72 ppi doesn't look any better printed at a printer resolution of 600 dpi than it does at 1200 dpi. So be sure that your image has an adequate image resolution to start with.

- ✔ **Don't use a higher resolution than you need.** All you'll do is create an unnecessarily huge file with a slower print time. In addition, the printer may be incapable of reproducing all the detail in the image. In some cases, higher-than-necessary printer resolution settings may make your printout look muddier.

- ✔ **Remember that one printed dot doesn't correlate to one image pixel.** Most printers today use several dots per image pixel. Therefore, your printer manufacturer may recommend that you use a 300 ppi image to print at a printer resolution of 1440 or 2880 dpi.

You can easily calculate the maximum size to print an image at your desired print resolution based on the image's pixel dimensions. Simply divide the pixel dimension by the printer resolution to get the print size. For example, an image with the pixel dimensions of 640 x 480 yields a print of 2.1 x 1.6 inches at 300 dpi. Or an 8 x 10 print with a printer resolution of 300 dpi requires an image with a resolution of 2400 x 3000 pixels.

The term *image size* doesn't refer to pixel dimensions per se. Image size refers more to the physical dimensions and dpi of an image when it's printed. For example, a conversation at the local coffee house may go like this, "So what's the image size on that photo?" and the response would be "Well, it's 5 x 7 inches at 300 dpi."

Working with Camera Resolution

Many digital cameras allow you to select various resolution settings. Those settings may be in pixel dimensions, such as 1024 x 768, or in graphic display standards, such as VGA (Video Graphics Array, usually 640 x 480) and XGA (Extended Graphics Array, usually 1024 x 768). The settings may even take on generic terms like Fine, Hi and Basic. To understand the resolution settings your camera offers, check the manufacturer's documentation.

Depending on your type of camera, the manufacturer may refer to resolution settings as Image Size.

Some manufacturers also tie in image quality with resolution and file format. For example, if you choose a Hi setting, your image will be stored as a TIFF, not a JPEG. (For more on file formats, see "Working with Different File Formats," later in this chapter.) And that Hi setting is only available if you choose Full resolution (which is equal to 2560 x 1920 pixels).

After you're familiar with your camera's settings, consider what setting is optimum for your intended output:

✔ For high-quality printed images, shoot your photos at a higher resolution.

   If you take the resolution setting in pixels and divide it by the recommended resolution of the printer (described in the preceding section), you get the size of your image when printed.

✔ If the image is intended for the Web, be sure and take into account the demographics of your audience. Are they imaging professionals with 21-inch monitors or are they your friends and family with a 15- to 17-inch monitor?

Table 3-1 is a guide to the settings.

Table 3-1   Camera Resolution, Print Size (at a Printer Resolution of 300 dpi), and Screen Display

Camera Resolution	Print Size	Screen Display
2560 x 1920	8.5 x 6.4	Full — too large to display on any monitor
2560 x 1710	8.5 x 5.7	3:2 — too large to display on any monitor
1600 x 1200	5.3 x 4	UXGA (Ultra Extended Graphics Array) — displays full screen on 22- and 23-inch monitors
1280 x 960	4.3 x 3.2	SXGA (Super Extended Graphics Array) — displays full screen on 21-inch monitors
1024 x 768	3.4 x 2.6	XGA (Extended Graphics Array) — displays full screen on 17-inch monitors
640 x 480	2.1 x 1.6	VGA (Video Graphics Array) — displays full screen on 13-inch monitors

---

Understanding megapixels

You often hear cameras described or rated in terms of the number of megapixels they can capture. A *megapixel* is a unit of measurement equivalent to 1 million pixels and is used to quantify the resolution of digital cameras. The number of megapixels is calculated by multiplying the height and width of the image in pixels. For example, 2590 x 1920 pixels is 4,915,200 pixels, or the number of pixels my 5-megapixel Nikon is capable of capturing in full-resolution mode. More pixels means higher resolution, greater detail, and better quality. It also means big files. You will also find a "megapixel-dollar" relationship — the greater the number of megapixels, the more expensive the camera. For details about print sizes in relationship to the megapixels of a digital camera, check out Chapter 14.

Run your own test prints to see what your camera, and either your home printer or service provider, is capable of.

The size of the images when printed depends on the printer's resolution setting. The higher the printer resolution, the smaller the final print size. Similarly, if you reduce the print size of an image, the resolution of the image increases.

Working with scanner resolution

Just as your camera has resolution settings, so does your scanner. Scanning resolution corresponds with output resolution. Here are some suggestions for working with scanner resolution:

- **Skim the manual that came with your scanner for resolution settings and any tips on getting the best scan for your particular scanner.** Typically, for scanners, the maximum *optical* resolutions start at 600 ppi and go up to 2400 ppi.

- **Never scan beyond the scanner's maximum optical, also called *true*, resolution.** Anything higher involves the nasty process of interpolation. Standard scanning software allows you to scan anywhere from 72 ppi on up.

- **Consider the end usage for your images before you scan and use resolution that is appropriate.** If you're planning to print your images at 100 percent of their original size, a good rule to follow is to scan them at 300 ppi.

Some Web designers swear that you'll get a better image if you scan your Web images at 144 ppi (2 x 72 ppi, the standard screen resolution) and then downsample them in an image-editing program like Photoshop or Photoshop Elements. If you don't own an image editor, go ahead and scan your Web images at 72 ppi.

Photoshop Album, in conjunction with your scanner's plug-in, allows you to get photos directly from your scanner. For more specifics on acquiring images from scanners, see Chapter 4.

Working with monitor resolution

Monitor resolution is measured in the number of pixels that are displayed on the screen. Monitors have various preset pixel settings that you can choose from, depending on the size of your monitor and the amount of video RAM you have. Common monitor resolutions are 640 x 480, 800 x 600, 1024 x 768, 1280 x 820, and 1600 x 1024 pixels. Monitor resolution settings are also referred in graphic display standards such as VGA, UXGA, and so on (refer to Table 3-1).

When viewing screen images, output resolution settings really don't a play a role. Because the display of images on-screen is based on a one-to-one ratio (one image pixel per screen pixel), what matters is that you want your image to fit inside your monitor when viewed at 100 percent.

Unlike printer resolution, monitor resolution is a one-to-one (1:1) ratio.

This is where pixel dimensions come into play. When you view an image on-screen, the display size is determined by the pixel dimension, plus the size and setting of the monitor. For example:

- A 17-inch monitor usually displays 1024 by 768 pixels. When you view an 800 x 600 pixel image, the image fills only part of your screen.

    However, change your monitor setting to 800 x 600, and the same image fills the screen (of course, each pixel appears larger).

- An 800 x 600 pixel image fills the screen of a 15-inch monitor.

    But if you were to view a 1024 x 788 image, it wouldn't fit inside the screen; you would have to scroll to see the image.

Bottom line: Establish the level of your audience and use the appropriate pixel dimensions. I recommend using a pixel dimension of 800 x 600 as your default image size. That way the majority of the people will be able to view your image adequately.

For images to be viewed on-screen, you may see recommended output resolution settings of 72 to 96 ppi. That's because monitors display at 72 to 96 dpi, which is an easy number to remember. But keep in mind that when you change the dimensions of your image, it will always be at a one-to-one ratio with the monitor.

If you view an image whose resolution is higher than the monitor, the image appears larger on-screen than in its printed state. For example, try opening a 300 ppi JPEG file into a browser window. It spills way past the screen boundaries. That's because the monitor can only display 72 to 96 ppi at a time, and it would need a lot higher resolution to show all the pixels in the image.

Understanding Color

Peruse the computer graphics section of your local bookstore, and you're bound to see several books on the topic of color — I'm talking, big, thick, expensive books on color. The array of books may lead you to the logical conclusion that color must be a big deal in the world of digital imaging. It is.

Why? Well, sometimes you might hear a friend, colleague (or yourself) say, "Geez, the oranges in my photo of the sunset are so vibrant." Of course, the comment may be worded a little more like, "#$%&*, what in heck happened to the print of my sunset? The orange is much more vibrant on-screen!"

If you find yourself getting serious about digital photography and digital imaging, I recommend plunking down some cash for a good book that tackles the sole topic of color in depth. Because this book is primarily about Photoshop Album, I'm just going to provide you with the short version of color theory.

Album allows you to import images that possess RGB, CMYK, Grayscale, Indexed Color, or Bitmap *color modes* (you may also hear *image mode* or just *mode*).

You'll come across other color modes, such as Duotone, Lab, and Multichannel, if you do any editing in programs such as Photoshop and Photoshop Elements. But if you stick with just Album, I've covered all the modes you need to be familiar with.

Color modes define the color values used to display an image and affect the number of colors shown, the size of the files, and other characteristics. For the lowdown on each type of color, read on.

RGB color

Light, like you get from the sun or from a flashlight, can be broken down into three colors — red, green, and blue. These colors are referred to as the *primary colors* of light. They are also the colors that correspond to the three types of receptors, or *cones,* inside your eyes. Each cone, red, green, or blue, in your eyes senses the amount of red, green, and blue light, respectively. When that information reaches your brain, it is translated into millions of different colors. I mean millions literally. And I don't just mean a couple million, either. When you mix just these three colors, you can produce up to 16.7 million colors.

If you have ever visited a children's museum or science center, they always have a display where the kids can shine three spotlights, red, green, and blue into the same spot. They are amazed to find that the resulting color is white. Turn off all the lights, and the color is black. Move the light up or down and create blue, green, orange, and every color in between. By moving the light, the intensity of the light is being varied. In the digital world, we call the intensity of the light *brightness value.* Each color — red, green, and blue — contains 256 (from 0 to 255) levels of brightness. These brightness values are contained in what we call *channels.*

Think of channels as holding tanks of color information. Getting down to the nitty-gritty, each individual pixel in the channel in your image is assigned its own brightness value ranging from 0 (black) to 255 (white). When you view them separately, as shown in Figure 3-5, each channel appears as a grayscale (black and white) image. But when you view the pixels from each channel together, the pixels mix to form colors, which, in turn, provide you with a *composite,* or full-color image.

A value of 255 from all three channels produces white while a value of 0 from all three channels produces black. Different values produce all the other colors. Because RGB colors combined at 255 create white, they are known as *additive colors.* If your digital image is comprised of these three colors, it is called, not surprisingly, an *RGB image.*

Digital cameras, scanners, computer monitors, and even television screens all display colors in RGB. Many desktop inkjet printers, such as Epson, also print RGB images beautifully. RGB is the primary color mode (with Indexed Color being secondary) to use on any images to be viewed on-screen, whether on the Web, or in any kind of multimedia presentation such as slide shows and video CDs.

CMYK color

CMYK color is very different from RGB. It is based on the light-absorbing quality of ink on paper. When white light hits these inks, some visible wavelengths are absorbed while other wavelengths are reflected back to your eyes.

CMYK images are comprised of various percentages of only four colors of ink — cyan, magenta, yellow, and black. Darker colors have higher percentages, and lighter colors have lower percentages. These colors correspond to the inks used in the offset printing process that is used for professional, high-end printing of magazines, books, and sales and marketing materials. Full-color images that are printed on an offset press must be in the CMYK color mode.

Cyan, magenta, and yellow are called *subtractive colors*. That's because colors are produced by subtracting various percentages of cyan, magenta, and yellow from white. Technically, if you combined these three inks, you would produce black. But because of ink impurities, they create a nasty brown color. Therefore, K (or black) is added to produce black.

CMYK colors are also known as *process colors*. When all four inks are set to 0 percent, pure white is produced. A CMYK image contains four channels, one for each process color. The greater the number of channels, the larger the image. High-resolution, CMYK images are usually the behemoths of digital images.

Figure 3-5:
The red, green, and blue channels in an RGB image appear as grayscale images when viewed independently, but combine to produce a full-color image.

Grayscale

Black-and-white images are referred to as *grayscale* images in the digital realm. They only have one channel, which contains up to 256 levels of gray. Each pixel in the channel has a brightness value ranging from 0 (black) to 255 (white). Some digital cameras allow you to adjust the color saturation (intensity or vividness) to black and white, which allows you to take grayscale photos. You also can scan an image in grayscale mode, or you can convert color images to grayscale in a program like Photoshop or Photoshop Elements.

Although Photoshop Album doesn't allow you to convert color images to grayscale, you can reduce the color saturation in the Fix Photo dialog box. For more details on this technique, see "Using Manual Fixes" in Chapter 11.

Indexed Color

Indexed Color uses 256 colors or less, what we call *8-bit color*. When an image is converted to Indexed Color, in a program like Photoshop or Photoshop Elements, a *Color Lookup Table* (CLUT) is built that stores and indexes the color. If a color in the original image isn't in the table, the program chooses the closest match or makes a new one from the available colors.

The low number of colors in Indexed Color really trims the size of an image file, which is why this mode is used for the popular file format for Web graphics, GIF. Because of the small file size the graphics download quickly from Web servers.

Just be aware that a format with only 256 colors usually isn't sufficient to display photographic images with any quality. Dithering (the technique of emulating colors by varying the pattern of dots) occurs, and too much detail is lost in the process of discarding colors, as shown in Figure 3-6. Photographic images for the Web are better displayed in RGB color rather than Indexed.

Bitmap

Bitmap images contain pixels that are either black or white, no shades of gray in between. Bitmap images consist of one channel and are very small in file size, so this mode is best used for scanned line art and signatures, shown in Figure 3-7, to place in letters and page layouts. Occasionally, you may use this mode for photos where you want a special effect.

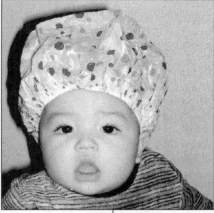

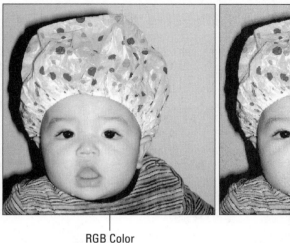

Figure 3-6: Indexed Color reduces your color palette to 256 colors and causes dithering and loss of details.

RGB Color
16.7 million colors

Indexed Color
256 colors or less

Figure 3-7: Use bitmap mode for line art and signatures. Use it for photos only for special effects.

Working with Different File Formats

Photoshop Album can handle a variety of file formats for graphics, sound, and video. A file format is the way a file's data is represented and saved. It is a specific way of structuring the information into bytes.

All digital data is stored through a series of 0s and 1s, each known as a *bit*. And 8 bits create a unit of storage called a *byte*.

No need to worry about the technical jargon. Just know that each format has its strengths and weaknesses, and some are better at certain tasks than others.

Graphic file formats

Most of the files you will be importing into Album will probably be graphic, or still image, files. Fortunately Album can work with quite a few different graphic formats. Certain formats are designed for print purposes, and others are specifically tailored for the Web.

JPEG

JPEG (Joint Photographic Experts Group) is a file format that is the standard format used by digital cameras. It is also one of the formats used for Web graphics.

JPEGs uses *lossy* compression, which means it squeezes your file size down to the minutiae by discarding image data. The actual technical mechanics of the compression algorithm are too complex to get into in this book. But suffice to say that during the compression, colors are averaged in blocks of 8 x 8 pixels to save space. When you open the file again, the original colors cannot be recovered by the program. During a single working session, this compression won't hurt because JPEG works from the on-screen version. But if you close, reopen, and resave or re-export a file in JPEG format, quality degradation occurs. You might not see the nasty results right away, but you may over time, because the damage is cumulative.

Leave your image in either TIFF or PSD formats while performing any editing function like red eye removal, contrast adjustment, and the like. After you're finished with all the editing, export the image as a JPEG. Strangely, you will not find a Save command in Album. Instead Album has you export a file and then presents you with various file formats from which to choose. Choose the File➪Export command in Album to open the Export Selected Items dialog box, shown in Figure 3-8. Here you have several export options:

✔ **Photo Size:** This option allows you to keep your image at its original dimensions or choose from a number of presets, such as 320 x 240 pixels and 1280 x 960 pixels.

You also have the option of choosing Custom, which allows you to enter your desired height and width in pixels. Be aware, however, that although Album lets you enter any value you want, it retains the original proportions of the image. In order for Album to maintain the proportion, it may throw out one of your dimensions. For example, if you enter a custom size of 100 x 100 pixels and your original photo is rectangular, you may end up with a size of 100 x 66 pixels.

✔ **Quality:** For JPEGs, you have a Quality slider, which offers 13 compression settings from 0 to 12. A compression setting of 0 squeezes your file size to a few bytes, but the quality suffers tremendously as a result. On the other hand, a compression setting of 12 retains good image quality but won't compress your file as significantly. And of course, you have all the settings in between — trade offs between quality and level of compression. JPEG compression works best with *continuous-tone images*, such as photographs, which have a wide range of colors. But because the compression is lossy, I don't recommend this format for high-quality printing. Reserve JPEGs for Web images.

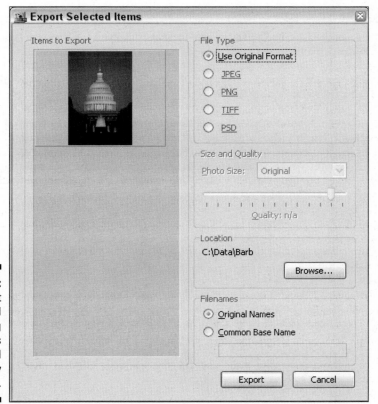

Figure 3-8:
The Export
Selected
Items dialog
box offers
Size and
Quality
options.

> ✔ **Location:** Click the Browse button to navigate to the desired location on your computer or external media, such as a Zip disk.
>
> ✔ **Filenames:** Keep it simple and keep the Original Name of your file, or provide a generic Common Base Name. For example, if you are exporting a bunch of photos from the latest Westchester dog show, you may want to give the base name of Dogs. Each photo you export will then be named `Dog-1.jpg`, `Dog-2.jpg`, and so on.

After you have established your options, click the Export button. For more on exporting, see Chapter 12.

TIFF

Some digital cameras allow you to shoot your photos as TIFFs. TIFF stands for Tagged Image File Format, was created by Aldus Corporation and is one of the most widely used file formats. One of the reasons TIFFs are used so widely is because they have always been usable across platforms. That means that whether your friends and family are using a Mac or a PC, they can always view your TIFF images.

Most programs, ranging from word-processing to image-editing programs, are able to import TIFFs. TIFFs are the format of choice for images that are to be ultimately printed.

Album can both import and export files as TIFFs. Like JPEGs, you have a Size option when you export the file.

The TIFF file format does support lossless compression (described in a moment), but you don't have an option to select it in Album; therefore, the TIFF files you create and modify in Album may end up being large. Also note that if you set your camera to capture images as TIFFs, you will quickly eat up the storage on your memory card. For example, using a 3 megapixel camera, a TIFF will take up around 9MB (megabytes) of storage.

As with JPEG, you specify the location and filename of your image in the Export As dialog box. The remaining file formats described in the next few sections also have options for Size, Location, and File Name in their Export As dialog boxes.

Lossless compression compresses files without deleting any vital data. LZW (named after the founders, Lempel-Zif-Welch) and Zip are two popular lossless compression schemes. Both work especially well with images that have large areas of a single color. If, during your forays in the computer world, you come across the option to apply these compression methods, you can use them without worrying that your gorgeous images will turn into mush after several dozen sessions of opening and saving.

BMP

BMP is a standard bit-mapped Windows graphics file format often used for images that you want to make part of your computer's resources, such as the wallpaper that you see on the Windows desktop. Although Album can import BMP files, it cannot export any images in the BMP format.

PNG

Another file format for Web graphics, PNG stands for Portable Network Graphic. Like GIFs, PNG files offer good lossless compression, but are usually 10 to 30 percent smaller than GIFs.

Here are the various PNG graphics options:

- ✔ **PNG-8:** Supports only 8-bit color, which is fine for graphics such as logos and other illustrations with areas of solid color.
- ✔ **PNG-24:** Supports 24-bit color and is suitable for photos.

PNGs also support *transparency,* which allows an image to be silhouetted against background of the Web page, rather than appearing on-screen surrounded by a white box.

GIF

GIF (Graphics Interchange Format) is a commonly used file format for Web graphics. GIFs use the Indexed Color mode (described earlier in the chapter), which uses a color palette of 256 colors or less. It also utilizes the LZW lossless compression scheme.

This limited color palette is great for creating miniscule files for Web downloads, but is not suitable for continuous tone images (such as photos) in which the number of colors displayed is critical.

Like PNG-8 files, GIFs are well suited for images with areas of solid colors, as shown in Figure 3-9. You may want to export an image as a GIF only if it is of an illustrative nature such as a logo, or if the color quality of the photo is not critical.

PSD

PSD is Photoshop's native file format. Album allows you to export an image as a PSD file. The Photoshop format supports all image color modes, is the fastest format for opening and saving files in Photoshop or Photoshop Elements, and uses a lossless compression process (although it's invisible to you). Just don't expect to get the same kind of compression you get with JPEG or PDF.

Figure 3-9:
Images with
solid areas
of color
make ideal
GIFs.

Besides being the format of choice if you (or the recipient of your image) want to work on the image in Photoshop or Photoshop Elements, almost all drawing and layout programs now support the importing of native Photoshop files.

PDF

PDF stands for Portable Document Format and is the native format of Adobe Acrobat. PDFs can contain text, images, sound, motion, and video, which make them an ideal format to save Photoshop Album creations. Here are a few other advantages to using PDFs:

- ✔ They're flexible. They are one of the few file formats that are suitable for both viewing on-screen and for printing.

- ✔ They're often used for electronic documents that are downloadable from the Web (like your IRS forms) and are a great format for e-mail attachments and exchanging files between people.

- ✔ Anyone with a computer running Windows, Mac OS, or a Unix operating system can read a PDF. All you need to view a PDF file is Adobe Acrobat Reader, which is available as a free download on Adobe's Web site (www.adobe.com). The recipient of your file doesn't need to have the same operating system, program, or fonts as you do. All he or she needs is the reader.

- ✔ PDFs have an automatic compression scheme that crunches down the file size and makes them ideal for e-mail and Web transfer.

When you make a creation in Album — such as an album, slide show, video CD, or even an e-mail attachment — and want to save it, the format of choice is PDF. PDFs are small in size and allow you to e-mail a single attachment rather than numerous, individual images. Album offers various Size and Quality options for optimizing the PDF: for viewing on-screen, for printing, or for utilizing the full resolution of the images.

After you choose one of these three options (as shown in Figure 3-10), Album presents you with one of two dialog boxes, depending on whether it deems the size and resolution of your images are satisfactory for your intended creation:

- **Satisfactory:** Album presents you with the Export PDF dialog box where you can enter the filename and location to save the file. Then click the Save button, shown in Figure 3-10.

- **Unsatisfactory:** You get a dialog box that presents you with "issues," as shown in Figure 3-11. These issues may be that your images are either below the optimum resolution for printing at this size or that they are low resolution and will not display well at this size on-screen. For more on resolution, see the section "Getting a Handle on Resolution," earlier in this chapter.

Figure 3-10:
Album offers three options for optimizing PDFs.

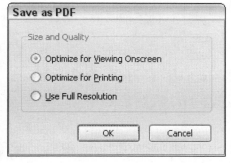

When you're sending creations as e-mail attachments, Album also displays the file size and download times after the creation has been saved as a PDF. You can reduce the size of PDF e-mail attachments by changing the settings in your e-mail preferences.

Like JPEG files, size and quality have an interrelationship: the smaller the file, the lower the quality. For more details on file size and resolution, see Chapter 13.

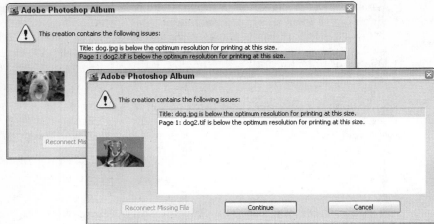

Figure 3-11:
Album
warns you
when an
image's
resolution is
too low for
its intended
use.

PDD

PDD files are catalogs created in Adobe's PhotoDeluxe program. Album allows you to import the PDD images, but you are unable to export them in the PDD format. Adobe stopped delivering PhotoDeluxe in July 2002 (tech support continues until mid 2003). It won't be missed; Photoshop Album does everything PhotoDeluxe did and a ton more.

Choosing a format for your digital photos or scanned images

Before I leave the topic of graphic file formats, let me just briefly cover what file format you should choose when taking digital photos or when scanning images. Many digital cameras offer the option of choosing either JPEG or TIFF as a file format for the photos you take. Some even offer their own proprietary formats unique to the camera's manufacturer.

When choosing a format, take your intended usage for those photos into account:

- ✔ If you plan on making a photo book or you want high-quality prints, I recommend capturing your images as TIFFs. Just remember, TIFFs will result in larger files.

- ✔ If you just want to create slide shows or albums to view on-screen or you want to e-mail your photos to family and friends, stick with the more compressed JPEG format.

- ✔ If you aren't sure and just want the photos in your library for future projects, then it is okay to stay with JPEGs; just don't continually open and re-export them.

The lossy compression scheme used by JPEGs will deteriorate the image over time. Better to make a copy of the image (Edit⇨Duplicate Item) and keep your originals unmolested.

✔ Avoid using any proprietary format. Not that proprietary formats are bad; it's just that the format might not be supported by Album and other software programs. For example, if your camera allows you to choose between JPEG and Camera RAW or CCD RAW, choose JPEG. Album doesn't support the Camera RAW or CCD RAW formats.

It may not be completely obvious how to choose the file format for your camera. Some cameras go by settings. A setting of High saves your images as TIFFs, while other settings, such as Medium or Low, save your images as JPEGs. If you're not sure which setting does what, refer to the documentation that came with your camera. I know, "manual reading" isn't fun, but it is a necessary evil sometimes.

When acquiring a scanned image, Album prompts you to choose a file format in which to save your scanned image. You have the choice of three: JPEG, TIFF, and PNG. Again, using the criteria I listed earlier in this section, consider your intended usage. For the specific mechanics of scanning an image, see Chapter 4.

Converting one file format to another

Although Album doesn't have the sophisticated file conversion capabilities of Photoshop or Photoshop Elements, you can change one format to another by choosing File⇨Export and selecting your desired format, as shown in Figure 3-12. This feature can come in handy when you have a JPEG file, and you want to perform some editing magic on it. Export it as a TIFF *before* you begin your editing session if your editing session will take awhile, and you need to open and save it repeatedly.

When you fix a photo in Album, Album leaves the original file intact and saves the file with the word *edited* after the filename. But it doesn't allow you to the save the file in any format but the original format. On the flip side, if you have a TIFF that you want to post on the Web, you will have to convert it to a PNG or JPEG, since TIFFs cannot be used as Web graphics. Again, choose the TIFF and choose File⇨Export.

Album doesn't support the Camera RAW file format used by some digital cameras. If you want to import these files into Album, you will have to use the manufacturer's software that came bundled with your camera to convert the files into a format Album can handle. If the software isn't capable of doing the conversion, you may have to invest in a program that does graphic conversions. See Chapter 21 for more information.

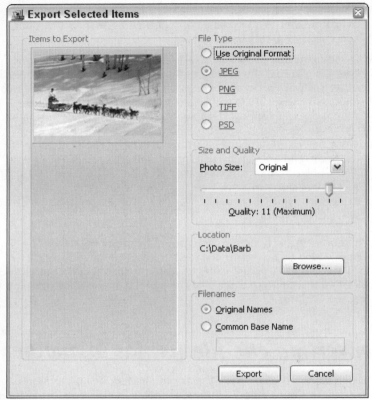

Figure 3-12:
Change
your file's
format by
using the
Export
command.

Audio file formats

If you're one of those folks who aren't satisfied with just using one of your senses, Photoshop Album graciously allows you to incorporate one more. The program can handle a couple of different audio formats.

Not to get too technical, but audio file formats essentially store digital audio data that contains information about waveform characteristics and how they're stored.

Audio files are great for jazzing up slide shows or desktop videos with music or narration, such as audio captions. (For more on incorporating audio files, see Chapters 6 and Chapter 18.) Album supports two audio file formats: MP3 and WAV.

MP3

The popular MP3 audio file format has been the rage of late, prompting software companies to develop players and consumer electronic manufacturers to produce personal MP3 devices. Musicians and record labels have also embraced MP3 and offer online samples of their music in this format.

MP3 is a great format for several reasons:

- ✔ It compresses the file size significantly (a 1:12 ratio) without sacrificing sound quality. The compression scheme reduces the number of bytes in the file by deleting sounds that the human ear cannot hear, much like JPEG reduces the size of a graphic by deleting pixels. A one-minute song only requires 1MB or so of storage.

- ✔ The quality approaches CD quality or near CD quality depending on the compression scheme used.

- ✔ Any platform, Windows, Mac, or Unix, can handle MP3 files.

The disadvantages of MP3 files are

- ✔ They need to be decompressed when played. Decompression requires processing muscle.

- ✔ A 16-bit sound card is a minimum system requirement.

- ✔ You need a software player like Winamp, Windows Media Player, or Real Audio QuickTime to play MP3 files.

Just a bit of techno geek trivia. MP3 is an abbreviation for its real name — Moving Picture Experts Group, Audio Layer 3. MP3 refers to its method of compression, with Layer 3 providing the highest level of compression (in contrast MP1 and MP2 files where Layer 1 and Layer 2 provide a lower level of compression). MP3 is one of a family of standards (you'll meet more in the next section) used for digitally coding audio and video data created by the MPEG folks. I use the term "folks" loosely. MPEG consists of a group of over 70 international organizations.

WAV

Every beep, chirp, and clang you hear from a Windows computer is essentially a WAV file. That's because WAV is Microsoft's native audio file format for the Windows operating system. This format is a great way to store voice data because the format is simple, easy to create files with, widely used, and creates files of good quality.

Many sound effect clips that you download from the Web (such as www.partnersinrhyme.com) are in the WAV format. In addition, no special software players or plug-ins are needed to play WAV files.

On the down side, WAV files tend to be very large. While some compression algorithms are available for WAV files, they are almost always uncompressed when you download them from various sound Web sites. Uncompressed data is more easily decoded and can therefore be played easily by most everyone. Therefore, a one-minute song may require as much as 10MB of storage.

Video file formats

If you have a hard time keeping still, you'll probably want to experiment with bringing motion to your images. In its simplest form, motion can be achieved by incorporating transitions into a slide show. But if that doesn't satiate your need to move, you can try importing video clips into Album and incorporating them into your video CD projects or Web sites. A video file is an integrated package of sound and lots of still images. Album allows you to import a few video file formats.

Here are a few points to keep in mind when creating video files:

- ✔ Video files can eat up memory like Godzilla ate up Tokyo. If you want to use the video for a Web site, choose a format that offers excellent compression.
- ✔ If you want to share your videos with family and friends, be sure everyone who will be viewing the videos has the necessary plug-ins or players to play the video file.
- ✔ Be sure that the media you choose to store or burn your video clips (your hard drive, a Zip disk, CD, or DVD) provides adequate storage space.

Motion JPEG

Also known as MJPEG, this format is an extension of the JPEG standard. In an MJPEG file, each frame in the video is stored with the JPEG still-image lossy compression applied. Because each frame is captured, the quality is high, and you can easily edit the files in a desktop video-editing program such as Adobe Premiere. MJPEG is a common format used by digital video recorders and often used in security surveillance cameras.

Here are a few other characteristics of the MJPEG format:

- ✔ Produces compressed AVI files that are smaller, easier to play and e-mail than regular AVI files. Audio/Video Interleaved, or AVI, is the native file format for Windows-based video.
- ✔ Offers a variety of compression rates ranging from 2:1 (broadcast quality) to 12:1 (consumer grade).

    ✔ Requires large amounts of storage in comparison to MPEG files and does require fairly large bandwidth.

    ✔ Is not a standard, so the MJPEG file format can vary across different vendors.

The newer MJPEG 2000 format is an international standard and has found a market in professional video production, especially in the fields of medical imaging, mapping, remote surveillance and sensing, and mobile phones.

MPEG-1

MPEG-1 was the original file format used in CD-ROMs and video CDs. MPEG-1 offers high-quality and good (although lossy) compression (50:1 ratio). Unlike MJPEG, the MPEG-1 file format only captures the differences between one frame and the next, a technique called *interframe compression*. Because every frame isn't captured, editing is more difficult, since the frames in between have to be re-rendered. In addition, a plug-in is required to view the movies.

On the upside, the file sizes are small and can be streamed over the Web. MPEG-1, however, has seen its hey day and has been replaced with MPEG-2 (better quality and smaller file sizes, 150:1 ratio of compression), which is the standard used for DVD movies, and the MPEG-4, which is the latest standard for multimedia, offering the most compression and highest quality, on the Internet.

Streaming video (or streaming media, which also includes audio) in Web circles has nothing to do with water. It refers to the technique of processing data as a *continuous stream*. In other words, the file plays *while* it is being downloaded. With streaming video, your browser starts displaying the video *before* the whole file has been downloaded. It is not necessary to download the file, open it, and then view it in a browser or application. Remember, however, that the files do require streaming servers to deliver the video.

MOV

Originally for Macs, the MOV format, or Apple QuickTime movie shown in Figure 3-13, is now available for all platforms. The format delivers great quality, is *streamable,* but tends to produce large file sizes (depending of frame rate and quality). Of course, the result is longer download times and the need for more bandwidth to download the files. In addition to video, QuickTime is also capable of creating or viewing virtual reality files, like those used in sophisticated computer games.

The QuickTime plug-in is required to view MOV files. (You can download the plug-in for free from www.apple.com.) The latest version of QuickTime also supports the MPEG-4 file format, among a host of 200 media types.

Figure 3-13:
Album
allows you
to import
video clips,
such as
MOV files.

AVI

Audio/Video Interleaved, or AVI, is the native file format for Windows-based video. This simplest of video file formats was the big dog on the block before the advent of the Web. It is still a common format found on CD-ROMs.

AVI files are basically comprised of a string of JPEG images brought together in a glorified slide show. The quality of AVI files is pretty good, and the format doesn't need any special software or plug-ins to play.

Unfortunately, the file sizes are monstrous and therefore not practical for loading onto the Web unless they are highly compressed. The problem is that the compression scheme is lossy, so you have to sacrifice quality to compress the files.

AVI files are also not streamable. Advance Streaming Format, or ASF, is the successor to AVI.

Album can import video in PAL format, but the files cannot be used in any Album creations. For more on creations, see Chapter 18.

Part II
Importing, Organizing, and Managing Photos

In this part. . .

Album's got features coming out of its proverbial ears, but in order to use them, you have to bring your files into the program. Album can get photos from just about anyplace — digital cameras, scanners, CDs, hard drives. Unfortunately, it can't dive into those shoeboxes and storage totes full of snapshots and suck them into the monitor, but in Chapter 4 you find everything you need to know about importing your files from a multitude of sources. After you import your files, you can start to utilize one of Album's greatest strengths — its capability to identify, track, and organize your photos, clips, and creations. Chapters 5 and 6 show you how to create and use tags, captions, and notes to identify and organize your image inventory. Be sure to back up your catalog in case of a computer glitch or other type of catastrophe. Chapter 7 shows you to create backups of your catalog and also how to archive images onto CD or DVD to make more space available on your hard drive.

Chapter 4

Importing Files

After you've successfully installed Album and have a feel for how it works, it's time to wrangle your files and get them into the program. If you have a large inventory of files or if your images are scattered about, this process may take a good chunk of time. But the feeling of well being and peace of mind that comes from knowing all of your images are in one centralized, well-organized location is well worth any time you invest.

You can get your files into Album many ways, depending on the source they're coming from — your hard drive, CDs, your digital camera, your scanner, and so on. Album gives you a lot of assistance in finding and importing files and makes the process extremely simple. However, Album isn't quite able, at least not yet, to hook up your camera or scanner for you or look on your shelves for CDs. That manual labor is still up to you, and it's the first step toward getting stuff organized in Album.

Gathering Your Source Materials

Before you start importing your files into Album, it's a good idea to gather all your source material. Granted, you don't have to get every digital image you've gathered over the years into Album in one sitting, but may find the process to be more time efficient if you have some materials handy before you get started on the first import session. Here are some items you may want to round up:

- **Digital camera:** If you have images stored in your camera, connect your camera to the computer. Or if you're using a memory card (CompactFlash, SmartMedia and so on), insert the card into your reader or adapter, which should also be connected to the computer. If you have a digital video camera, connect that to your computer as well.

- **Photo CDs:** If you have had images burned to a Photo CD by your photofinisher or service bureau, and you want to have a record and thumbnail of those images, be sure and import them into Album. You can store the actual, high-, or full-resolution files offline, which means Album retains only the low-resolution proxy version of the files on your hard drive, and prompts you for the Photo CD when it needs to access the actual file.

  A *proxy* is like a stand-in image for the real thing. For more on storing images offline, see the section, "Importing Photos from CDs, DVDs, and Adobe Sources," later in this chapter.

- **Picture CDs:** These CDs, which are offered by Kodak photofinishing centers, contain digital copies of your prints. You may even have some really old digital copies of your prints on, gasp, floppy disks. The images are low resolution and in JPEG file format, which is great for posting on the Web or e-mailing. But they may not be appropriate for creations that you will ultimately print.

  If the only digital version of an image that you have is a low-resolution JPEG, you may want to rescan the prints yourself at a higher resolution. For more on resolution and format, see Chapter 3.

- **Stock photography CDs:** If you have acquired any stock photo CDs, you may want to have a record of the images within Album. As with Photo CDs, you can store the full-resolution files offline so your hard drive space isn't eaten up.

- **CDs and DVDs:** Dust off those CDs and DVDs to which you dutifully burned archived photos, video clips, and audio clips. Although you can't import music directly off a music CD, Album does recognize MP3 files. So any music that you have either converted to or downloaded in the MP3 format can be imported. For more on acceptable file formats, see Chapter 3.

- **Prints, slides, or negatives that need scanning:** It's time to dig out those photo albums, binders, and shoeboxes that contain years of memories. You can scan and store the images in a folder on your hard drive and import them from your hard drive, or you can import them directly into Album via the scanner. For details, see "Getting Photos from a Scanner," later in this chapter.

  If you have a lot of photos to scan, you might want to hire a sharp, quick-learning neighborhood teenager (or maybe you have one in the family) who will scan for meager wages. However, before anyone scans anything, be sure to check out Chapter 3 on resolution. Believe me, you don't want to do this job twice.

- ✔ **Videotapes that need digitizing:** Those priceless home movies need to be digitized in order to get them into Album. If you don't have the hardware and software to digitize tape, some service centers will do it for you for a reasonable fee. Album accepts Motion JPEG (commonly saved as AVI), MPEG-1 (MPG), QuickTime (MOV), and Audio/Video Interleaved (AVI) formats.

- ✔ **URLs of Web sites that contain images you want:** If you and your family and friends have shared photos online on Web sites such as Shutterfly.com, MSN Photo.com, and others, you may want to have those URLs handy so you can download those images and import them to Album.

- ✔ **Removable disks:** If you have files stored on Zip disks, Jaz disks, Bernoulli disks, or even floppy disks, have them at the ready so you can "insert and import."

- ✔ **External hard drives:** If you have any external hard drives that you use for data storage, make sure they're connected and ready to go.

Importing Files from Your Hard Drive

After you've completed the "hunting and gathering" of source materials, you're ready to start importing files into Album. When you import files from your hard drive, Album creates a *link* to those files. This means that the file itself isn't copied or embedded into the program. Instead, a low-resolution version, called a *proxy,* is imported, and the thumbnail is displayed in the Photo Well. A link is created from the proxy to the full-resolution file on your hard drive. When you need to use the full-resolution file — to print a copy or make a creation, for example — Album goes out and gets the full-resolution data and uses it.

Because the files are just links, it is important that you don't move the files from their original folder locations after importing them. If you move a file, Album will not be able to find it and will consider it a "missing file." You will then have to reconnect the file to its new location. (For more on reconnecting missing files, see Chapter 7.)

Importing photos by using menu commands

Here's how to get files into Album from your hard drive:

1. **Choose File⇨Get Photos⇨From Files and Folders.**

   You also can click the handy Get Photos button in the Shortcuts bar and choose From Files and Folders from the pop-up menu. Or you can choose Help➪Quick Guide and click the Get Photos button or the Get Photos tab. From there, click the File Folders button.

The Get Photos from Files and Folders dialog box appears (see Figure 4-1).

 2. **Navigate to the folder that contains the photos you want to import.**

    You have three choices in the types of files that will display in the list:

    - **Media Files:** Shows any photo, audio, and video files that are in formats compatible to Album.

    - **PDF Files:** Shows files in the Portable Document Format (PDF), such as those you created with the Creations Wizard (albums, slide shows, and so on).

    - **All Files:** Shows, well, everything, whether Album can import it or not. If you choose a file format that Album can't work with, a message that says "Unsupported File Format" appears where the thumbnail preview would be in the dialog box. For more on the file formats that Album supports, see Chapter 3.

 3. **Choose the method that relates to the number of files you want to import:**

    - **Single file:** Select the file from the folder. Note that if you hover your mouse over a file, info about the photo (file type, date/time, and size) displays. After you select the file, you see a thumbnail preview. If you're satisfied with your selection, click the Get Photos button, shown in Figure 4-1.

Figure 4-1:
You can import one or multiple photos into Album using the Get Photos From Files and Folders dialog box.

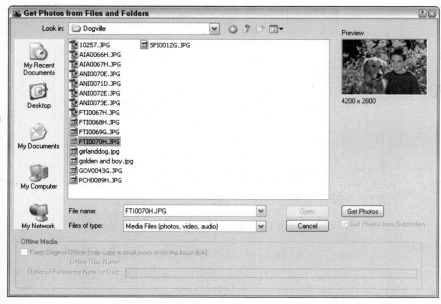

- **Multiple photos:** Select the first file you want to import, hold down the Ctrl key, and select additional files. Or you can select the first file, hold down the Shift key and click a second file, and you will select those files and all the files in between. Then click the Get Photos button.

- **All the photos in a folder:** Navigate to the folder, select it, and then click the Get Photos button.

- **All the photos stored in multiple subfolders:** Navigate to the main folder and select it. Select the Get Photos from Subfolders check box on the right side of the dialog box (refer to Figure 4-1).

4. **When you're finished selecting files, click the Get Photos button.**

   Album imports your photos into the Photo Well. Album may display a dialog box that tells you that only newly imported files are being displayed. Click OK, and if you don't want to keep seeing this dialog box, check the Don't Show Again option.

   To see all your images, click the Show All button in the Shortcuts bar or the Clear button in the Find bar above the Photo Well.

If you accidentally try to get an image you previously imported, Album tells you it wasn't imported because it already exists in your catalog, as shown in Figure 4-2.

Figure 4-2:
Album tells you which files weren't imported and why.

Items Not Imported

The items listed were not imported.

Reason	File
The file already exists in the catalog	C:\Data\Barb\Photoshop Album Images\WTR0057E.JPG

OK

You can't import a PDF creation that was made in Album, such as a Slide Show or Calendar (for example, if a relative or friend who also owns Album sends you a PDF creation). Album imports the individual files (photos, video clips, and audio clips) used in the creation, but not the actual creation. If you want to keep the creation, you will have to recreate it. For more on creations, see Chapter 18.

Importing photos by dragging and dropping

If you're a drag-and-drop kind of person, you'll be happy to know Album supports this method of importing photos. To import photos into your catalog, just drag and drop them into the Photo Well. Album creates a new file with the image, just as it does when you import using the menu commands.

You can drag and drop from your desktop, from Windows Explorer, or from image editors, such as Photoshop Elements:

- ✔ If you drag and drop from the desktop or from Windows Explorer, the file appears in the Photo Well immediately.

- ✔ If you drag from an image editor, the Getting Photos dialog box briefly appears, and then the photo appears in the Photo Well.

    Not every image editor allows you to drag photos into Album. Try it, and if it doesn't work, you can always go the conventional route and use the menu commands.

Click the Show All button in the Shortcuts bar or the Clear button in the Find bar to view all your images.

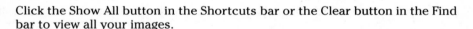

You also can export image files by dragging and dropping. See Chapter 12 for details.

Searching for files on your hard drive

Getting photos from your hard drive is fine and dandy, if you know where everything is. But what if you were a little lapse on your file housekeeping, and items are scattered high and low on your hard drive?

Being the wonderful organizer it is, Album provides a way to search for files on your computer and then allows you to pick and choose what you want. Album can find photos and video clips, but not audio clips or creation PDFs (for more on creations, see Chapter 18).

Album cannot search CDs and DVDs or network drives (like a server). But it can search external media such as Zip disks.

Here are the steps to get photos into Album by searching your hard drive:

1. **Choose File➪Get Photos➪By Searching.**

    The Get Photos by Searching for Folders dialog box appears.

2. **Select one of the following search options from the Look In drop-down menu:**

   - **All Hard Disks:** Finds all the files on your computer, which includes all installed and connected hard drives.

   - **Drive C:** Searches only the main hard drive, which is usually the C drive.

   - **My Documents:** Searches for files in the My Documents folder and its subfolders only.

   - **Browse:** Allows you to navigate and pinpoint specific locations on your computer.

3. **Deselect the Exclude System and Program Folder option, if desired.**

   By default, this option is checked, so Album searches all the folders on your computer except for System and Program folders. This relieves Album, and you, from looking through folders that probably don't contain photos and video clips. On the other hand, if you have really bad file management practices, or if someone else who uses your computer does, you may want Album to search every nook and cranny for possible rogue images.

   Files that you are using for your Windows wallpaper reside in the System folder. And sample images supplied by programs like Photoshop Elements live in the Program folder. If you want to have these files included in your catalog, then you will want to deselect the Exclude System and Program Folder option.

4. **Deselect the Exclude Files Smaller than 100K option, if desired.**

   By default this option is checked so Album ignores any file smaller than 100K. The reasoning behind this option is that any files that small are too low in resolution to be of any significance. This assumption may not be true, however, if you prepare a lot of images for to display on the Web, because such files are smaller in size by nature. You can enter in your own size criteria or uncheck the option altogether.

5. **Click the Search button.**

   Depending on your search option and the number of files you have, the search may take a couple minutes. Take a break and get a beverage or click the Cancel button if you want to end the search.

   When Album has finished its search, it displays a list of folders that contain photos and video clips in the Search Results section of the dialog box, as shown in Figure 4-3.

   If, like me, you have a bazillion folders with files, you may be a bit overwhelmed when you see the search results. My head spun, anyway.

6. **If you decide you just want to browse the folders on your own and navigate to a particular folder, click the <u>Take me there</u> link at the bottom of the dialog box.**

   The Search dialog box transports you to the Getting Photos from Files and Folders dialog box. See the section, "Importing Files from Your Hard Drive" earlier in this chapter.

7. **Select one or more folders that contain files you want to import.**

   When you select a folder, Album thankfully gives you a preview (on the right side of the dialog box) of the first few files in the folder so you can get an idea of what's in it, in case your memory is a bit foggy.

8. **Click the Import Folders button.**

   Album retrieves the files and imports them into your Photo Well.

You also can use the Quick Guide to search for files on your computer. Choose Help⇨Quick Guide. Click the Get Photos button or tab. Then click the Search Drive button. From there, follow Steps 2 through 4 above.

Figure 4-3:
You can have Album search your computer for folders containing photos and video clips.

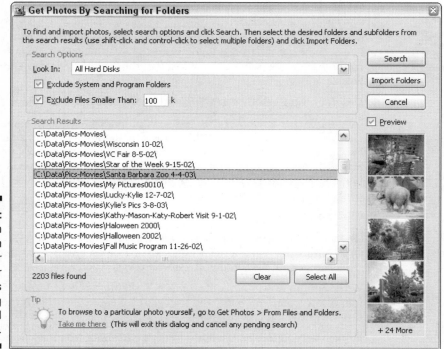

Importing Photos from Cameras and Card Readers

If you are connecting your camera directly to your computer, via a serial, USB or FireWire cable, first make sure that you have all the necessary drivers that came with your camera. If you are running Windows XP, drivers for some cameras (models of Nikon, Kodak, Olympus, and others) are already installed. Still, I recommend installing the drivers that actually came with your camera. If you don't know where the disk containing the drivers is, you should be able to download the drivers from the camera manufacturer's Web site.

 If this is the first time connecting your camera, I recommend reading the documentation that came with your camera. As dry as most manuals are, the information is usually useful. And let's face it, if the camera isn't talking to the computer, there's no way the images are getting into Album.

The exact steps you take to import photos from a digital camera also depend on the kind of driver your camera uses:

- **TWAIN drivers:** TWAIN is a universal software standard that links applications and devices, such as cameras and scanners. If your camera came with a TWAIN driver, it must be installed so that the computer and Album can talk to the camera. Also, if you are running Windows 2000 or 98SE, you will have to work with TWAIN drivers.

- **WIA (Windows Image Acquisition) drivers:** WIA can be used only if you're running Windows XP or ME. If your camera is WIA-enabled, you can get photos from your camera by clicking a single button in Album.

Some cameras mount directly to your computer like a hard drive. Getting photos from a mounted camera is similar to getting photos from a hard drive, so follow the steps in the section "Importing Photos from Your Hard Drive," earlier in this chapter.

If your camera uses a flash card or memory card, like a CompactFlash or SmartMedia, or another kind of card and you have a reader attached to your computer, Album also can import images from the reader. In fact, importing from the reader is usually faster, quicker and pretty much hassle-free. If you have a choice between importing from the camera or from the reader, I recommend going with the reader.

To get photos directly from the camera or the reader, follow these steps:

1. **Make sure that your camera or card reader is connected to the computer.**

If you are unsure how to connect the camera or card to the computer, check the documentation that came with your camera. Most likely a USB cable was included in the box along with your camera or card reader.

Manufacturers recommend that you keep the camera turned off while cabling it up. Card readers usually don't have any on and off switch, so don't worry about those being off.

If you're connecting your camera via a serial cable, turn off your camera and your *computer,* as well. If you don't, the computer may not recognize that the camera is connected.

2. **Turn on your camera.**

   At this point, some juice is needed.

   Note: If you're running Windows XP or Me and using a WIA-enabled camera, Album may begin importing your photos automatically, so you can skip the rest of the steps. Your newly imported images appear in the Photo Well. Click the Clear button to see your entire catalog.

3. **Choose File⇨Get Photos from Camera or Card Reader.**

   You also can use one of these methods:

   • Click the Get Photos button in the Shortcuts bar and choose From Camera or Card Reader from the drop-down menu.

   • Choose Help⇨Quick Guide and click the Get Photos button or tab. Click the Camera button.

   The Get Photos from Camera or Card Reader dialog box appears, as shown in Figure 4-4.

4. **Choose the name of the camera or reader from the Camera pop-up menu, if necessary.**

   If you have already established your settings in the Preferences dialog box (described in the next section), you bypass the dialog box, and your photos are imported directly into the Photo Well.

   Album may not distinguish between the camera or reader in the Camera pop-up menu. Both may appear as <Camera or Card Reader> rather than the specific name of the device. And to make matters more confusing, if you happen to have a Zip drive, it may also be called <Camera or Card Reader>. If you're not sure what device belongs to what drive letter, use Windows Explorer and check and see what contents are on each drive letter.

5. **Click the Browse button if you want to save the imported photos in a particular folder on your hard drive. In the Browse for Folder dialog box, navigate to the folder and then click OK.**

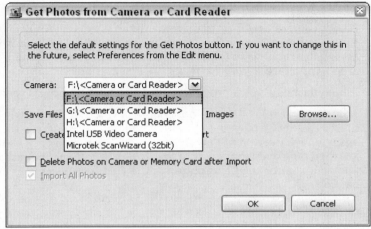

Figure 4-4:
Choose your
camera or
card reader
from the
appropri-
ately named
Get Photos
from
Camera or
Card Reader
dialog box.

By default, Album stores the files at `C:\Documents and Settings\My Pictures\Adobe\Digital Camera Photos\`. You also can create a new folder if desired.

6. **If you want to import your photos into a new subfolder, which is named using the date and time of import, select the Create Subfolder Using Date/Time of Import option.**

   This subfolder is saved inside the folder that appears in the Save Files In field. This option can come in handy if you have other folders on your computer identified by date and time, and you want to be able to readily identify this new batch of images.

7. **If you want to delete the files from your camera after they have been imported into Album, select Delete Photos on Camera or Memory Card after Import option.**

   If you choose this option, Album displays a prompt when you click OK, asking you if this is really what you want to do.

   I really don't recommend selecting this option, just in case something goes awry in the importing process. You can always delete the images later, after you're sure they have been imported successfully.

8. **The Import All Photos option is available only if you have a WIA-enabled camera. Select it if you want to import all the images on the camera.**

   If you want to select only certain photos, don't check this option.

9. **Click OK and watch the magic happen.**

   If your camera uses TWAIN drivers, Album may launch the manufacturer's software that came with your camera. If so, just follow the on-screen instructions to import the photos from your camera. If there aren't any, consult your camera's documentation.

   Album flashes a quick preview of the images as it imports them.

   Album may display a dialog box that tells you that only newly imported files are being displayed. Click OK. If you don't want to see this message again, check the Don't Show Again option before you click OK. They are then displayed in the Photo Well. Click the Shortcuts button in the Shortcuts bar or the Clear button in the Find bar to see your entire catalog.

Getting Photos from a Scanner

Album allows you to scan images and immediately import them into Album in one fell swoop. You can import photos from either a USB or an older SCSI scanner (at least I was able to). If you have problems importing with a SCSI scanner, scan your images to the hard drive and then import using the method described in the section, "Importing Files from Your Hard Drive" earlier in this chapter. Also, you can always resort to this measure if the steps below prove to be too frustrating, for whatever reason.

Before you get started, make sure that you have installed all the software (drivers and so on) that shipped with your scanner. Some scanners use TWAIN drivers (described earlier in the camera and card reader section). Other scanners use WIA (Windows Image Acquisition) drivers, which are only available on Windows XP or ME. The software enables the scanner to communicate with the computer. It is a good idea to make sure that your scanner is, in actuality, able to talk to the computer after you install the software. If necessary, run a couple of test scans using the stand-alone scanning software that came with the device.

Here are the ins and outs of importing photos from a scanner:

1. **Turn on the scanner.**

   I know this is a no-brainer, but I have to mention this step just in case it's early, and you haven't had your morning coffee. Also, it is a good idea to make sure your scanning bed is clean from dust, fingerprints, chocolate smudges and any other debris. Remember, unwanted garbage gets scanned along with your image.

2. Choose File➪Get Photos➪From Scanner.

You also can use either of these commands:

- Choose Help➪Quick Guide and click the Get Photos button or tab. Then click the Scanner button.

- Click the Get Photos button in the Shortcuts bar and choose From Scanner from the drop-down menu.

The Get Photos from Scanner dialog box appears, as shown in Figure 4-5.

3. Select your scanner from the Scanner pop-up menu.

If Album annoyingly responds with a "None Detected" message, make sure that the scanner is on and all connections are well seated.

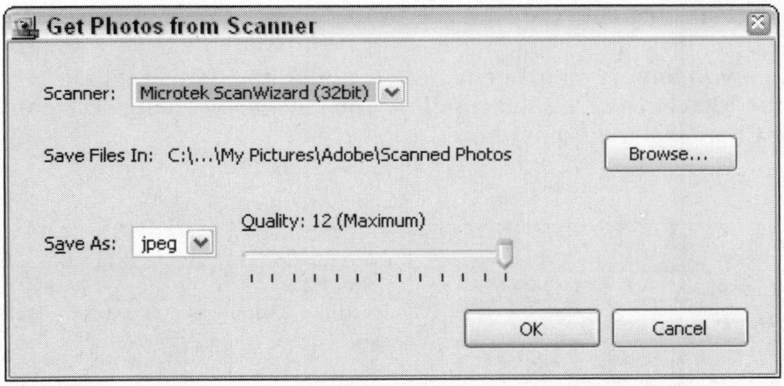

Figure 4-5:
Album
allows you
to scan and
import your
images
directly.

4. If you want to save your file in a location other than the default path shown, click the Browse button.

Navigate to your desired folder on your computer or create a new fold.

5. Choose a file format from the Save As pop-up menu.

If you are unfamiliar with file formats, check out Chapter 3.

6. If you're using the JPEG format, drag the slider to establish the quality of the image.

Album's default quality setting is Medium. A higher value results in a better quality image but larger file size. If you plan on using the file just for display on-screen, you can get away with using a lower value. However, if you plan on using the image for print, be sure and save it at a higher value. For more on JPEGs and quality settings, see Chapter 3.

7. Click the OK button.

If you're using a scanner with a TWAIN driver, Album launches the driver, and your scanning plug-in software appears. My scanning software appears in Figure 4-6. If you're familiar with using the software, you're all set. If not, read the instructions that came with the scanner to capture the scan. If you have questions on size, resolution, and color mode, refer to Chapter 3.

If you're using Windows XP, Album may launch the Windows XP scanning interface. If you're unfamiliar with using it, check your Windows documentation for details.

8. When the scan is completed, close the scanning software, if necessary.

The Getting Photos dialog box briefly flashes, and then Album imports the scan into the Photo Well.

Album may display a dialog box that tells you that only newly imported files are being displayed. Click OK. The scanned image is then displayed in the Photo Well. Click the Shortcuts button in the Shortcuts bar or the Clear button in the Find bar to see your entire catalog.

When you import an image using a scanner, the date and time of the scan is embedded in the file's information. You can easily change the date and time. See Chapter 5 to find out how.

Figure 4-6:
Album launches your scanning software to enable you to capture your image.

Importing Photos from CDs, DVDs, and Adobe Resources

When importing images from a CD or DVD, you have two options:

✔ You can import the files and have a full-resolution copy stored on your hard drive and displayed in the Photo Well.

✔ You can import them and have a proxy (a low-resolution copy) stored, while leaving the original, full-resolution image on the CD or DVD.

This is known as storing them *offline*. A proxy is like a stand-in image for the real thing. It is linked, or points to, the original, full-resolution image, and Album prompts you to insert the CD or DVD when it needs to pull that information to execute a command like printing and making creations and so on. At that time, you can choose to insert the disk to import the master image, use the low-resolution proxy, or cancel the command. Storing images offline is a good idea if you are short on hard drive storage.

Follow these steps to import files from a CD or DVD:

1. **Insert your CD or DVD in the appropriate drive.**

2. **Choose File⇨Get Photos⇨From Files and Folders.**

   Or you can use one of the following options:

   • Choose Help⇨Quick Guide and click the Get Photos button or tab. Then click the CD button.

   • Click the Get Photos button in the Shortcuts bar and choose From Files and Folders from the drop-down menu.

   The Get Photos from Files and Folders dialog box appears, as shown in Figure 4-7.

3. **Navigate to your CD or DVD drive.**

4. **Select the photos you wish to import.**

5. **If you want to copy only a proxy of the photo to your catalog, check the Keep Original Offline option. If you want to copy the full-resolution original, leave this option unchecked.**

   If you select this option, Album creates a link to the full-resolution original image on the CD/DVD.

6. **If you checked Keep Original Offline, you can choose to type in an optional Reference name for the CD or DVD for easier identification later.**

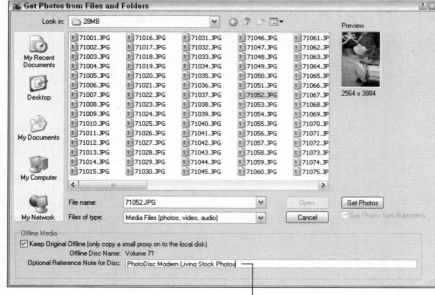

Figure 4-7:
You can
store
images from
CDs or
DVDs as
proxies or
copied
originals.

Reference name for easier identification

Although it is optional, I recommend providing a descriptive reference name so that when Album requests the master file, as described in the first paragraph, it will provide the reference name of the disk, making it easy for you to retrieve. Generic names like "Volume 71" or "Photo CD" leave a lot to be desired. Choose something more descriptive, such as PhotoDisc Modern Living Stock Photos.

7. Click the Get Photos button.

The Getting Photos dialog box appears briefly, as shown in Figure 4-8, and your images are imported in to Album.

Album may display a dialog box that tells you that only newly imported files are being displayed. Click OK if you desire, and also the Don't Show Again option to turn this prompt off.

The images are then displayed in the Photo Well. Click the Shortcuts button in the Shortcuts bar or the Clear button in the Find bar to see your entire catalog.

A photo stored offline has a CD icon on its thumbnail in the Photo Well, as shown in Figure 4-9. The link information is also referenced in the Properties pane also shown in the figure.

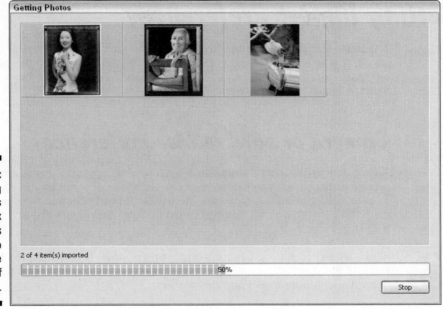

Figure 4-8:
The Getting
Photos
dialog box
appears
briefly to
show the
status of
your import.

CD icon

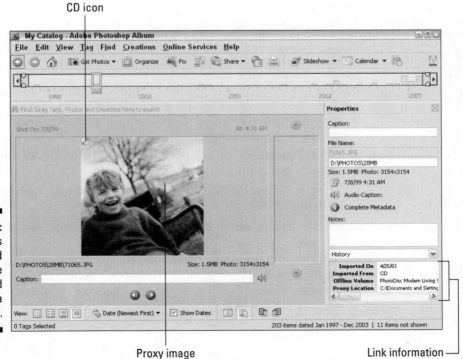

Figure 4-9:
Photos
stored
offline are
annotated
with a
CD icon.

Proxy image   Link information

Setting Import Preferences

It is helpful to set the import preferences for your various devices. Once you do so, Album will use those preferences as the defaults for all of your importing tasks. The only time you will have to change your preferences is if you want to import from another device.

Camera or card reader preferences

After you identify your camera to Album by setting your camera and card reader preferences, you can bypass the Get Photos from Camera or Card Reader dialog box when you execute the Get Photos command (unless you click the Restore Default settings button). Your photos are imported directly into the Photo Well.

If you are experiencing difficulty importing photos, try clicking the Restore Default Settings button in the Preferences dialog box to return to the original defaults, which may alleviate the problem.

Here's how to set the preferences for your camera or card reader:

1. **Choose Edit⇨Preferences.**

   The Preferences dialog box appears.

2. **Choose Camera or Card Reader from the list on the left side of the dialog box, as shown in Figure 4-10.**

3. **Choose the name of your camera from the Camera pop-up menu.**

   If you've used more than one camera, or a camera and card reader, all devices will appear in the list. If you connect a different camera, you need to select it from the list.

4. **Specify the location you want to save imported files. Also check any of the options you want.**

   For more on these options, see "Importing Photos from Cameras and Card Readers," earlier in the chapter.

5. **Check the Always Ask to Become Default Application option.**

   This action ensures that Album automatically launches when WIA-enabled cameras are attached to your computer, and your computer is running Windows XP or ME. Select this option even if you don't have a WIA-enabled camera.

6. **Click OK to close the Preferences dialog box.**

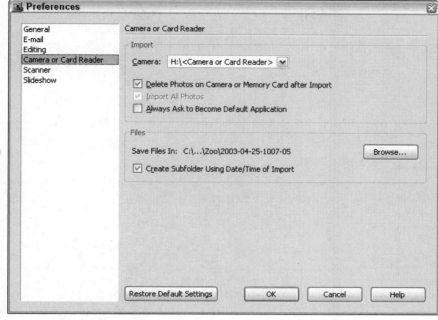

Figure 4-10:
Establish
the defaults
for your
camera
and card
reader
in the
Preferences
dialog box.

Scanner preferences

After you set your scanner preferences, the scanning process is streamlined. Essentially, you bypass the Get Photos from Scanner dialog box and are transported directly to your scanning software interface.

You will lose the flexibility in choosing file formats and Quality settings for various scans. All images are scanned to the settings established in your Preferences. If you need to change the settings, as well as the default location you are saving your scanned images to, you have to change your Preferences settings.

Here's how to set the preferences for your scanner:

1. **Choose Edit➪Preferences.**

   The Preferences dialog box appears.

2. **Choose Scanner from the Preferences list on the left side of the dialog box, as shown in Figure 4-11.**

3. **Choose your scanner from the Scanner pop-up menu.**

   If you connect your computer to a different scanner, you have to go back to the Preferences and select that scanner from the list.

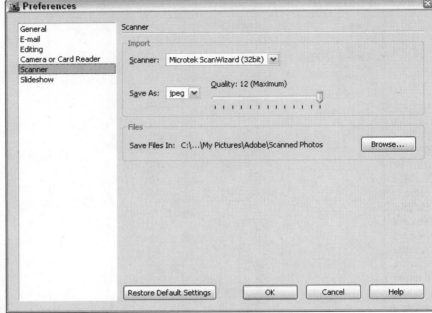

Figure 4-11:
Choose
your default
settings
for your
Scanner
in the
Preferences
dialog box.

4. **Choose a file format from the Save As pop-up menu. If you choose JPEG, select a Quality setting.**

   For more on the Quality setting, see "Getting Photos from a Scanner," earlier in this chapter. For real details, see Chapter 3 for more on file formats and Quality settings.

5. **Click the Browse button to select the location of the folder where you want your scans to be stored.**

    You can skip this step if you're satisfied with the default location.

6. **Click OK to close the Preferences dialog box.**

Preferences for offline photos

In the General section of the Preferences dialog box, you can choose a default size of the proxy images you want to store in Album. Here's how:

1. **Choose Edit⇨Preferences and click General in the list on the left side of the dialog box, as shown in Figure 4-12.**

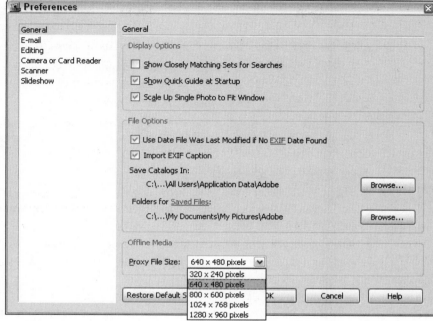

Figure 4-12:
You can
choose
a default
size for
proxy
images
whose
masters
are stored
offline.

2. **Choose the default pixel dimension for the Proxy File Size in the Offline Media section.**

   Album's default size is 640 x 480, which is a good middle-of-the-road size. A larger size (such as 1024 x 768) provides better quality, and a smaller size (such as 320 x 240) saves disk space. For particulars on pixel dimensions, see Chapter 3.

3. **Click OK to close the dialog box.**

Getting Photos from Adobe PhotoDeluxe or Adobe ActiveShare Albums

If you are a current, or most likely a former, PhotoDeluxe or Adobe ActiveShare user, Album can import images from those catalogs. I recommend consolidating your entire inventory of images into one program. Trying to remember which image resides where is just too tedious for even the most fastidious among us.

Follow these steps to import photos from Adobe PhotoDeluxe or ActiveShare:

1. **Choose File⇨Get Photos⇨PhotoDeluxe Album or ActiveShare Album.**

   Either the Finding PhotoDeluxe Albums dialog box (shown in Figure 4-13) or the Finding ActiveShare Albums dialog box appears.

2. **Choose which folders Album should search.**

   Leave the default folder to search for catalogs only in the folders associated with PhotoDeluxe or ActiveShare. Or click the Browse button to navigate to a particular folder.

3. **Click the Search button.**

   When Album is done searching, any folders containing PhotoDeluxe or ActiveShare albums appear in the Search Results list. Click a folder to preview its contents.

4. **Select a single or multiple PhotoDeluxe or ActiveShare album.**

5. **Click the Import Album button.**

   Album imports the PhotoDeluxe or ActiveShare catalogs, and the photos appear in the Photo Well.

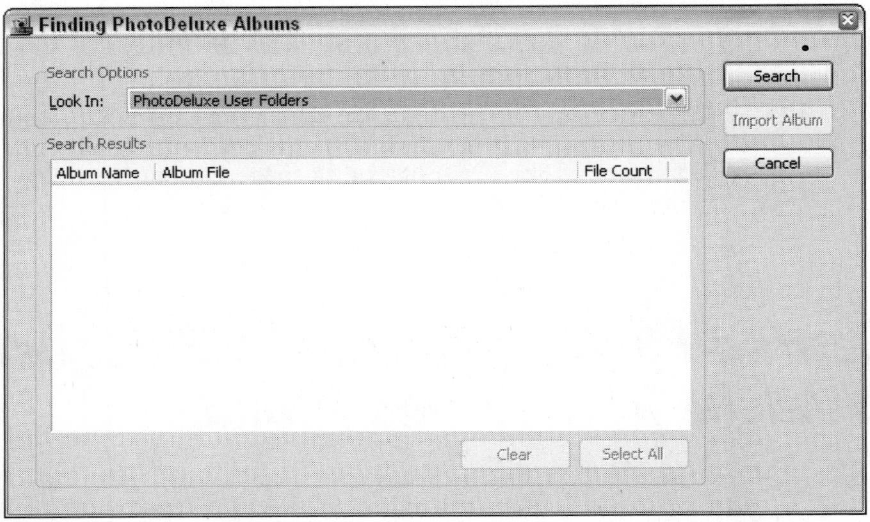

Figure 4-13:
You can seamlessly import files from Photo-Deluxe or ActiveShare albums.

Getting Images Off the Web

Album does not have a direct way to import images from the Web. If you want to bring Web images into your catalog, you must save them to your hard drive and then use the method described in the earlier section "Importing Images from Your Hard Drive."

Most images that you download from the Web, unless otherwise noted, are low resolution and not really suitable for any applications, such as printing, which require higher resolutions. They are fine for displaying on alternate Web sites, for viewing in e-mail messages, or for slide shows to be displayed on-screen.

Make sure that any images you get from the Web are not copyright protected. There are numerous sites that offer free or inexpensive, copyright-free images for your personal use. And of course, there are also great sites such as Getty Images, Corbis, ThinkStock, and PhotoSpin, all of which offer high-quality, high-resolution photos (priced accordingly of course) for business and personal use.

Chapter 5

Organizing, Categorizing, and Cross-Referencing Photos

Album's greatest strength, in my humble opinion, is its ability to help you organize all your digital images. Album allows you to sort and view your images in the Photo Well by a particular date or range of dates, import batch, folder locations, color similarity, media type and tags. How you sort and view your images is totally up to you, and you may find one particular method works better than others depending on what you are doing or looking for. In my opinion, one of the best organizational tools is the tagging function. Tags are like keywords that you attach to your file.

Although you can organize your files by date and use the timeline and calendar to track down files, tags kick it up a notch by adding descriptive information to help identify and later find your files quickly and efficiently. For example, say you have no idea when you took such-and-such image. After the 1,000th snapshot, dates can begin to blur. Having to scroll through a year's worth (or even a few months' worth) of images can be time consuming, especially if you have a lot of files.

Using tags also can unburden you from assigning pertinent filenames to your images or grouping them into folders by topic. You can actually get lazier while getting more organized. What a concept.

TIP

This chapter focuses on using the Photo Well and the tag categorization system to organize files. You also can organize your files by adding information to them in the form of captions, notes, and audio annotations. This additional method for keeping your digital images straight really works and isn't a whole lot of extra effort. To find more information about using captions and notes to identify, organize, and find your photos, see Chapter 6.

Organizing Photos in the Photo Well

Album allows you to view your whole collection of images in one central location — the Photo Well. (See Chapter 2 for more on the Photo Well.) This fact is true no matter where your files reside — on the hard drive, on a CD, on a CompactFlash card, and so on.

Album automatically organizes your photos in the Photo Well by the following criteria:

- Date (Newest First)
- Date (Oldest First)
- Import Batch
- Folder Location
- Color Similarity

Select a different viewing arrangement or a different range in the timeline, and your photos will be organized and displayed accordingly in the Photo Well.

Selecting a viewing arrangement

I cover sorting by these criteria in detail in Chapter 9, but I'll give you the condensed version here. You can select a viewing arrangement a couple ways:

- Choose View➪Arrangement and select one of the sorting criteria.
- Click the Photo Well Arrangement button (also known as the Sort button) in the Options bar and do the same.

Either way, Album displays your images in the Photo Well accordingly. For example, if you choose Date (Newest First), your images are organized from the newest creation date to the oldest, as shown in Figure 5-1. Choosing Folder Location organizes and displays your images by the name and location in which they are contained.

Timeline   Endpoint markers

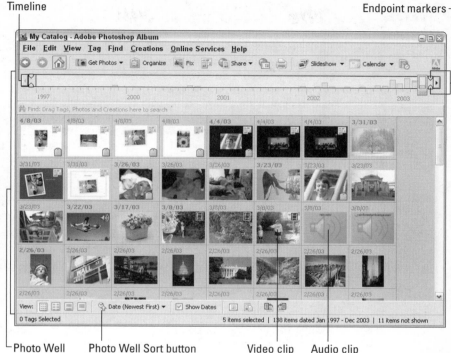

Figure 5-1:
You can
organize
and display
your files in
the Photo
Well based
on date,
folder
location,
import
batch, or
color.

Photo Well   Photo Well Sort button   Video clip   Audio clip

Using the timeline

You also can organize your photos by using the timeline. The timeline, which
appears above the Photo Well, displays bars that represent the number of
photos you have in a given month, folder, or batch, depending on how your
photos are organized in the Photo Well. Using the timeline, you can find and
organize photos based on a range you establish by dragging the endpoint
markers at either end. For example, if your images are organized by date, you
can drag the endpoint markers to set a range of time in the timeline. Album
then displays photos with dates that are within that timeframe. For more on
the timeline, see Chapter 8.

I use the word "photos" loosely in the preceding paragraph. Depending on
what media types you have selected (View➪Media Types), you may see creations, video clips, and audio clips, in addition to photos (refer to Figure 5-1).
Of course, if you want to narrow down the media types that are displayed in
the timeline, just choose the file type you're interested in from the
View➪Media Types menu.

Changing the Date of a Photo

Dates are used extensively in Album to identify, find, and organize your files. Most digital cameras automatically embed the date and time when you take a photo, and when you scan an image, the date and time of the scan is recorded by your computer's operating system, so using dates as a sorting criteria makes a lot of sense and shouldn't waste too much of your time.

At some point, you may need to change the date of a file. Maybe your camera's clock was wrong or the photo you took on vacation was in another time zone from your camera. Or you may have scanned some vintage shots of your great grandparents and want the date to reflect 1900 instead of 2003. Or possibly, you just want to make a group of photos reflect a certain fixed date for organizing and locating purposes. Whatever the case, you can adjust the date and time of a file by following these steps:

1. **Select your desired photo(s) in the Photo Well.**

   You also can change the dates of video and audio clips and creations.

2. **Choose Edit⇨Adjust Date and Time.**

   You also can use any of these options:

   - Click the date or time on the file's thumbnail. Your mouse pointer looks like a pointing finger.

   If you don't see any dates, be sure and check the Show Dates option in the Options bar. Or choose View⇨Show Dates and Tags. The thumbnail method works for all Photo Well views. For more on views, see Chapter 9.

   - Right-click an image thumbnail and choose Adjust Date and Time from the context-sensitive menu.

   - If you have selected a single photo, you can click the Adjust Date and Time button in the Properties pane, shown in Figure 5-2. For details on the Properties pane, see Chapter 6.

   The Adjust Date and Time dialog box appears, as shown in Figure 5-3.

3. **Select one of the following options:**

   - **Change to a Specified Date and Time:** Select this option to manually change the date and time, and then click OK. In the Set Date and Time dialog box, enter your desired date. If you don't know the date, you can select the question marks from the pop-up menu. Choose the time, if you know it. If you are unsure (or aren't that picky), you can select Unknown. Click OK when you're done.

Figure 5-2:
You can
change the
date and
time of
a single
photo in the
Properties
pane.

- **Change to Match File Date and Time:** Select this option to have Album change the time to the modified date of the file, and then click OK. For example, you may have shot an image on March 23, 2003, and cropped it and removed red eye in Album on April 10, 2003. The date of the image is March 23, but if you select the Change to Match File Date and Time, the date of the image changes to April 10.

- **Shift by Set Number of Hours (Time Zone Adjust):** Select this option to adjust the time by a certain number of hours, and then click OK. In the Time Zone Adjust dialog box, select either Ahead or Back and select the number of hours you want to adjust. Click OK when done. This is a great option if you want to adjust the date and time of those vacation photos you took in Europe or Asia.

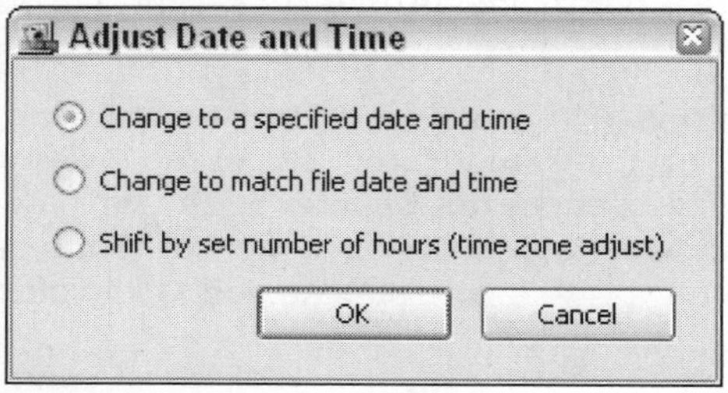

Figure 5-3:
Select your
desired
option in the
Adjust Date
and Time
dialog box.

Adjust Date and Time

- Change to a specified date and time
- Change to match file date and time
- Shift by set number of hours (time zone adjust)

OK   Cancel

Album adjusts the date and time and embeds the new information in the image's metadata. Metadata is information about the image, such as information about your digital camera settings, that is stored along with the file. Depending on the new date and time, the file dutifully takes its new position in the Photo Well.

Occasionally, you may see a file that has a question mark instead of a date. This indicates that the date is unknown. Maybe the clock on your digital camera wasn't cooperating at the time you shot your images. Don't worry; you can assign the date and time of your choice using the above steps. If you want to round up all those stray doggies, choose Find➪Items with Unknown Date or Time.

Creating Subcategories and Custom Tags

In Album, calling yourself a tagger is a good thing and won't result in the City Graffiti Removal Unit paying you a visit. While you can organize your images by date, folder, batch, or color and be perfectly content, attaching tags to your files puts you in the major leagues of organization.

Tags are tidbits of descriptive information that you attach to your files. You can use tags to group types of images together for easy access. For example you may want to tag some images with a keyword, such as Family or Places. By default, Album categorizes tags into four categories of tags: People, Places, Events, and Other.

When you attach a tag to a file, the tag appears as an icon on your image thumbnail, as shown in Figure 5-4, and the descriptive keyword displays in both the Properties and Tags panes and in the Large Thumbnail and Single Photo views (also shown in Figure 5-4) in the Photo Well.

Tags are powerful for several reasons:

- ✔ The additional identifying information makes finding and organizing your files easier, quicker, and more specific.
- ✔ You don't have to remember the name, date, or location of your files.
- ✔ You don't have to go through the hassle of filing your images in folders by topic. Album performs the manual labor for you and wrangles the tagged files from wherever they're located. To get the lowdown on using tags to locate your images, check out Chapter 9. The next few sections take a look at the Tags pane, which manages the world of tags, and tag categories. You find out how to create subcategories and custom tags.

Tags can be applied not only to photos, but also to video and audio clips and to creations.

Tag icon Tag

Tag

2/26/03

Find: Drag Tags, Photos and Creations here to search

Shot On: 2/26/03   At: 9:47 AM

Europe

Figure 5-4:
Tags
displayed
in Large
Thumbnail
and Single
Photo
views.

Europe-01.jpg   Size: 2.4MB Photo: 2565x3885

Caption:

Europe

Large Thumbnail view   Single Photo view

Using the Tags pane

To display the Tags pane, choose View⇨Tags. (You also can click the
Organize button in the Shortcuts bar.) The Tags pane is control central for
working with tags. By default, tags fall into four categories of tags: People,
Places, Events, and Other. If you don't have a large inventory of files, these
default categories may be sufficient. But if you need more specificity, you can
add your own subcategories. And if you need even more identification, you
can create your own custom tags under a category or subcategory.

You can attach one or more tags to a file. For example you may have all of
your family photos tagged with the Family tag. Within that group of family
photos, some may also be tagged with a Christmas tag or a Vacation tag.
This cross-reference allows you to quickly find all family photos or just the
family photos that were taken at Christmas or while on vacation, as shown
in Figure 5-5. And like I mentioned above, these files can be stored in different
folders or on CDs or elsewhere in your system.

If you make a mistake or decide you aren't happy with the way you have
tagged and organized your images, you can always edit your tags, or even
delete them and start over.

The Tags pane displays and manages all of your various tags, including category tags, subcategory tags, and the custom tags you create within those two groups.

As you can see in Figure 5-6, you can use the Tags pane to click buttons to create, attach, edit, select, and delete tags. You also can choose various viewing options; for example, you can choose small, medium, or large icons for your tags, and organize the tags in alphabetical order. Click the triangle to the left of the tag name to view or hide subcategories or custom tags.

Working with tag categories

As I mention earlier, Album provides you with four default tag categories: People, Places, Events, and Other, as shown in Figure 5-7. These four categories cannot be edited or deleted, so learn to love them. You also cannot create a new tag category.

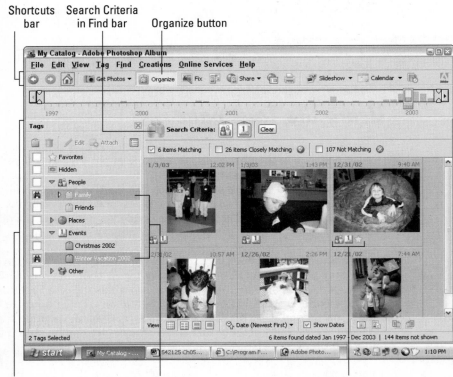

Figure 5-5: Attaching multiple tags enables you to pinpoint the images you're looking for.

New
tag   Delete   Edit   Attach   View options

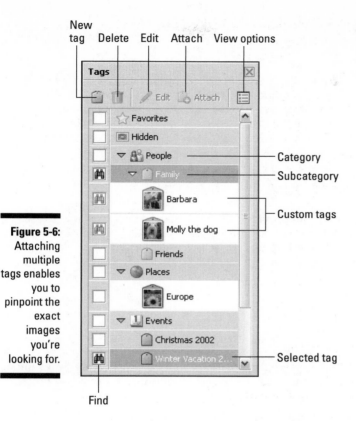

Category

Subcategory

Custom tags

Figure 5-6:
Attaching
multiple
tags enables
you to
pinpoint the
exact
images
you're
looking for.

Selected tag

Find

But don't let this fact deter you from taking advantage of the ample organizational opportunities that the existing tag categories give you. You can create and organize your own subcategories and custom tags, arranging them in countless permutations in the default categories.

Although you can attach category tags to files, category tags are best used as organizational headings for other more descriptive subcategories or custom tags. For example, the People category doesn't really tell you a whole lot, except that human beings are involved. A subcategory of "Family" or "Friends" is a little more descriptive. And a custom tag of "Joe" is more descriptive yet.

Here are a few tips on how you can use the four default categories:

✔ **People:** The People category is for tags featuring, well, humans. (If you consider the family pet worthy of the People category, I'm certainly not going to argue with you.)

Figure 5-7:
There are
four tag
categories.

By default, Album graciously provides you with two subcategories under People — "Family" and "Friends" (refer to Figure 5-7). But if you prefer, you can either edit or delete these subcategories.

✔ **Places:** You can use the Places category for tags that tell where a photo was taken. You can create tags based on particular destinations, such as "Japan," "New York City," or "Vacation Cottage, Lake Winnebago." Or you may want to add Places tags that represent generic locales, such as "The Beach" (which contains every picture you ever took of anyone at any beach) or "School" (which contains every school picture, from kindergarten to law school graduation).

You can create custom tags under the subcategories as well. For example, if the subcategory is Japan, you could then create custom tags such as "Mt. Fuji," "Tokyo," and "Kyoto" to further identify the images.

✔ **Events:** The tags you can create in the Events category are endless. For example, holidays, birthdays, reunions, graduations, sporting events, competitions, performances, and vacations are all possible Events subcategories.

Although you could then create separate custom tags for the year of each event, for example, "First Birthday," "Second Birthday," and so on, you don't have to. You can just use the timeline to select your desired date. Then only those tagged photos with that specific date will appear in the Photo Well. For more on using the timeline, see Chapter 8.

✔ **Other:** I am sure you have a few files that don't fit nicely in the preceding three categories. That's where the Other category comes in handy. You can create subcategories for "Work," "Hobbies," "Church," "Volunteering," "Barn Raisings," or plain old "Miscellaneous." And, of course, you can have lots of custom tags under those and other subcategories.

Using the Favorites and Hidden tags

In addition to the four default categories, Album provides you with two special tags — the Favorites and Hidden tags (refer to Figure 5-7). Here's the scoop on these tags:

✔ **Favorites:** The name of this tag pretty much says it all. Attach this tag to your most beloved files. The unique thing about the Favorites tag is that it instantly whittles down your search results with a single click of the mouse. For example, say you created a tag with your child's name, as described earlier in this chapter, in "Working with tag categories." You can then tag your favorite pictures of your child with a Favorites tag. When you want to gather images of your child to create an Album to send to the grandparents at the holidays, simply select the child's tag and the Favorites tag as your search criteria. In an instant, your favorite images of your child appear in the Photo Well for you to use in your creation, as shown in Figure 5-8. No more scrolling through screens of photos. For more on finding images, check out Chapter 8.

TIP

Organizing family photos

You may want to create custom tags under the Family or Friends category with the specific names of family members or friends. Here's an example scenario to get your organizational juices flowing.

Say you attach the Family tag to all family members. Makes sense, right? Well, why not have custom tags called "Dad" and "Mom" that you attach to all photos with either Dad or Mom in them? If you have photos of dad and mom together, you can attach both the "Mom" and "Dad" tags to those photos.

Here's how this organization can really help you down the line. When you're planning mom and dad's golden wedding anniversary party, you will be able to locate any photos of them both within micro seconds. A few more micro seconds and you could create an eCard invitation to the anniversary party and e-mail it to all of the guests. No doubt, you will earn family hero status for that.

Favorites tag

Figure 5-8:
Attaching
a Favorites
tag enables
you to find
your favorite
tagged
photos.

✔ **Hidden:** If you have files you don't want to see or sort through, but that you still want to keep, attach the Hidden tag to them. Files that you attach Hidden tags to only appear in the Photo Well when you perform a search with the Hidden tag as a search criteria.

Examples of candidates for the Hidden tag may be those mediocre shots that you want to keep as backups, or photos that are similar but not exact (different poses of a person). Or maybe you have some files that are embarrassing, like those video clips you've considered sending to "America's Funniest Videos."

The Hidden tag can be attached in addition to other tags. But unlike the Favorites tag, it does not carry a preference in searches. For example, if you use Family and Hidden as your two search criteria, your results will show *all* photos with the Family tag, including images that have been tagged as Hidden. Your search results will *not* show just those Family tagged images that are also tagged with Hidden.

After attaching a Hidden tag to a photo, you still see the photo in the Photo Well until you refresh the Photo Well. You refresh the Photo Well by choosing View➪Refresh or by pressing F5. Or you can select a different view of the Photo Well by using the View buttons in the Options bar.

Creating tag subcategories

Because Album gives you only four main categories and doesn't allow you to add any more, you have to rely on creating subcategories to help further identify, organize, and find your files. Here's how to create new subcategories:

1. **Choose Tag⇨New Sub-Category.**

   You also can right-click a tag category and choose Create a New Sub-Category from the context-sensitive menu.

   The Create New Sub-Category dialog box appears.

2. **Type the name of your subcategory.**

   For example, type **Clowns** if you have a large collection of clown photographs that you'd like to group together.

3. **Choose the category under which you would like to place your subcategory from the Category pop-up menu, shown in Figure 5-9.**

   For example, if the clowns are members of your family, choose Family.

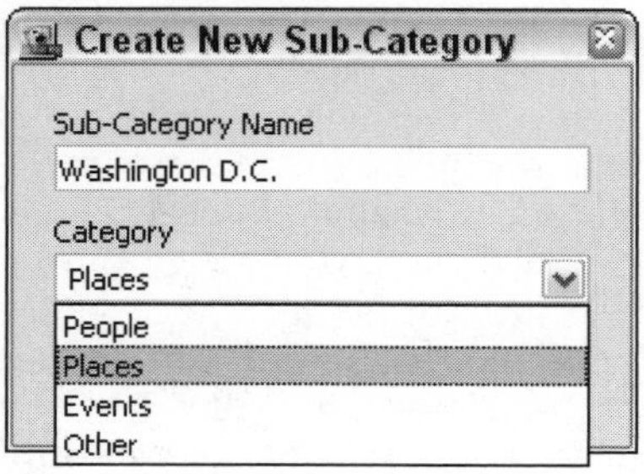

Figure 5-9:
Creating subcategories helps to further define and organize your photos.

Create New Sub-Category
Sub-Category Name
Washington D.C.
Category
Places
People
Places
Events
Other

4. **Click OK.**

   Your new subcategory now appears in the Tags pane.

   The icon of a subcategory tag always appears as a plain tag. It cannot display a photo like a custom tag can. (See the next section for more on creating custom tags.)

Creating custom tags

The most definitive kind of tag is one that you create to fit the photos you have in your repertoire. Tags that you create with specific, personalized descriptions help to categorize and organize your inventory of files into groups that have a common element and allow you to locate and gather them on your system quickly and efficiently.

You can use custom tags in addition to, or in lieu of, subcategorical tags. What counts is that the tags are useful and meaningful to you and that they enable you to be as organized — and as productive — as possible.

To create a custom tag, follow these steps:

1. **Click the Create New Tag button in the Tags pane.**

   You also can choose Tag⇨New Tag. Or you can right-click a category or subcategory tag and choose Create New Tag from the context-sensitive menu.

   The Tag Icon Editor dialog box appears.

2. **From the pop-up menu, choose the Category or Subcategory under which you want the tag to be organized.**

   For example, you can choose the Events category.

   You also can choose New Sub-Category from the pop-up menu to create a subcategory for this custom tag.

3. **Type the name of the custom tag in the Tag text box.**

   For example, type **Vacation 2003**.

4. **Type a note if you wish to provide more descriptive information regarding the tag.**

   For example, if your tag is "Vacation 2003," you may want to add a note that says, "Summer family vacation in Washington, D.C., June 2003."

5. **Click OK to close the dialog box.**

   You won't see a photograph on the tag icon when you first create it. Instead, you see a question mark, as shown in Figure 5-10. When you attach the tag to your files, the first file in the Photo Well supplies the thumbnail photo for the icon. You also can edit the icon photo if you want. See the section "Modifying and deleting tags" later in this chapter.

Using folders to create subcategories and tags

If you have your music CDs alphabetized and you feel faint if someone returns a CD out of that alpha order, you probably already have your digital image files grouped in appropriately named folders on your hard drive.

You can extend your tagging system to your pre-existing folder structure by using the Folder Location command to display your files and then create tags.

Figure 5-10: Custom tags display a question mark icon until you attach them to files.

Here's how to apply tags to an entire folder of images in one fell swoop:

1. **Choose View⇨Arrangement⇨Folder Location.**

   You also can choose Folder Location by using the Photo Well Arrangement button in the Options bar. For more on viewing files, see Chapter 9.

   Your files are then displayed in the Photo Well by the folder where they reside. The folder's pathname appears above the thumbnails, as shown in Figure 5-11.

2. **Scroll through the Photo Well until you see the folder of images you want.**

3. **Using the Tags pane, create the tag for your folder. Or you also can create a subcategory by choosing Tag⇨New Sub-Category.**

   Details on how to do either are described above in the sections "Creating tag subcategories" and "Creating custom tags."

4. **Click the folder pathname in the Photo Well to select all the images in that folder.**

5. **Click the Attach button in the Tags pane.**

   The tag is now attached to all the images in that folder. See the next section for more on attaching tags.

Folder pathname

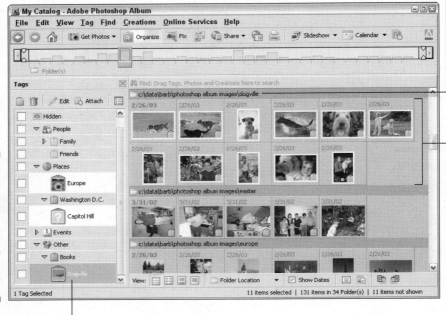

Figure 5-11:
You can use images already grouped in folders as a basis for your tagging system.

Tag

Selected photos in folder

Attaching, Editing, and Deleting Tags

Coming up with really descriptive tags is the hardest thing about tagging. Attaching, editing and removing the tags once they are created is a cinch. In the next few sections, you find out how to attach, edit, and remove the tags.

Attaching tags to photos

Attaching tags is a no-brainer. You can drag a tag from the Tags pane onto a file or select the file in the Photo Well and click the Attach Selected Tag(s) to Selected Photo(s) button in the Tags pane.

Here are the specific steps for attaching tags:

1. **Select your desired photo(s) in the Photo Well.**

2. **In the Tags pane, select the tag you want to attach to those files.**

   If you want to select more than one tag, Ctrl+click to select multiple tags.

3. **Click the Attach Selected Tag(s) to Selected Photo(s) button in the Tags pane.**

   Or you can use one of these methods:

   - Drag the tags from the Tags pane onto the photo (or onto any one of the multiple photos) in the Photo Well.

   - Choose Tag⇨Attach (1) Selected Tag. If you have more than one, the command will read (2) or (3) and so on.

   The tag is now attached to the photo(s). If this is the first time you have attached the tag to a photo, the photo becomes the icon for that tag. If you select multiple photos, the first photo in the Photo Well becomes the icon for that tag.

You also can select your photo(s) in the Photo Well and then choose Tag⇨Attach Tag. Select your desired tag from the sub-menu. However, this method only allows you to select one tag at a time.

In the Small and Medium Thumbnail views, to identify which tags are attached to a file, position your mouse over the tag icon on the thumbnail in the Photo Well. The name of the tag displays on-screen.

Removing tags

The process of removing tags is easy and pain-free. Removing a tag from a file is not the same thing as deleting the tag category altogether. When you remove a tag, you merely detach the categorization from that particular file or files. When you delete a tag, you remove the tag entirely from your catalog.

To remove a tag, you can be in any of the views — the Single Photo, Small, Medium, or Large Thumbnail view. Right-click a tag and choose Remove Tag from the context-sensitive menu. For more on viewing your files, see Chapter 9.

If you want to remove tags from multiple photos, select your desired photos in the Photo Well. Then right-click any of the selected photo thumbnails and choose Remove Tag from Selected Items from the context-sensitive menu that appears. Choose the tags you wish to remove from the sub-menus. You also can choose Tag⇨Remove Tag from Selected Items and choose the tags from the sub-menu.

Modifying and deleting tags

After you create a tag or two, you may decide that what you came up with wasn't that descriptive after all and needs a little refining. Or maybe you want to add a note to an existing tag or change the photo that is being used for the tag icon. You may just want to delete the darn tag altogether. No problem. Just remember you can't touch the four main tag categories; nor can you modify or delete the Favorites or Hidden tag.

Here's how to modify your tags:

1. **Select the tag in the Tags pane and choose Tag⇨Edited Selected Tag.**

   You also can click the Edit button at the top of the Tags pane. Or you can right-click your chosen tag and choose Edit Tag from the context-sensitive menu that appears. The name of your tag appears in the Edit command.

   The Tag Icon Editor dialog box appears.

2. **Edit the tag information to your heart's desire.**

   - **To modify the category:** Choose a category or subcategory from the Category pop-up menu. If you choose New Sub-Category, you will get the Create New Sub-Category dialog box where you can enter your information.

   - **To modify the tag's name:** Type the new name in the Tag Name text box.

   - **To add or change the note:** Type in the Notes text box.

   - **To change the photo being used for the tag icon:** Click the Edit Icon button, shown in Figure 5-12. Click the Find button to open the Select Icon dialog box. Scroll through all of the images that use that tag, select the image you want, and click OK.

     You also can click the arrows to the left and right of the Find button to browse through the tagged images and select the one you want. Adjust the *cropping marquee* (the moving dashed line) by dragging the corner handles (your mouse icon changes to a double-headed arrow) to frame the photo to your liking. To move the entire marquee, place your cursor inside the marquee and drag. Click OK. For more on cropping, see Chapter 11.

3. **When you're done modifying the tag, click OK in the Tag Icon Editor dialog box.**

If you would just rather delete a tag and start fresh, you can do so. Select the tag in the Tags pane and click the Deleted Selected Tag button. Or you can choose Tag⇨Delete Selected Tag.

You can't delete more than one tag at a time.

Figure 5-12:
You can change the photo used for the icon of your tag.

When deleting tags, don't press the Delete key on your keyboard. Album will try and delete *actual* photos. A warning will appear on-screen telling you that you need to select the photos first, however, so you have a chance to cancel the command.

Chapter 6

Giving Your Photos a Better Identity

*I*f you have been poking around in Album a bit, I am sure you have gotten the feeling that this program loves to provide you with data. Without trying too hard, you can find all kinds of data about your images, from where they originated, to when they came into existence, what you did with them, and where they are currently stored. Album is like a digital private detective when it comes to identifying your files.

You can contribute to that profiling of your images by adding additional information. Album lets you give descriptive names to your files and add captions, notes and audio captions. You'll find many opportunities to add descriptive tidbits. For example, you can add data directly in your images, in creations, galleries, and contact sheets. Captions and notes help you not only identify and find your images, but also to enhance your presentations. Use them in a fun and creative way, and they can make your images and creations really come to life.

You also can use captions, notes and annotations as a basis to search for your files. For details on how, check out Chapter 8.

Renaming Your Photos

As wonderful as digital cameras are, their naming conventions leave a little to be desired. I mean `DSCN0423.jpg` really doesn't tell you much about the image. And if you have traditional images that have been converted from film to a Photo CD you also have funky names like 834044.pcd or something equally useless when all you want is to find a picture of Roger, your pet cockatiel.

Although it isn't mandatory to rename your files for Album to find and manage them, you may want to do so in order to have the easily identifiable to you.

Renaming is a snap in Album. You can rename a single file or a group of files in one fell swoop. The following sections give you the skinny.

Renaming a single file

To rename a single file, select your desired item in the Photo Well and choose one of these two options:

1. **Choose File⇨Rename.**

   The Rename dialog box (shown in Figure 6-1) appears.

2. **Type a name in the New Name text box and click OK.**

Or

1. **Choose View⇨Properties to display the Properties pane.**

   You also can click the Show Properties button in the Options bar beneath the Photo Well.

2. **Enter a new name in the File Name text box.**

   If the photo has been edited, it will say Edited File Name.

If you change your mind, you can undo by pressing Ctrl+Z immediately after renaming.

Renaming a group of files

Your files will be *batch-renamed.* This means that after you assign something called a *common base name,* each file gets that base name along with a numeric suffix. For example, if you assign the common base name Europe, the first photo is named Europe-1, the next one Europe-2, and so on. Note that Album renames the files according to the order in which they appear in the Photo Well.

If you batch rename an edited or duplicated photo, it loses its "_edited" or "_copy" suffix. The name of the original file remains undisturbed.

Figure 6-1:
Renaming files allows you to make obscure camera-assigned names more descriptive.

And if, by chance, you already had an existing file with a batch rename name (say that five times fast), Album adds an additional suffix. For example, if a filename Europe-1 is already in your catalog, the renamed file is Europe-1-1.

To rename a group of files, follow these steps:

1. **Select your desired files in the Photo Well.**

   Ctrl+clicking allows you to select both adjacent and nonadjacent items.

2. **Choose File⇨Rename.**

3. **Enter a name in the Common Base Name text box, shown in Figure 6-2, and click OK.**

Figure 6-2:
Batch rename your files to give grouped images sequential order.

Using Captions with Your Images

There are utilitarian reasons for adding captions to your photos. Captions provide descriptions of the image, such as who is in the image, who took the image, where and when the image was taken, and so on. Captions also are great if you want to add a personal touch to your images and to preserve a memorable occasion. Add a caption with some humor or sentimentality. You are limited to 63 characters, so short and sweet is the ticket. You can add a caption when you first import your images or at any time thereafter.

Adding a caption

You also can use captions in creations, such as eCards, Web and 3D Atmosphere galleries, calendars, photo books, video CDs, slide shows, instant slide shows, and albums.

If you plan to use captions in a creation, you have to add the captions *before* you make your creation. If you don't, no captions will appear with your images. (For more on making creations, see Chapter 18.) Also, when you print a contact sheet, you can choose to include captions. But again, the captions must be added before you print the sheet.

Here's how to add captions to your files:

1. **Select a file and double-click the thumbnail to open the image in Single Photo view in the Photo Well.**

   Or you can choose View⇨Properties to display the Properties pane. Then select a thumbnail in the Photo Well.

2. **Enter your caption in the Caption text box, as shown in Figure 6-3.**

When you duplicate a photo, you also duplicate any captions, notes, and tags attached to that image. Be sure to apply all those extras before you duplicate your image to save time. For more on duplicating photos, see Chapter 7.

Editing and deleting captions

Editing or deleting a caption is a no-brainer. Use one of these methods:

- Select the image in the Photo Well, and in the Properties pane, highlight the text in the Caption text box and retype your caption. To delete the text, simply highlight the text and press the Delete key.

Caption

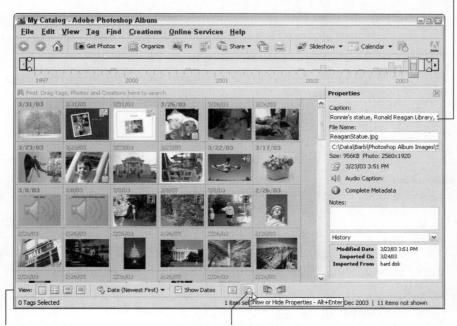

Figure 6-3:
Adding
captions
helps to
identify and
personalize
your photos.

Options bar   Show Properties button

✔ Double-click the image, and in the Single Photo view, edit or delete the text in the Caption text box below the image.

✔ Select one or more images and choose Edit⇨Clear Caption for a single image or Edit⇨Clear Captions of Selected Items to delete several captions at a time.

Adding Notes to Photos

The Notes function in Album is great for identifying your photos and adding information related to the images. You can have up to 1,023 characters in a note. Or on the more practical side, you could enter information such as the lighting conditions or camera settings (that aren't part of the embedded metadata) you used to capture the image.

If you have images that represent unforgettable events, try adding a personal recollection or short story about the image in the form of a note.

To add a note to an image, follow these short steps:

1. **Choose View⇨Properties to display the Properties pane.**

   You also can click the Show Properties button in the Options bar.

2. **Select your desired image in the Photo Well.**

3. **Enter your text in the Notes text box in the Properties pane, as shown in Figure 6-4.**

Note

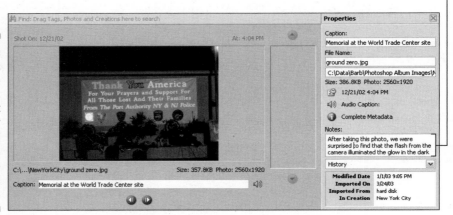

Figure 6-4:
Use notes
to include
memories,
short
stories, or
practical
information
such as
camera
settings.

REMEMBER

Unlike captions, you can only view your notes on-screen. You can't print them along with your images. You also can't include notes in your creations. However, like captions, you can search for your images based on keywords in your notes.

Adding Audio Captions

If you have a microphone attached to your computer, you can easily add audio captions to your files. You can add them in addition to, or in lieu of, written captions and notes.

Like other kinds of captions, you can use audio captions to provide practical information such as descriptions (who took the picture, what the picture is of, and when and where it was taken). Or you can use them to preserve a memory with sound.

Here's how to add an audio caption:

1. **Select your desired photo in the Photo Well.**

2. **Choose View➪Properties to display the Properties pane.**

   Or click the Show Properties button in the Options bar under the Photo Well.

3. **Click the Record Audio Caption button in the Properties pane, shown in Figure 6-5.**

   The audio window, also shown in Figure 6-5 appears.

4. **Click the Record button in the audio window and begin speaking into your microphone.**

   If you have an existing audio clip you want to use as your audio caption, choose File➪Browse from the audio window menu, locate your file and click Open. The audio clip is imported into your audio window. Note the filename of the audio clip at the top of the audio window.

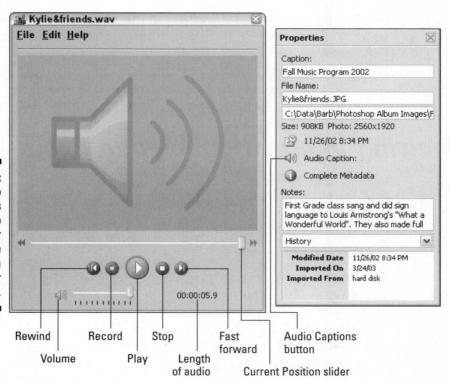

Figure 6-5: Audio captions can help to further preserve the memory of a milestone or occasion.

5. **Click the Record or Stop button when you're done recording your audio caption.**

6. **Click the Play button to listen to your audio caption. If you want to do a second take, click the Record button again.**

7. **Click the Close button to close the audio window.**

You also can choose File⇨Close from the audio window menu. This action automatically saves the audio caption and attaches it to your photo.

Here's some useful information for handling your audio captions:

✔ **Playing an audio caption:** You can play captions in a couple of ways:

• Double-click the image thumbnail to display the photo in the Single Photo view. Click the Play Audio Caption button (which looks like a mini speaker icon), located immediately to the right of the written Caption text box.

• Select your photo and click the Record Audio caption button in the Properties pane.

In either case, the audio window appears. Click the Play button to hear the caption. Close the window when you're done.

✔ **Editing an existing audio caption:** Repeat all of the steps above.

✔ **Deleting an audio caption:** Follow Steps 1 through 3 above. Then choose Edit⇨Clear to delete the audio caption from the image.

Viewing Information About a Photo

Earlier in this chapter I showed you how to add captions, notes, and audio captions. I referred to the Properties pane as one vehicle to use when adding these identifiers. But I didn't give the Properties pane its full due. In addition to displaying your captions and notes, the Properties pane lets you see everything you've done with the file, from when and where it came from to whom you shared it with and more.

Here's how to use the Properties pane to find all the vital statistics about your files:

1. **Select your desired photo in the Photo Well.**

2. **Choose View⇨Properties to bring up the Properties pane.**

You also can right-click and choose Properties from the context-sensitive menu or click the Show Properties button in the Options bar.

You immediately see any caption attached to the image, the filename, the location of the file, the size of the file, and the date and time of the file.

3. **To play an audio annotation, click the audio button (the speaker icon), and click the Play button in the audio window.**

4. **Click the Complete Metadata button (the "i" icon), if it is available, to see all EXIF (Exchangeable Image File) data in a separate window, shown in Figure 6-6.**

   Metadata is extra information that some software programs or digital cameras store as part of the image's file format.

   Metadata includes the caption (if there is one), the camera's make and model, resolution, and other data. EXIF is a variation of the JPEG file format (see Chapter 3 for more on formats) and contains information such as your camera's aperture, shutter speed, exposure and other settings.

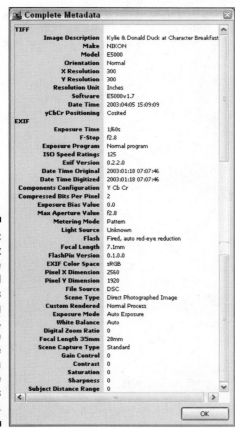

Figure 6-6:
To get all the technical details regarding your image, click the Complete Metadata button in the Properties pane.

5. **Choose one of the following options from the pop-up menu, shown in Figure 6-7:**

   - **Brief Metadata:** This option gives you an abbreviated version of the Complete Metadata profile.

   - **History:** This setting shows you the date a photo was imported and modified, where you imported it from, any creations that use the image, when and how it was shared, and if and when it was printed. I bet you didn't know your images were under surveillance, did you?

   - **Tags:** Selecting this option displays any tags attached to the file. For more on tags, check out Chapter 5.

You also can view information about a file by double-clicking the image thumbnail in the Photo Well to display the image in a Single Photo view. Make sure the Show Dates option is checked in the Options bar (or choose View↪Show Dates and Tag). You can then see the caption, the file's location, the size of the photo, any attached tags, and the date and time the photo was taken (see Figure 6-8). You also can listen to an audio caption if one exists.

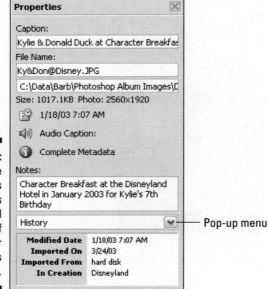

Figure 6-7:
The Properties pane gives you a full history of where your image has been.

Pop-up menu

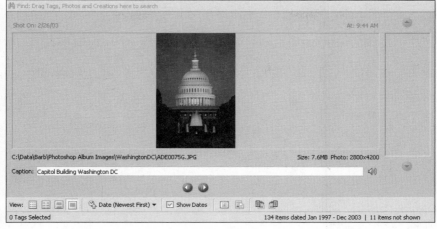

Figure 6-8:
The Single
Photo view
gives you
some, but
not all, data
about your
image.

If the only information you're interested in is the date, time, and tags of an image, you can get that in either the Medium or Large Thumbnail views in the Photo Well. The Small Thumbnail view yields only the date and time a file was created. For more on viewing images, see Chapter 9.

Chapter 7

Managing Your Photos

*T*he more you use Album, the more you'll discover its exceptional ability to gather data about your files, store that information, and update it when directed to. Album is also excellent in its ability to track the uses, or what is referred to as the *history,* of the file (see Chapter 8). For example, with Album's tracking system, you can see just what you've done with an image and when you did it. And last, but not least, Album provides a great way to allow you to identify your files by using tags (Chapter 5), captions, and notes (Chapter 6). All of this file data, along with the history, tags, captions, and notes, gives Album a wealth of information to help identify, organize, and modify your files.

Organizing Files into Catalogs

When you launch Album and import files — photos, video clips and audio clips — a catalog is automatically and invisibly created. You don't have to lift a finger.

A *catalog* is a database of information that keeps track of everything about your files — file formats, locations of files, dates and times, edits, tags, captions, and so forth. This vital data is linked to your files (the important word being *linked*).

When data about a file is linked to a catalog, that means that although the catalog contains this information about your files, it doesn't contain the actual photos, video, or audio clips themselves. Instead, the catalog references the files on your computer (or external media like CDs and DVDs) and displays a thumbnail in the Photo Well. Adobe uses the analogy of a catalog being like a phone book. The catalog contains important information about people and businesses, but not the actual people and businesses themselves.

Here is a laundry list of the info that the catalog stores about your files:

- The path and filename of the photo, video clip, or audio clip.

- The path and filename of any audio file attached to a photo (such as an audio caption) or creation (such as background music).

- If the original file is being stored offline (on a CD, DVD, or external media such as a Zip disk), the catalog stores the path, filename, and volume name of the original, full-resolution file.

- If a file has been edited, the catalog stores the path and filename of the original, unedited file.

- If you imported a batch of files from a digital camera or scanner, the catalog stores the name of the camera or scanner.

- Any captions, notes, or tags that you've added to a photo.

- The media type of the file and whether it's a photo, video clip, audio clip, or creation.

- The date and time the photo was taken.

- The file's history, such as if it was e-mailed, shared online, printed, exported, sent to an online service provider, used in a creation, or Web or Atmosphere gallery.

- Edits, such as contrast and color adjustments, that have been applied to the image.

- The pixel dimensions of photos and video clips.

- Details on creation settings, such as the type of creation, selected style, whether you've included captions and page numbers, transitions, and so on.

Creating new catalogs

Like me, you may be perfectly content to live with a single catalog. With all the great organizational tools Album provides, you can have your entire inventory of photos and clips neatly identified and categorized. But, just in case you want to, Album allows you to create additional catalogs.

For example, maybe you don't want to mix business with pleasure and feel better if your business and personal files reside in two separate catalogs. Or, if you share a computer with the family, you may want your kids to have their own catalogs, especially if they want to use their own tagging system. Why clutter your Tags pane with tags like "Lollapalooza Mosh Pit?"

If you decide to go the multiple catalog route, be warned that you can't move photos or tags between catalogs. You also cannot search across more than one catalog at a time. For more on locating files, see Chapter 8.

Here's how to create a new catalog:

1. **Choose File⇨Catalog.**

   The Catalog dialog box appears, as shown in Figure 7-1. Note that if you want Album to import free music files (these files are installed when you install Album) into your new catalog, select the check box at the bottom of the dialog box.

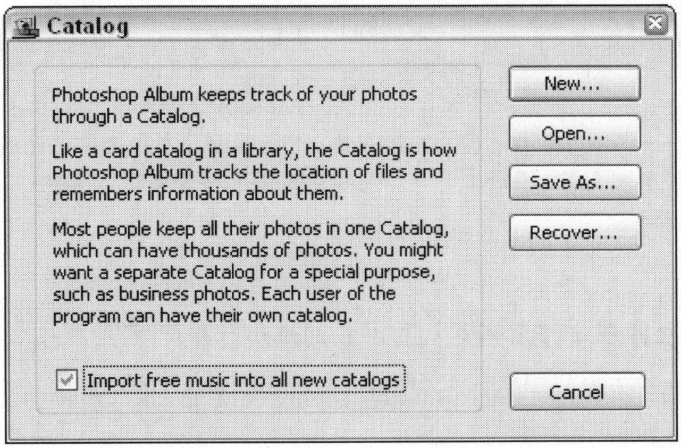

Figure 7-1: Creating multiple catalogs allows you to divide your files for different purposes or for different Album users.

Catalog

Photoshop Album keeps track of your photos through a Catalog.

Like a card catalog in a library, the Catalog is how Photoshop Album tracks the location of files and remembers information about them.

Most people keep all their photos in one Catalog, which can have thousands of photos. You might want a separate Catalog for a special purpose, such as business photos. Each user of the program can have their own catalog.

☑ Import free music into all new catalogs

New...

Open...

Save As...

Recover...

Cancel

2. **Click the New button.**

   The New Catalog dialog box appears.

3. **Select a location for the catalog or use the default Catalogs folder, shown in Figure 7-2.**

   I recommend using the default Catalogs folder. You will remember where it's stored because it simply makes sense to store a catalog in the Catalogs folder. However, if you have a really large catalog and need to store it on a separate hard drive, you can do so.

   If you want to change the default folder to any catalog you create, check out the next section "Changing the default catalog folder."

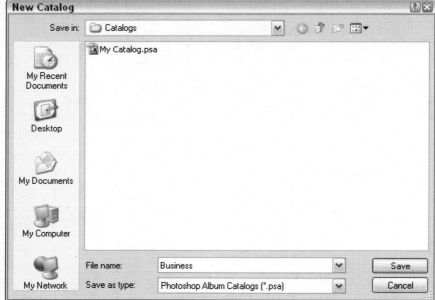

Figure 7-2:
You can
store your
catalog in
the default
Catalogs
folder or
create a
folder to
your liking.

4. **Enter a name for the catalog in the File Name text box and make sure the Save as type says Photoshop Album Catalogs (*.psa).**

5. **Click Save.**

Changing the default catalog folder

To establish a different default folder to any catalog you create, follow these steps:

1. **Choose Edit➪Preferences.**

2. **In the General pane of the Preferences dialog box, click the Browse button for the Save Catalogs In section, shown in Figure 7-3.**

   The Browse for Folder dialog box appears.

3. **Either select an existing folder or create a new folder in your desired location. Click OK.**

   If you change your mind or made a mistake, simply click the Restore Default Settings button to get back to the original folder pathname.

4. **Click OK to exit the Preferences.**

   The next time you create a new catalog, your new default folder will appear in the New Catalog dialog box.

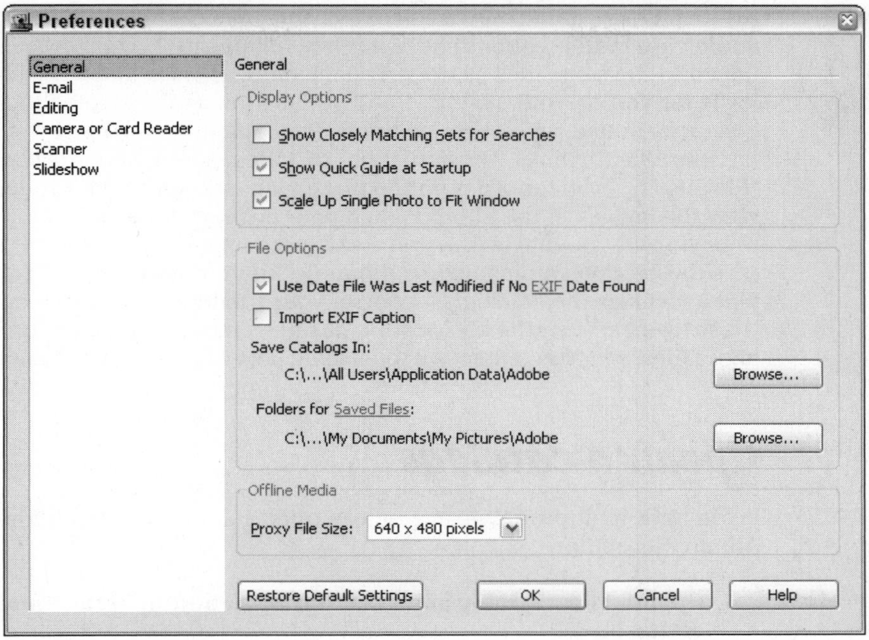

Figure 7-3:
Album
allows you
to change
the default
folder you
use to
save your
catalogs.

Copying catalogs

Instead of creating a new catalog from scratch, you can create one by making a copy of your existing catalog. For example, say you currently have personal and work files in one catalog. You can make a copy of your existing catalog, rename it Business, and then remove your personal files, while leaving your work files intact.

Or you may want to give a copy of your catalog to someone who admires your elaborate, yet efficient tagging system and wants to use it for organizing his or her own catalog. You shouldn't have to reinvent the wheel if you want your catalog like someone else's, right?

Here's how to copy a catalog:

1. **Choose File⇨Catalog.**

2. **In the Catalog dialog box that appears, click the Save As button.**

3. **Keep the new catalog in the default folder or choose a new location and folder.**

4. **Give your new catalog a name in the File Name text box.**

5. **Click Save.**

    Your new catalog opens in Album, and your old one closes.

Although the catalog has been copied, the physical files (photos, video clips, audio clips, and creations) have not been duplicated. The new catalog is linked to the same files as the original catalog. This is fine if the copied catalog is for you on your system. But if you are giving the catalog to a friend or colleague to use on another computer and you don't also give your friend or colleague the links (the actual photo, video, audio, and creation files), a "file missing" icon appears on the thumbnail as soon as your friend tries to view the images in the Photo Well. If your colleague doesn't want your files to begin with, no biggie. He or she can just remove the files from the catalog (see the section coming up in a minute). But your friend needs copies of the files as well as the catalog. Of course, your friend will have to reconnect to those files because the file location has been moved. For more on reconnecting to files, see "Reconnecting to missing files," later in this chapter.

Opening catalogs

If you have multiple catalogs, you can open a different catalog from within Album. Here's how:

1. **Choose File⇨Catalog and click the Open button in the Catalog dialog box.**

2. **Select your catalog.**

   If your catalog is stored in a location other than the default folder, navigate to that folder.

3. **Click Open.**

Your current catalog closes to accommodate opening another one. Album only allows you to work in one catalog at a time.

Removing items from the catalog

If you don't want a file to show up in your catalog, you can remove it without deleting the original file. You are simply removing the link to the photo, video clip, or audio clip. You also can remove creations.

Here's the scoop on removing a file from your catalog:

1. **Select one or more files in the Photo Well.**

2. **Choose either Edit⇨Delete from Catalog (for a single file) or Delete Selected Items from Catalog (multiple files).**

   The Confirm Deletion from Catalog dialog box appears, as shown in Figure 7-4.

Figure 7-4:
You can
remove
items from
your cata-
log with
or without
removing
the actual
file.

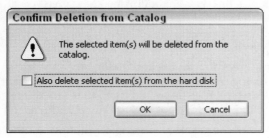

3. **If you want to delete the actual file in addition to the link, select the Also Delete Selected Item(s) from the Hard Disk check box.**

4. **Click OK.**

Keeping Your Catalog Safe and Sound

After you've painstakingly imported, identified, and organized your files, you definitely want to protect them. Fortunately, you don't need to hire a body guard to watch over your catalog; you can ensure its safety by using the tools in Album along with a blank CD or DVD or additional hard drive.

Using Album's Backup command and burning your catalog and all associated files (both original and edited versions) onto a CD or DVD keeps them safely stored in a location other than your hard drive. You also can back up your catalog and files to another drive, for example, a drive that you have dedicated for data storage. Although you may never need to use a backup, you'll be so very thankful if the unimaginable does occur. Recovering or restoring a catalog is a piece of cake if you have a backup handy.

Make a habit of burning a backup once a month or so, or after you have imported a significant number of files or have performed a major tagging reorganization. The hard-core computer troubleshooting experts say that you should store those backup CDs and DVDs offsite, in another location other than where your computer resides. That way if a fire, earthquake, or other act of Mother Nature destroys your possessions, you'll be covered.

Backing up your catalog

Album's Backup command makes it quick and easy to back up your catalog and all the linked files — photos, video clips, and audio clips.

You can back up the catalog to another hard drive or external media such as a Zip disk, Jaz disk, CD, or DVD. The following steps give you all you need to know:

1. **Choose File⇨Backup.**

   The Missing Files Check Before Backup dialog box appears, as shown in Figure 7-5. This dialog box warns you that if you have moved the location of your files since you've imported them that Album may not be able to find them and therefore not include them in the backup.

   Album backs up only your current catalog. If you have multiple catalogs, be sure to perform separate backups for all of them.

Figure 7-5: Be sure to reconnect any files you have moved so they will be backed up properly.

Missing Files Check Before Backup

If photo files have been moved since they were imported into your catalog, Photoshop Album will not be able to find them and they will not be backed up. To ensure that all files are properly located, select Reconnect button below before contining with backup.

☐ Don't Show Again

[Reconnect] [Continue] [Cancel]

2. **Click the Reconnect button in the dialog box.**

   In the Reconnect Missing Files dialog box, shown in Figure 7-6, a list of your missing files appears on the left, along with the file's thumbnail. If you don't have any missing files, proceed to Step 4.

3. **Select a file and then locate the file's new location by clicking the Browse button on the right side of the dialog box. If it is a match, click the Reconnect button. Repeat this step until all files have been reconnected.**

   You also can view a thumbnail of the file you have located.

   The reconnected files are removed from the Missing Files list.

4. **Click the Close button in the dialog box.**

   The Backup dialog box appears.

5. **Select the hard drive or external media to which you want to back up your catalog.**

   Choose Burn onto a CD or DVD Disc to burn your backup catalog to a writeable CD or DVD. Or choose Specify Backup Drive and then choose the particular drive onto which you would like your backup. If you're backing up the files to external removable media such as a Zip or Jaz disk, choose the letter of the Zip or Jaz drive.

6. **Select the type of backup you want.**

    Choose Full Backup to create a copy of the catalog, along with all the associated, linked files — photos, video clips, and audio clips. Choose Incremental Backup to make a copy of the catalog and any new or modified files since the last full or incremental backup.

7. **Click OK.**

8. **If you selected Burn onto a CD or DVD Disc, follow the instructions presented to you. If you selected Specify Backup Drive, navigate to the specific location on your hard drive or external media you want your backup to reside (see Figure 7-7). You can, of course, also create a brand spanking new folder as well.**

    If you're performing an incremental backup, insert the media or locate the hard drive that has your last backup and follow the instructions presented to you on-screen. If your backup is too large, Album gives you a gentle heads up, and you can either insert new media or locate another hard drive if available.

    Album informs you when the backup has been completed. That's it. Label your backup and keep it in a safe location. You are officially backed up and ready for computer crashes and any other unfortunate events.

Figure 7-6: Be kind enough to show Album where you moved your photos, and it will reward you with a complete and accurate backup.

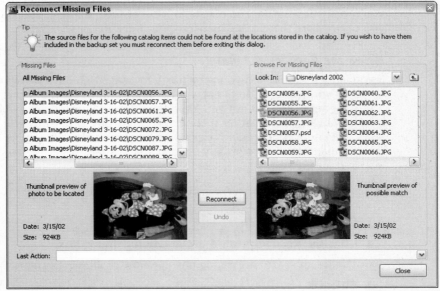

Figure 7-7:
Specify the
location you
want your
backup
catalog and
files to live.

Recovering and restoring your catalog

Say the unfortunate does happen. The first thing you may want to try before you break out your backup disk is to recover the catalog. If that doesn't work, you can restore the catalog by using your backup copy.

Using the Recover command

If you launch Album and you get a nasty message that says you have a problem with your catalog, don't call your computer the first foul word that pops into your head. At least not yet. Your catalog could have been damaged by a power outage or some other technical gremlin, but is possibly still salvageable. The Recover command tries its best to repair the catalog. As a bonus, the command also removes any unused space, thereby getting your catalog lean and mean.

Here's how to recover and repair a catalog:

1. **Choose File⇨Catalog.**

2. **Click the Recover button in the Catalog dialog box.**

   The Recover Catalog dialog box appears, as shown in Figure 7-8.

3. **Click OK.**

If the catalog was recovered and repaired successfully, a dialog box appears, also shown in Figure 7-8.

If you get another nasty message instead, you might want to proceed to the next section.

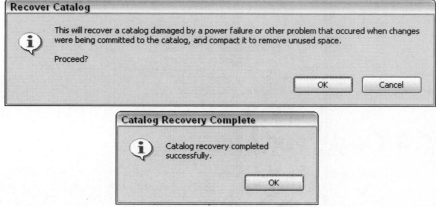

Figure 7-8:
Use the
Recover
command
to repair a
damaged
catalog.

Restoring your catalog

If your catalog couldn't be recovered, you need to restore it instead. You may also want to restore your catalog to a previously saved version if you inadvertently deleted some files or did something equally as irritating. And finally, you also can use the Restore command to move your catalog and files to another computer. The Restore command installs the backup copy of your catalog, along with all the associated, linked files — photos, video clips and audio clips.

Follow these steps to restore your catalog and all its files:

1. **Insert your backup media (CD, DVD, or other external media).**

   If you had to back up your catalog and files onto more than one disk, Album prompts you to insert the additional disk(s). Just follow the instructions on-screen. If you made your backup to an external hard drive, make sure it is connected to your computer.

2. **Choose File⇨Restore.**

   The Restore dialog box appears, as shown in Figure 7-9.

3. **Choose Restore from CD or DVD or Restore from hard disk or other storage volume.**

4. **Select the backup copy of your catalog in the list and click the Restore button.**

   Your backup is installed, and your catalog is restored and back to normal.

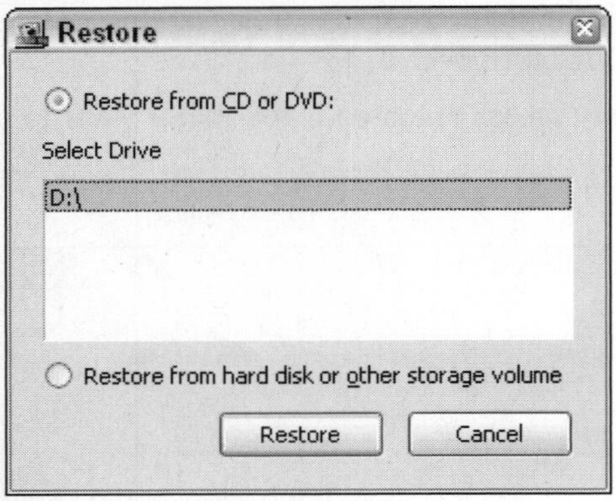

Figure 7-9:
Restore
your catalog
from your
backup
copy if
things have
gone awry.

Archiving Your Photos

There may be instances when you don't want to back up a catalog, but you want to make a copy of just the files themselves. The Archive command is the ticket. This command allows you to make a copy of your files (photos, video clips, and audio clips) and burn them onto a CD or DVD.

You might use the Archive command when you want to give a family member or friend a copy of a bunch of photos for him to use as he pleases, for example, to print or make his own creations. This is especially handy if the files are high resolution and large, and you don't want to (or can't) e-mail them. For more on resolution, see Chapter 3.

Or you may want to free up your hard drive by archiving the high-resolution originals of your photos onto a CD or DVD. Remember that Album lets you store your physical files offline (on media) as well as on your system. The Archive command actually has an offline option where the master files are burned to a CD or DVD, and a low-resolution proxy is saved to your hard drive. The master files are then deleted from your hard drive. The files still appear in the Photo Well, but now they have a CD icon on their thumbnails. If you try and make a creation or print an image whose master is offline, Album politely prompts you to insert the CD or DVD with that master.

Here's how to archive your files:

1. **From the Photo Well, select the items you wish to archive.**

   If you don't select any items, all files in your catalog will be archived. Note that you cannot archive creations. If they are among the items selected, they will be listed in the "Items Not Archived" dialog box.

2. **Choose File⇨Archive.**

3. **Name your archive in the Archive Set Name text box.**

4. **If you want to delete the high-resolution photos from your hard drive after the archiving is done, select the Move items offline option.**

   You cannot use this option for video clips and audio clips.

5. **Select the CD or DVD drive where you're burning the archive and click OK.**

   Album asks if you really want the items removed permanently from your computer or forever hold your peace.

6. **Click Yes or Chicken Out (er, No).**

   Album does a quick analysis and lets you know how many disks are required for the archive. Album then directs you to insert a CD or DVD.

7. **Click the Burn button.**

 As in most CD- or DVD-burning sessions, you have the option of verifying the disk. Even though it takes a couple additional minutes, I highly recommend verifying. Once in awhile the burning process hiccups, and the CD or DVD isn't burned properly. You don't want to find that out after you have mailed the media to your family member or friend or when you need the high-resolution image to make a print and the disk is corrupted, especially if you deleted the high-resolution original from your hard drive.

Working with Different Versions of Photos

Album is very methodical when it comes to managing various versions of photos — originals, edited images, duplicates, and so on — giving them descriptive names to identify whether they are edited or copied versions. The program also errs on the cautious side by retaining the original in case you want to revert back to it. But as with any other program, fully understanding how Album manages all of your files and their various iterations can help you avoid confusion and prevent management mishaps.

Naming edited files

When you edit a photo — for example, when using the Fix Photo dialog box — any changes you make are applied to a copy of the file, not to the original. Album provides a new name for the edited version. This little trick can be annoying if you've done a lot of correction and retouching and would rather just dump the original. But don't worry; you can dump the original as well, as I explain in the upcoming section, "Replacing an original photo with an edited version."

If the format of the edited file is JPEG, PNG, TIFF, or PSD, Album adds the word "_edited" to the filename. For example, my original is called `statueofliberty.jpg`, and the edited version is called `statueofliberty_edited.jpg`, as shown in Figure 7-10. For more on file formats, see Chapter 3.

Figure 7-10: Album retains your original file and appends the name for edited versions.

If your file is in a format that Album can't work with, you can save the edited version in one of the approved formats listed above. Album also adds "_edited" to the original name.

Reverting to an original photo

If you decide later that it isn't really a good idea to submit the photo of your boss with his head cropped off to the company newsletter, you can always return to the original, unadulterated version of the image. Here's how:

1. **Select one or more images in the Photo Well.**

2. **If you chose only one image, choose Edit⇨Revert to Original. If you selected multiple photos, choose Edit⇨Revert Selected Photos to Original.**

   You also can right-click and choose the commands from the context-sensitive menu.

Replacing an original photo with an edited version

Say you performed digital magic on your original image and want the edited version to forever replace the mediocre original. Album allows you to make this switch, but make sure you're positive that you want to make the switch yourself, because after the original is replaced with the edited file, the original is gone forever. And, with the exception of rotating, you can't undo any changes made in the editing process.

If disk space, not image quality, is the issue and you want to delete the original to save room, archive your files first so that you have a copy if you should ever need it (see the section on archiving in this chapter).

Follow these steps to replace your original photo with the edited version:

1. **Select one or more photos in the Photo Well.**

2. **If you selected a single image, choose Edit⇨Replace Original with Edited. If you selected multiple images, choose Edit⇨Replace Selected Originals with Edited.**

    You also can right-click and choose the commands from the context-sensitive menu.

Duplicating photos

The Duplicate command is pretty self-explanatory — it creates a copy of your image. The power to duplicate photos can come in handy if you want one or more copies to edit differently. For example, you may want to crop an image a couple different ways — one version that only shows a single person and another that shows the group shot. Or maybe you want a copy that is color corrected and another copy that is desaturated so it appears as a black-and-white image. For more on editing photos, see Chapters 11 and 12.

To duplicate a photo, follow these steps:

1. **Select the photo in the Photo Well.**

    You can only duplicate one file at a time.

2. **Choose Edit⇨Duplicate Item.**

    You also can right-click and choose Duplicate Item from the context-sensitive menu.

    The duplicated photo is a new file, with the word "-copy" appended to the name. It is also a new catalog entry. The duplicate appears near the original in the Photo Well. It is, however, no longer linked to the original photo.

The Duplicate Item command copies both the original file of the photo and, if there is one, the edited version as well. For example, I duplicated my "Europe-01.jpg" file, but as you can see in Figure 7-11, it also duplicated my "Europe-01_edited.jpg" file as well.

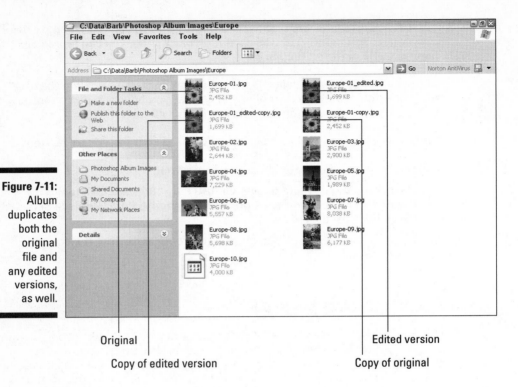

Figure 7-11:
Album
duplicates
both the
original
file and
any edited
versions,
as well.

Original

Copy of edited version

Edited version

Copy of original

Any tags, captions, and notes attached to the original are duplicated with the file. So be sure and do all your tagging and caption/note writing before you duplicate to maximize your time.

Updating thumbnails

As long as you do all your editing within or through Album, the program keeps a good record of your photo's vital statistics and history. If you edit a photo in Album, it makes an edited version, keeps the original, and it knows exactly what's going on. If you need to edit your image in another image-editing application, like Photoshop Elements or Photoshop, be sure and launch the program from within Album. If you do so, Album will *still* know what's going on and will be able to track all versions of your file.

If you don't launch an image-editing program through Album, the thumbnail in the Photo Well and the file information will not reflect the edited image. In this case, you have to perform an additional step to update the thumbnail and file info. Here's how:

1. **Select one or multiple images in the Photo Well that have been edited outside of Album.**

2. **If you selected a single image, choose Edit⇨Update Thumbnail. If you chose multiple photos, choose Edit⇨Update Thumbnails for Selected Items.**

   You also can right-click and choose the commands from the context-sensitive menu.

Reconnecting to missing files

In your zeal for organizing, you may move a file, such as a photo, video, or audio clip, from its original location in Album to a new one that is outside the Album realm. If you do so, Album will not be able to find it and will consider it missing. It will then place a File Missing icon on top of your thumbnail in the Photo Well. This is not a disaster, by any means, but it is a minor inconvenience. All you have to do is use the Reconnect Missing File command and show Album where the file now resides.

You may choose to ignore the file missing icon thinking you know darn well the file isn't missing. But the next time you try and print, export, e-mail, edit, or do anything that requires the original file, the Reconnect Missing Files dialog box will appear automatically, forcing you to take action to direct Album to the file's new location.

To reconnect a single missing file, follow these steps:

1. **Select a file that has a file missing icon in the Photo Well.**

2. **Choose Edit⇨Reconnect Missing File.**

   You also can right-click and select the command from the context-sensitive menu.

   The Reconnect Missing Files dialog box appears, as shown in Figure 7-12. The missing file, along with a thumbnail preview and file info, appears on the left side. The right side of the dialog box shows the original folder where the image was once stored.

3. **In the Browse for Missing Files section of the dialog box, navigate to folder where the file now resides and click the Reconnect button.**

   A thumbnail preview of a possible match is displayed when you select a new folder.

   The Last Action pop-up menu lists the file that has been reconnected.

   The Reconnect Missing File command does not work for files that have been renamed outside of Album or deleted.

4. **Click Close to exit the dialog box.**

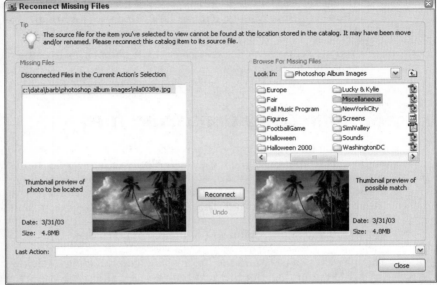

Figure 7-12:
Reconnect
files that
you have
moved into
different
folders so
Album can
track them
properly.

Here's how to reconnect multiple missing files:

1. **Choose File➪Reconnect All Missing Files.**

   You don't have to select the images in the Photo Well. Album checks through your catalog, and all files it finds as missing are listed in the Reconnect Missing Files dialog box that appears.

2. **Select one or more of the missing files in the list.**

   As with a single file, Album displays the thumbnail preview and last known folder location on the left side of the dialog box (refer to Figure 7-6).

3. **In the Browse for Missing Files section, navigate to the folder containing the missing files and then click the Reconnect button.**

4. **Repeat Steps 2 and 3 for all missing files.**

   The Last Action pop-up menu shows a list of the files reconnected. Any files that couldn't be reconnected remain in the missing files list. If you mistakenly reconnect to the wrong file, click the Undo button right away. Or, later, once back in the Photo Well, you can rename the erroneous file or delete it from the catalog.

5. **Click Close to exit the dialog box.**

Part III
Finding, Viewing, and Editing Photos

The 5th Wave   By Rich Tennant

NATIONAL ENQUIRER PHOTO IMAGING WORKSHOP

"Remember, your Elvis should appear bald and slightly hunched. Nice Big Foot, Brad. Keep your two-headed animals in the shadows and your alien spacecrafts crisp and defined."

In this part. . .

When you've gotten your files into Album and organized them to your liking, you can find, sort, and view images without much strain. Those days of rummaging through shoeboxes and scrolling through folders on your hard drive are over! You also find information on the different ways you can view your images. Choose from thumbnails, Single Photo view or take a gander at images using instant slideshows.

The very first step in fixing digital images is to set up the best editing environment possible. After you optimize your editing environment, Chapter 11 shows you how to use Album's Fix Photo dialog box to eliminate red eye, flatten contrast, and eliminate color casts, all with a click or two of the mouse. You'll be amazed at the large amount of improvement that can be gained from such little effort. If you need heavier-duty capabilities, I cover using Album with an external image editor, such as Photoshop Elements.

Chapter 8

Locating Your Photos

*P*hotoshop Album is chock full of ways to help you find the exact photos you want. One method isn't necessarily better than another; it's a matter of how you've organized your images and how you like to work. If you haven't organized your images, you might want to check out Chapters 5 and 6 for the lowdown. Although you can find your images by date, filename, and media type without any prior organizing, working with tags may be the ticket for getting a handle on your digital shoebox of images. But no matter which method you use or which search criteria you choose, you'll find Album does a great job in bringing you the files you're looking for.

Finding Photos by Date

One of the most popular criteria to find any kind of file is by date. I know I often find myself hunting for the latest version of a particular file by having Windows arrange my files by date modified. Fortunately, Album gives you a couple of methods to find photos by date — using the timeline and the calendar.

Using the timeline

To view images using the timeline, it isn't necessary to attach tags to them (although you can). Album automatically arranges your photos in the timeline. The timeline is divided into years and months, as shown in Figure 8-1. You can click the month you desire, or you can drag the slider. Hold your mouse over a bar in the timeline, and the name of the month appears. To find and view photos within a select range of time, move the end points of the timeline.

Drag endpoint markers
to select range of time

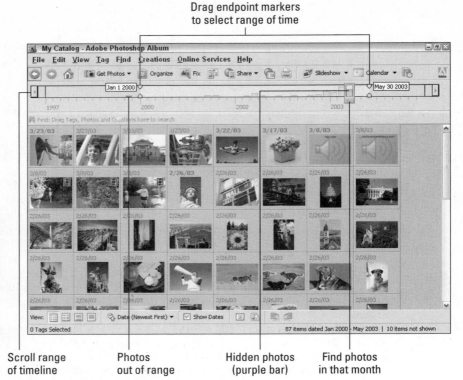

Figure 8-1:
Use the
timeline to
find your
images
by month
and year.

Scroll range
of timeline

Photos
out of range

Hidden photos
(purple bar)

Find photos
in that month

Here are the specific steps to find and view photos using the timeline:

1. **Choose View➪Timeline to bring the timeline into view.**

2. **Choose View➪Arrangement and then choose a sorting criteria.**

   You can sort by criteria such as newest date first, oldest date first, import date, folders, or color. Album's default sorting option is newest date first. For full details on sorting, see Chapter 9.

   After you choose a sorting option, Album displays blue bars in the timeline. The height of each bar corresponds to the number of images per your sorting criteria. For example, if you've sorted by newest date first, the height of the bars corresponds to the number of photos in each month (refer to Figure 8-1). If you sort by folder location, the height corresponds to the number of images in each folder (as shown in Figure 8-2), and so on. Hover your mouse over a bar in the timeline to display the name of the respective folder containing the images.

3. **Choose Find➪Set Date Range.**

   The Set Date Range dialog box opens, as shown in Figure 8-3.

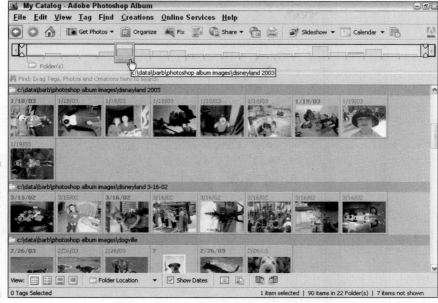

Figure 8-2:
The height
of each bar
corre-
sponds to
the number
of images in
each folder.

4. **Enter start and end dates to further refine your search. Click OK.**

   You also can drag the endpoint markers to set the date range. Only those photos with dates within the range specified appear in the Photo Well. If a photo doesn't have a date, it appears with a question mark in both the Photo Well and the timeline. You can assign a date to a photo by choosing Edit➪Adjust Date and Time. For details on changing the date or time, see Chapter 9.

Using the calendar

You also can use the calendar to find photos by date. Of course, it is a good idea to know the approximate date of the photo(s) you want, or you may spend quite a bit of time clicking through images, depending on the size of your catalog.

It's extremely simple to find photos using the calendar. Here are the steps you need to follow:

1. **Choose View➪Calendar.**

   You also can click the Calendar button in the Shortcuts bar. The calendar window (shown in Figure 8-4) initially displays whatever photo is selected in the Photo Well or, if none is selected, the first photo in the Photo Well.

Figure 8-3:
Specify the
date range
of the
photos you
want Album
to locate.

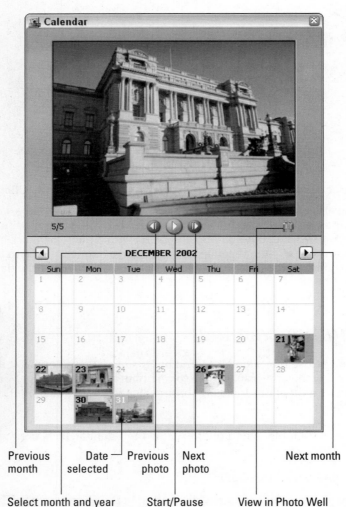

Figure 8-4:
Using the
Calendar is
a fun and
easy way to
locate your
photos.

Previous
month

Date
selected

Previous
photo

Next
photo

Next month

Select month and year

Start/Pause

View in Photo Well

2. **Navigate to your desired month by clicking the Next month or Previous month buttons.**

3. **Click the desired day in the calendar.**

   The Calendar shows the first photo on that day. It also displays the number of photos or videos taken on that day.

4. **If you select a day with more than one file, click the Next and Previous buttons to cycle through the images.**

   Or you can view a slide show in the calendar. Click the Start button to have the slide show automatically play.

5. **After you've found your desired file, click the View button.**

   The image displays in the Photo Well in a Single Photo view.

Finding Photos by Caption, Note, or Filename

Maybe you're not into dates, but instead are more of a wordsmith kind of person. You're in luck. Album lets you easily find photos by providing a word or phrase that you used in an image's filename, caption, or note. You don't even have to use the exact phrase.

Maybe you only remember a single word. No problem — Album brings up any matches that use the word in the data related to the file. Here's how to find files using similar words in captions or notes:

1. **Choose Find⇨By Caption or Note.**

   The Find by Caption or Note dialog box appears, as shown in Figure 8-5.

2. **Enter a word or phrase in the text box to find any files whose captions or notes contain that word or phrase.**

   The default option is set to match any part of any word in the caption or note. You also can choose to match only the beginning of words in the caption or note.

3. **Click OK.**

   Any matching files appear in the Photo Well.

To find a file by filename, follow these steps:

1. **Choose Find⇨By Filename.**

   The Find by Filename dialog box appears.

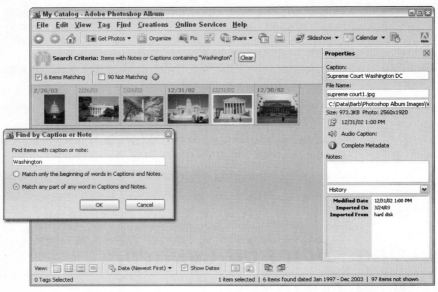

Figure 8-5:
Album lets
you locate
images by
entering
part of
a filename,
caption,
or note.

2. **Enter a word or phrase in the text box to find any files whose file-names contain that word or phrase.**

3. **Click OK.**

   Any matching files appear in the Photo Well.

   For full details on creating captions and notes, see Chapter 6.

Finding Photos by Their History

Album is truly a program for those of us who appreciate a meticulous tracking system. This program remembers where you got your photos, how you got them, when you received them, whether you shared, printed, or exported them, and how you've used them. So don't get any ideas about sneaking a photo in under Album's nose. It flat isn't going to happen. Album refers to all these details as a photo's *history*. And just as it captures and retains this history, it also allows you to locate photos via their history.

To find photos using their history, choose Find⇨By History and choose one of the following options, shown in Figure 8-6:

✔ **Items Imported On:** This option displays a list of devices you have imported images from, the date/time you imported files from those devices, and the number of files that were imported, as shown in Figure 8-7. Select your desired file(s) and click OK.

The selected files then appear in the Photo Well, as shown in Figure 8-8. If you have a single item highlighted in the list, you can simply double-click the file to have it appear in the Photo Well.

The search criteria you use to locate your images displays above the Photo Well in the Find bar.

Figure 8-6:
You can
locate your
images
by their
history —
when and
how you got
them, as
well as how
you used
them.

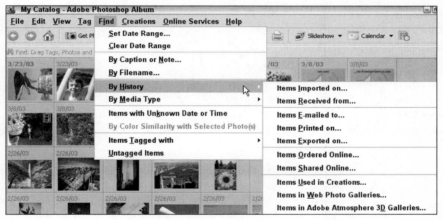

Figure 8-7:
Select your
desired files
from the
Imported
list.

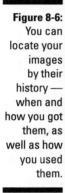

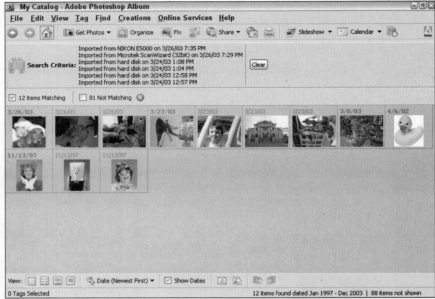

Figure 8-8:
Your
selected
files then
appear
in the
Photo Well.

✔ **Items Received From:** This option shows a list of who you have received files from via e-mail or from an online service, the date/time you received them and the number of files. Double-click your desired item or select several and click OK. The file(s) will appear in the Photo Well.

✔ **Items E-mailed To:** Album keeps a list of all files you have e-mailed to anyone in your contact book, as shown in Figure 8-9. If you want to view the file you e-mailed, double-click the item in the list. For more details on e-mailing files, see Chapter 13.

✔ **Items Printed On:** Select this option to see a list of all photos you have printed and the date and time you printed them, as shown in Figure 8-10. Double-click an item to see the photo(s) you printed on that day and time. This can come in handy if you're fulfilling numerous requests for prints for friends and family and can't remember if you printed a certain image or not. For more on printing images, see Chapter 14.

✔ **Items Exported On:** This option shows you a list of all the files you have exported, including the date and time. Double-click any item to view the file. For more details on exporting images, see Chapter 12.

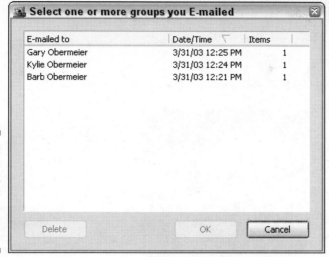

Figure 8-9:
Album
keeps track
of any files
you have
e-mailed to
friends.

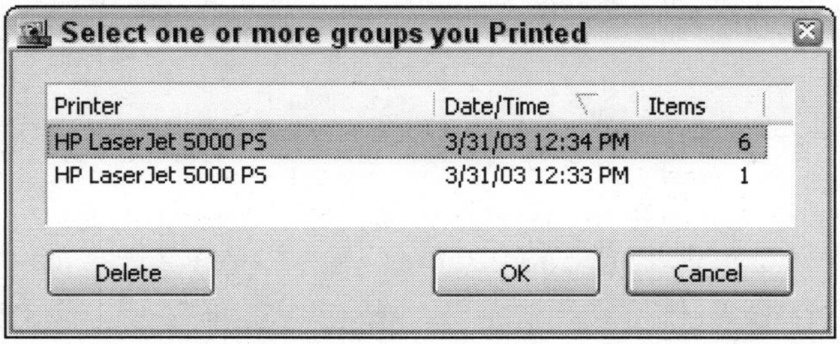

Figure 8-10:
A list of all
the files you
have printed
is kept
handy in
Album.

✔ **Items Ordered Online:** This option shows you a list of photos, such as prints or photo books, that you have ordered via online services, along with the date and time ordered. Double-click any item to view the file. For more on ordering online, see Chapter 15.

✔ **Items Shared Online:** This option offers a list of all the files that you have shared online via an online service, such as Shutterfly, along with the date and time you shared them (see Figure 8-11). Double-click any item to view the file. Details on sharing online can be found in Chapter 15.

✔ **Items Used in Creations:** This option displays a list of all creations you have made, when you made them, and how many items they include, as shown in Figure 8-12. Double-click an item to view the file(s). For more on creations, see Chapter 18.

Figure 8-11: Album can give you a list of files you have shared online with a service such as Shutterfly.

With creations, you have a few other ways to view items used:

- If you select a creation in the Photo Well, you can right-click and choose Show Photos in Workspace from the context-sensitive menu. Thumbnails of the files used in your creation appear in the Workspace window.

- You also can drag a creation onto the Find bar to display those files used. The files appear in the Photo Well. For more on the Find bar, see the section, "Searching with the Find bar and tags."

- You can see if a file was used in a creation by looking at its History in the Properties pane. Choose History from the pop-up menu at the bottom of the pane. If the file was used in a creation, the name of the creation is listed, as shown in Figure 8-13. For more details on using the Properties pane, see Chapter 2.

✔ **Items in Web Photo Galleries:** Select this option to view all items you have used in Web Photo Galleries and when you created those galleries. To see the files used, double-click any item in the list. For more on creating Web Photo Galleries, see Chapter 18.

✔ **Items in Adobe Atmosphere 3D Galleries:** Similar to the Web Photo Gallery option, this option shows all items you used in any Adobe Atmosphere 3D Galleries and when those 3D galleries were created. Double-click to display the files used in the Photo Well. For more on Adobe Atmosphere 3D Galleries, see Chapter 18.

Figure 8-12: You can easily access a list of creations you have made.

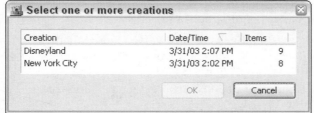

Figure 8-13: Checking out a file's history in the Properties pane lets you know if it was used in a creation.

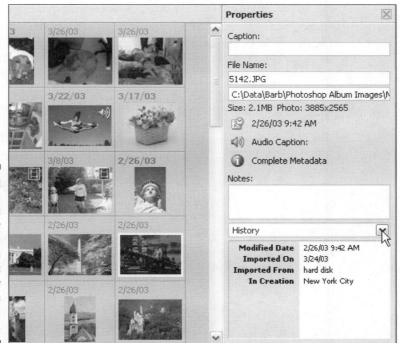

Tracking Down Files by Media Type

If you have any extensive catalog with various types of files — still images, video clips, audio files, and creations — you can have Album wrangle them into the Photo Well by media type. Unfortunately, you can choose only one type of media at a time. Choose Find➪By Media Type and select an option from the sub-menu. You have a choice of the following options:

- **Photos:** Displays photographs only.

- **Video:** Shows thumbnails of your video clips. Only the first frame of the clip is displayed. A small filmstrip icon appears in the top-right corner of the thumbnail, as shown in Figure 8-14.

- **Audio:** Displays your audio clips. An icon of a little speaker with the filename is shown.

- **Creations:** Displays in the Photo Well all creations you have produced. The first page or screen of any multi-page or multi-screen creation appears as the thumbnail with a small creation icon in the top right corner.

- **Items with Audio Captions:** Shows any photos and creations that you have attached audio captions to. A small speaker icon annotating an audio caption also appears in the top-right corner of the thumbnail.

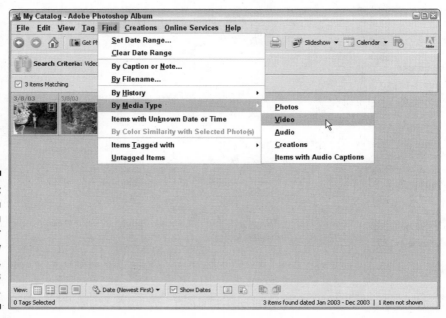

Figure 8-14: Album enables you to find your files by media type, such as video clips.

Even if you don't pay attention to the descriptive icons on your thumbnails, Album generously displays your chosen Search criteria in the Find bar above the Photo Well. And once you have narrowed down your search by media type, you can then apply other search criteria to further refine the search for your desired files.

Finding Files with Unknown Dates

Maybe the clock on your digital camera wasn't operating properly and didn't embed any dates and times on your photos. How do find those files that don't have a date or time they were created or imported? You can direct Album to round up those stray files by choosing Find⇨Items with Unknown Date or Time. Album then displays all the files without dates or times in the Photo Well. After you've rounded them up, you can easily change the date of the images by choosing Edit⇨Adjust Date and Time. For more details on date and time changes, see Chapter 5.

Photos with unknown dates are marked with question marks in the timeline and in the Photo Well.

Locating Images by Their Color

To find photos that have a similar color distribution, choose Find⇨By Color Similarity with Selected Photos. But before you can use this command, you have to select one or more images (up to four) so Album knows what to look for. Don't select any creations, Album will just ignore them anyway.

If you choose photos that are extremely dissimilar, you are going to basically get the kitchen sink thrown back at you. Even when choosing a single image, sometimes Album locates images that are not really all that similar, as shown in Figure 8-15. I chose a nighttime shot of New York City as my search criteria. Expecting only dark images to be found, I couldn't quite understand why I got some bright daytime shots among the images.

With all the other great search criteria available at your disposal, I would skip this one if you're trying to save time.

You also can find similarly colored images by dragging a photo onto the Find bar.

Figure 8-15:
Album
attempts
to locate
images that
have a
similar color
distribution
to your
selected
photo(s).

Using Tags to Find Files

You also can search for files by tags. Tags are descriptive keywords you attach to your photos to add additional information for organizing and managing purposes. Check out Chapter 5 to find out about these useful critters.

To find files using tags, choose any of these methods:

✔ Choose Find➪Items Tagged With, and then select a tag from the submenu. Your tagged images appear in the Photo Well. Click the Clear button in the Find bar to display all the files in your catalog again.

✔ Choose View➪Tags to bring up the Tags pane. In the pane, click the square to the left of the tag name(s), so the binoculars icon appears. Your tagged images appear in the Photo Well, as shown in Figure 8-16. Click the icon to cancel the search and display all files or click the Clear button in the Find bar.

✔ Drag one or more tags from the Tags pane onto the Find bar. The selected tag(s) appears in the search criteria window in the Find bar. Click the Clear button to cancel the search and display all catalog files.

Selected tag used to search

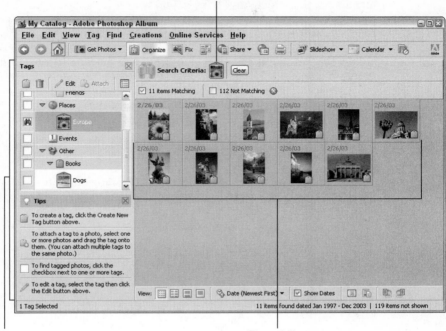

Figure 8-16:
Using tags
makes
searching
for images
quick and
easy.

Tags pane

Tagged files

> ✔ Right-click a Tag category in the Tags pane and select New Search using
> (Tag name) category.

You can work from the opposite perspective and choose any images that do
not have assigned tags. Choose Find➪Untagged Items to see all of the files in
your catalog that are don't have tags.

Using the timeline with tagged files

If using tags narrows down your search, but doesn't quite give you the exact
images you are looking for, try using the timeline along with your tags. For
example, say you're searching for images of family members taken around
the holidays. Of course, all your pictures of family have a nice "Family" tag
attached to them.

You could first do a search using the "Family" tag and then display the timeline and click in December bars to find winter holiday–related photos within the tagged images. Or you can drag endpoint markers to narrow the time range of photos you want displayed in the Photo Well.

Follow these steps to use tags along with the timeline to zero in a specific group of images:

1. **Choose View⇨Tags to display the Tags pane.**

2. **Drag and drop your selected tag onto the Find bar.**

3. **Drag the timeline endpoint markers to set the range you want to search.**

   All images with the tag found within the range of dates appear in the Photo Well, as shown in Figure 8-17.

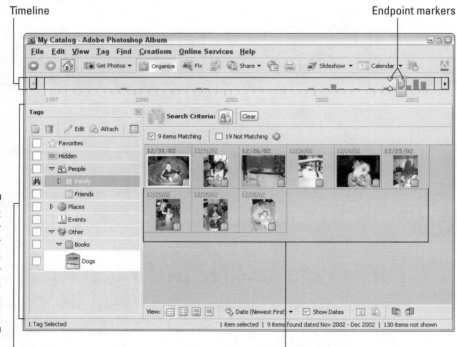

Figure 8-17: Further target your image search by combining tags with the timeline.

Timeline

Endpoint markers

Tags pane

Tagged photos within date range

Searching with the Find bar and tags

The fabulous Find bar, the thin blue bar directly above the Photo Well, allows you to quickly find files. When you drag a tag from the Tags pane onto the Find bar, the bar expands and displays a Search Criteria window that shows the tag you have used to search with. All tagged images then appear in the Photo Well. The Find bar also shows you how many items in your catalog exactly match the Search Criteria, how many closely match, and how many don't match at all. To display the items in any of these three categories, simply click in the check box. The default display are those items that match exactly. To cancel the search and display your entire catalog, click the Clear button.

Besides tags, you also can drag photos and creations onto the Find bar. You can find similarly colored images by dragging a photo onto the Find bar. And when you drag a creation onto the Find bar, all files used in the creation are displayed in the Photo Well.

Finding Favorite or Hidden files

Album allows you to attach a Favorites tag, which identifies your most prized images, clips, and creations. The methods to use when searching with the Favorites tag are the same as searching with other tags (described above); however, the Favorites tag has preference in searches when it is used with other tags.

For example, if you drag both the Family and Favorites tag onto the Find bar, only those images tagged with the Family tag that also have a Favorites tag attached to them appear in the Photo Well. For full details on creating and using tags, see Chapter 5.

You also can attach a Hidden tag to files, as shown in Figure 8-18. Maybe you have a batch of backup images or mediocre shots that you don't want to view in your catalog. Whenever you search for photos, any with a Hidden tag are not found. In order to find Hidden images, make sure you select both your desired tag and the Hidden tag in your search. And of course, if all you want to find are Hidden photos, simply select or drag the Hidden tag alone.

If a bar in the timeline is part purple, it means that you have Hidden photos in that month, batch, or folder.

Family tag

Hidden tag

Favorites tag

Hidden photos

Find bar

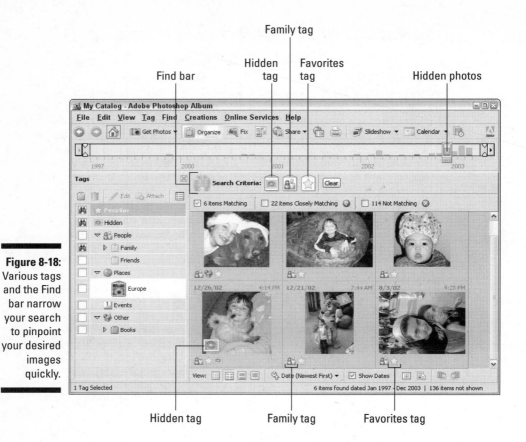

Figure 8-18: Various tags and the Find bar narrow your search to pinpoint your desired images quickly.

Hidden tag

Family tag

Favorites tag

Chapter 9

Viewing Your Photos

After you've located and imported your images into Album, I am sure you're more than ready to sit back and gaze at their awesomeness. Imported files, whether they're photos, video clips, audio clips, or creations, appear in the Photo Well in a grid of thumbnails. You can adjust the size of these thumbnails, as well as how your images are sorted.

Album also gives you the capability of displaying your images in an instant slide show. Slide shows are great if you want to preview images you've just imported or to show them off for family and friends as they huddle around the monitor and ooh and aah. For those of you who are more multimedia inclined, Album also has a built-in media player that allows you to play both your audio and video clips.

Choosing a Viewing Size

Album gives you the option of choosing how you want to view your files in the Photo Well. At times, you may want to see everything in your catalog so you would use the Small Thumbnail view. In other instances, you may just want to isolate the view to a single image, in which case the Single Photo view may better suit your needs. Changing the view is as easy as clicking your mouse, so feel free to do it as often as you want.

To change the view, choose View➪Size and select from the following options:

✔ **Small Thumbnail:** This option displays your files in the Photo Well in the smallest size. This is the best option if you need to see as many images at once as possible, as displayed in Figure 9-1. In addition to the thumbnail, the date, time, and tag icons (if tags have been attached) are displayed. For more on tags, see Chapter 5.

✔ **Medium Thumbnail:** This option is Album's default view. This view, shown in Figure 9-2, provides the best overall view for everyday browsing through your catalog. In addition to the thumbnail, dates, times and tag icons of the images are displayed.

✔ **Large Thumbnail:** This option shows just a few files at a time. This means you'll need to do a lot of scrolling, but you'll also see more details in the images than with the smaller views, as shown in Figure 9-3. This is a good choice if you have a sequence of images that look similar, and you need to distinguish between them. This view also displays the date, time, tag icon, and tag name for each image.

✔ **Single Photo:** This view shows only one photo at a time. To view the rest of the images in your catalog, click the Next Item or Previous Item buttons, shown in Figure 9-4. Not only do you get the largest view of the image, but you also get to see the metadata about the image (the file size and resolution are displayed on-screen below the image). You also can see the image's date, time, and any tags that have been attached.

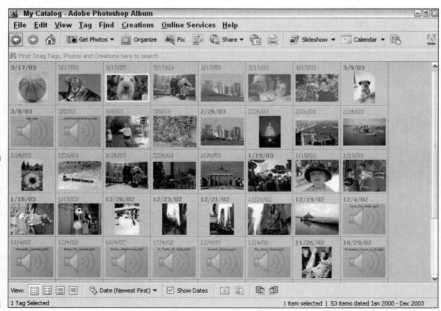

Figure 9-1:
To see as many images as possible, choose the Small Thumbnail view option.

Figure 9-2:
The Medium
Thumbnail
setting is
Album's
default
viewing
option.

If you don't see any metadata or tags, be sure that the Show Dates and Tags option is checked under the View menu (or check Show Dates in the Options bar at the bottom of the screen).

This viewing option also allows you to type a caption and attach or play an audio annotation. For more on captions and annotation, see Chapter 6.

You also can access the Single Photo view by double-clicking the image in the Photo Well (double-clicking an audio or video clip brings up the Album media player).

Here are a few other points to remember about views:

✔ You can change the date and time assigned to the photo by clicking either the date or time on-screen. For more on adjusting dates and times, see Chapter 5.

✔ You also can change your viewing options by clicking the icons in the Options bar.

✔ There is one other view you can select. Select your desired photo and choose View➪Show Full Screen. Your image will explode onto your screen. Any screen real estate not eaten up by image will be filled with black as shown in Figure 9-5. Click your mouse or press Esc to return to Album.

Figure 9-3:
To see more detail in your images, choose the Large Thumbnail view option.

Options bar   Date   Single Photo view   Metadata   Time   Tag

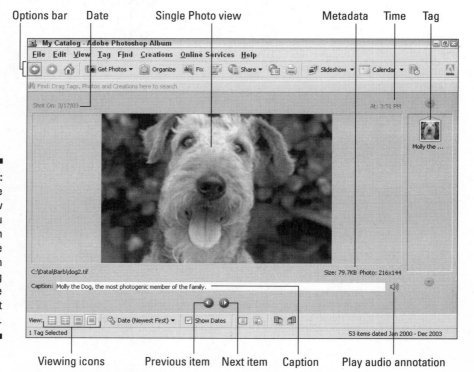

Figure 9-4:
The Single Photo view gives you metadata on your image in addition to showing you the largest view.

Viewing icons   Previous item   Next item   Caption   Play audio annotation

Figure 9-5:
To fill your screen with nothing but image, select the Full Screen view.

✔ Choose View⊏>Refresh to refresh your screen view. Sometimes commands you've performed on your image won't be displayed until you refresh. For example, if you attach a Hidden tag to a photo, the photo doesn't become hidden until the screen refreshes. For details on tags, see Chapter 5. You also can force a regeneration of all of your thumbnail images by right-clicking any photo, holding down the Ctrl key and selecting the Update Thumbnail command from the context-sensitive menu. Note that this process can take awhile if you have a large catalog.

Sorting Images in the Photo Well

You can specify how Album should sort the images you display. This option is truly made for us anal-retentive types who have a love for all things categorical and chronological.

Album lets you sort the files in your catalog using various criteria. You can sort by media type or you can sort by what Album refers to as arrangement. Sorting by arrangement allows you to sort your image by date and location among other criteria. After you choose your sorting criteria, Album retains this display until you decide to change it.

Sorting by media type

Sometimes you may want to view only images that are pertinent to a particular project. For example, say you're putting together a video CD and are concerned only with viewing video clips. Or maybe you're constructing a photo book and only want your photos to show in your Photo Well. Sorting files by media type allows you to selectively tell Album which kinds of files you want to display. Here's how:

1. **Choose View⇨Media Types.**

   The Items Shown dialog box appears, as shown in Figure 9-6.

2. **Select or deselect the types of files you want to display.**

3. **Click OK to close the dialog box.**

   Your chosen media types are now displayed in the Photo Well.

Figure 9-6:
You can
specify
which types
of files you
want to
display in
the Photo
Well.

Sorting by arrangement

Besides sorting by media types, Album also allows you to sort your files by date, how they were imported, location, and color. Sorting by the newest image first is probably the most popular arrangement, but each option has its advantages.

To sort by arrangement, choose View⇨Arrangement and select one of the options from the sub-menu, shown in Figure 9-7. You also can select a sorting option from the Photo Well Arrangement pop-up menu in the Options bar. Here's the lowdown on the options:

| View | Tag | Find | Creations | Online Services | Help |

Slideshow	Ctrl+Space
Show Full Screen	F11
Refresh	F5
Go To	▸
Size	▸
Arrangement	▸
Media Types...
✓ Show Dates and Tags	Ctrl+D
Contact Book...	Ctrl+Alt+B
Timeline	Ctrl+L
Tags	Ctrl+T
Properties	Alt+Enter
Workspace	Ctrl+W
Calendar	Ctrl+Alt+C

✓ Date (Newest First)	Ctrl+Alt+0
Date (Oldest First)	Ctrl+Alt+1
Import Batch	Ctrl+Alt+2
Folder Location	Ctrl+Alt+3
Color Similarity	

Figure 9-7:
You can specify which types of files you want to display in the Photo Well.

✔ **Date (Newest First):** This option shows the newest photos first, and includes either those images most recently taken or imported. Use this sorting option when you need to organize your most recently acquired images by renaming them, adding captions, or attaching tags. This option is Album's default.

✔ **Date (Oldest First):** This sorting option displays all of your files in chronological order, from the oldest to the newest.

✔ **Import Batch:** Choose this setting to display files in the batches in which they were imported. Each batch is separated by a dark gray line that includes information about the way the photos were imported into Album.

✔ **Folder Location:** This option displays photos by the folders in which they are located, as shown in Figure 9-8.

✔ **Color Similarity:** This option is grayed out unless you're viewing photos that have a similar color distribution. You can get this specialized view by selecting one or more photos in the Photo Well and choosing Find By Color Similarity with Selected Photo(s). For more on this option, see Chapter 8.

You also can view photos by date using the timeline and the calendar. Because this viewing option is closely tied to finding photos in Album, I cover it in detail in Chapter 8.

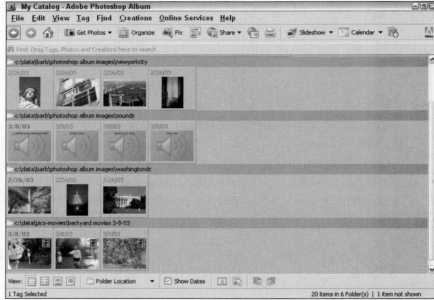

Figure 9-8:
Sorting by folder location displays your images in their respective folders.

Viewing Instant Slide Shows

A great viewing option in Album is the instant slide show. You can select the photos in your catalog and with a single command create a slide show that launches and plays on-screen. Each image in the slide show appears individually, gradually fades to black after a few seconds and then transitions into the next image. When the last image in the instant slide show is displayed, Album automatically closes the slide show and returns you to the Album application window.

Creating an instant slide show is a nice way to preview a folder or even a whole catalog of images. It is also helpful if you want to do a dry run of a slide show you ultimately plan on constructing and exporting as a PDF with the Creations Wizard (for more on the Creations Wizard, see Chapter 18). You also can control the pace of slide shows using the on-screen controls.

Viewing photos as a slide show

Follow these steps to view photos as a slide show:

   1. Select your desired photos in the Photo Well.

2. **Choose View⇨Slideshow.**

You also can click the Slideshow button in the Shortcuts bar, as shown in Figure 9-9.

You temporarily leave Album, and the slide show launches and takes over your screen, as shown in Figure 9-10. The show transitions through the chosen images automatically. Or you can use the on-screen controls to nudge the show along:

- You can pause the show by pressing the Stop button.

- If you don't see any controls, move your mouse to bring them to life. If the controls are not an aesthetically pleasing part of your presentation, you can close them by clicking the X in the top left corner of the controls.

- The slide show ends automatically; however to end it prematurely, press the Esc key.

If you're not happy with the timing, transitions, or background of the default settings for the slide show, you can change the slide show preferences (see the next section, "Setting instant slide show preferences," in this chapter).

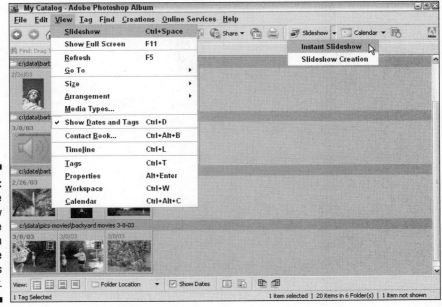

Figure 9-9: Choose Slideshow from the View menu or use the Shortcuts bar.

Figure 9-10:
Instant slide
shows are
a great
way to
preview
your
images.

Setting instant slide show preferences

If the default instant slide show settings aren't exactly to your liking, you can customize them by choosing new options in the Preferences dialog box. You can even jazz up your show by adding some background music. And if want your cat or dog to be entertained when you leave the room to do something else, you can set the show to repeat over and over and over . . .

Here's how to set your slide show preferences:

1. **Choose Edit➪Preferences.**

2. **Select Slideshow from the list of on the left side of the dialog box, shown in Figure 9-11.**

3. **Choose settings for the following options:**

   • **Background Music:** Choose an audio clip to play during your slide show. Select Play Audio Captions to play any captions that you have attached to the images in your slide show.

   • **Transition:** Select how the photos transition from one to the other in the slide show.

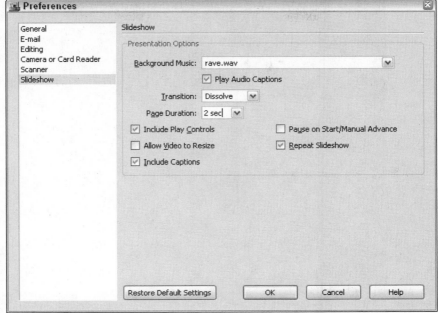

Figure 9-11:
Use the
Slideshow
Preferences
dialog box
to customize
your slide
.show.

Just a note of advice: Don't mix too many styles. Transitions are wonderful, but too much of a good thing has a tendency to make those of us with weak stomachs nauseous.

- **Page Duration:** Select the length of time that each photo stays on the screen. You can choose 2, 5, or 10 seconds from the pop-up menu or you can enter your own custom time duration.

- **Include Play Controls:** Choose this option to include the on-screen controls when you run your slide show.

- **Allow Video to Resize:** Select this option to allow video clips to resize to fill your screen. Be careful, however. If your image is small, allowing it to resize may result in a less-than-desirable screen quality, as shown in Figure 9-12.

- **Include Captions:** Choose this setting to include any captions you have attached to the images in your slide show.

- **Pause on Start/Manual Advance:** Select this option to pause the slide show when it starts so you can use the on-screen controls to run through the slide show instead of allowing it to run automatically.

Figure 9-12:
Don't
allow your
slide show
images
to be
resized
if they
are small.
Your results
may be the
blurry mush
shown here.

- **Repeat Slideshow:** Choose this option to put your slide show on a loop — have it repeat after it's made a run-through. The slide show will repeat (and repeat, and repeat) until you tell it to stop.

4. **When you're finished, click OK to close the dialog box.**

Viewing Video Clips

Because Album can't display thumbnails of moving images in the Photo Well, the thumbnails for video clips are displayed by their first frame. You can distinguish these thumbnails from still images because video clips have a film-strip icon that appears in the upper-right corner of the thumbnail.

Here are the steps to view a video clip:

1. **Double-click the video clip in the Photo Well.**

    The Photoshop Album media player launches, as shown in Figure 9-13.

2. **Click the Play button to start the video.**

   You can drag the position slider through the clip to view it frame by frame. But be aware that if your clip is long, this dragging method can jump over frames.

   If you need to control the volume, drag the volume slider.

3. **Click the Stop button to stop the clip.**

   If you find the urgent need to access Album's Help file, you'll be happy to know you can do it from the Media Player window.

4. **Click the Close button in the upper-right corner when you're done, which will close the Media Player.**

   You also can choose File➪Close.

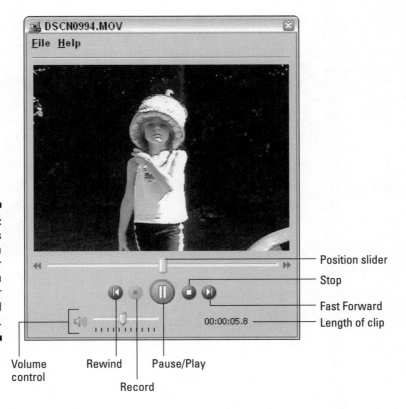

Figure 9-13:
Album's
Media
Player
allows you
to play your
video and
audio clips.

Position slider
Stop
Fast Forward
Length of clip

Volume
control
Rewind
Record
Pause/Play

Chapter 10

Setting Up Your Editing Environment

*B*efore you start a massive makeover of your images in Album, you might consider first taking inventory of your work area to see if it's conducive to image editing. I mean, you (or a delegate) spent a considerable amount of time setting up your computer, digital camera, and scanner to perform their assigned tasks, right? Similarly, consider setting up your workspace as an extension of your imaging equipment.

Not convinced? Well, let me add that setting up your workspace is free, easy, and takes very little time. I guarantee you'll get better-looking images as a result. As an added bonus, I throw in a couple of other tips in this chapter that help you manage your image-editing workflow.

After you have your workspace in ship shape, it's time to make sure your monitor is calibrated. The second step in working with digital images is to make sure that what you are seeing on-screen is as accurate as it can get. After that's been done you can move on to viewing, editing and sharing your photos with confidence.

Keeping Your Lighting Consistent

It is important to try and keep your lighting as consistent as possible:

✔ Try not to radically vary the level and intensity of the light while you are editing your images. For example, try to avoid working on an image in the bright afternoon sun and then again under the harsh light of a fluorescent bulb late at night.

✔ Try to view all of your images under the same intensity of light.

Looking at your source material, your on-screen images, and your prints under the same lighting can provide a consistent benchmark to use in your viewing and editing sessions. Variations in lighting can cause you to perceive color differently and result in color shifts in your output (both on-screen and in print).

If you happen to be stuck next to a window or skylight, you may want to purchase a monitor hood or visor. These tools help to shield your screen against glare and reflection and run in the neighborhood of $15 to $100.

Removing Distractions

No, I don't mean eliminating rambunctious kids, barking dogs, and cats hopping onto your warm monitor. (Of course, removal of the above could very well make you more productive.) The kind of distractions I am talking about are the ones on and around your monitor.

Stepping up to professional lighting devices

If you find yourself really getting into this digital imaging stuff, there are a couple of devices that the professionals use which may interest you:

✔ **Task lamp:** This is a lamp that provides consistent full-spectrum light that mimics sunlight. Task lamps allow you to see colors more accurately and with more clarity. They also offer low-glare lighting, run on less energy, and cut down on eye strain. Task lamps run from $50 to $200 or so.

✔ **Light box:** This is also called a *light booth* or *color viewing booth.* Professional-grade light boxes adhere to lighting standards developed by the ISO (International Standards Organization). Light boxes offer various lighting environments (depending on the make and model), such as fluorescent, incandescent, UV, daylight, and so on. Light boxes enable you to view images in a controlled, consistent environment so that you can see the images the way that your intended audience will. For example, if people will be viewing one of your pictures in an office setting (under fluorescent lights), you can adjust the settings accordingly — and adjust your output. Likewise, if people will be viewing the poster outside (in daylight), you just adjust the setting. Cost ranges from a few hundred dollars to several thousands, depending on the model.

Using a neutral background

If you've become attached to the dancing dinosaur wallpaper on your desktop, it's time to cut the ties. It might be painful, and it may seem oh so boring, but let go of the disco T. Rex and keep your desktop a neutral gray, which is better for image viewing.

Any colors and patterns behind your images will affect how you view those images, as shown in Figure 10-1. Think about it: When you display artwork, whether photographic or illustrative, it is usually framed against a neutral black, white, or gray background. That way the focus is on the work, and nothing is distracting your eye. Same principle applies for your digital photos.

If you're using Windows XP, follow the steps below to get your desktop to a neutral gray. If you're sporting another flavor of Windows, check your documentation if you're unsure of how to achieve a gray desktop. In Windows XP, follow these steps:

1. **Right-click the desktop. Select Properties from the context-sensitive menu.**

2. **In the Display Properties window, click the Appearance tab.**

3. **Click the Advanced button.**

4. **In the Advanced Appearance window, select Desktop from the Item pop-up menu.**

5. **Select Other from the Color pop-up menu.**

6. **In the Color window, enter a value of 128 in the Red, Green and Blue text boxes.**

   A value of 128 for Red, Green and Blue will yield a neutral gray color.

7. **Click OK.**

   You are now the proud owner of neutral gray background to help you with your image-editing tasks.

In fact, putting certain colors next to each other influences the way your eyes perceive a color. For more on color theory, see Chapter 3.

Choosing a work area with neutral walls

Like the computer desktop, keep the walls of your work area neutral as well. You don't have to paint the room gray (although, believe it or not, hard-core color and retouching experts do), but try to avoid lots of colorful artwork around and behind your monitor. Even objects and art that aren't directly next to your screen image may influence your perception.

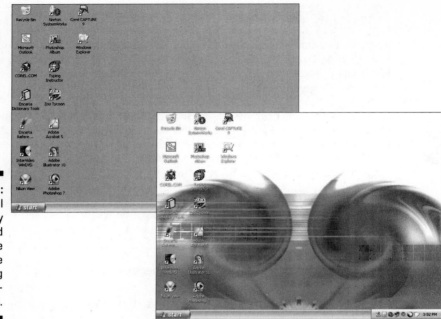

Figure 10-1:
A neutral
gray
background
is more
conducive
for editing
than moon-
flowers.

Sitting Pretty

If, by the end of a day of playing with your digital images, your arms are numb, your legs are cramped, and your back is screaming for a massage, it may be time to look at your desk and chair. Face it. If you aren't comfortable when you're parked in front of your computer immersed in imaging heaven, you're not going to be as productive.

At the very least, messing with your images isn't going to be as enjoyable. Invest in an ample desk and a chair with good support.

I find that propping my feet on a short wooden block under my desk helps my back tremendously. If you feel like you have carpal tunnel syndrome after a few hours at the keyboard, try using those cushy gel wrist rests for both your keyboard and mouse. Give yourself a little time to get used to them; you'll be surprised how much strain they absorb.

Find a Vendor and Stick with It

If you plan on buying imaging or printing services, either online or from a vendor near your home or office, spend some time finding the best service bureau or printer online or in your area. After you've found the one you like, stick with that vendor for all your prints, photo books, Photo CDs, and other products and services. Here are a few reasons why:

✔ You'll know what to expect, in terms of color and other quality characteristics.

✔ You will get better services by being a regular customer.

Sometimes jumping from vendor to vendor to save a few bucks isn't worth risking a good working relationship. After you have established a relationship with a vendor in your area (or online), ask questions. These people not only know their own business' products and services, but probably know a lot about digital imaging in general.

Running Tests, Tests, and More Tests

Take some time to test your workflow and your computer system. Take a lot of digital photos. You don't have to worry about film and developing costs so snap away. The more photos you take, the better photographer you'll be (check out Chapter 19 for tips on composition). Even if all you plan to be is the designated family vacation photographer, don't underestimate the significance of your function. Experience and a little knowledge behind the lens will make your photos all that more memorable, and that's a priceless gift. Here are a few other tests you can try:

✔ Scan images using multiple settings and see what kinds of results you get.

✔ Print images using multiple resolutions and different types of papers.

✔ View your images using different browsers on different monitors and different platforms.

Really become familiar with the ins and outs of every piece of your equipment in your workflow. No books, documentation, or advice comes close to the amount of knowledge gained from spending time on your system and experimenting. And play, play, play in Album. If friends and family start complaining about how they never see you now that you've become this digital fiend, you could always give them a beautifully printed photo of yourself!

Calibrating Your Monitor

If your images appear too dark, too light, or have a weird bluish, yellowish, or reddish cast, your monitor probably needs *calibrating*. Even if your images look pretty good, it is still a good idea to calibrate.

By calibrating your monitor and creating a characterization, or profile, of your monitor, you ensure that you are getting rid of any color casts and providing as neutral a gray screen as possible. By doing so you are standardizing the display of images — how you view your images today will be the same as how you view them next week.

Calibrating your monitor is the first step in trying to get consistent color from all input (cameras, scanners), and output devices (screen, printer).

You can calibrate your monitor by using any of several methods. If you hunt on the Internet, it seems every digital expert or photographer has his or her preferred method. Photoshop Album ships with a program called Adobe Gamma.

It's a good idea to display an image with known color values while calibrating your monitor. In other words, use an image that you have worked with before and for which you have a good print. Then use that image each and every time you calibrate.

Some experts say you should calibrate your monitor weekly; others say monthly because monitors can drift and even degrade over time.

Using the same image every time you calibrate enables you to more closely match what you see on-screen to match the printed output. For more on getting optimum prints, see Chapter 14.

Using Adobe Gamma

Follow these steps to use Adobe Gamma to calibrate your monitor:

1. **First, turn your monitor on and let it warm up at least 60 minutes.**

    This action allows your monitor to stabilize before calibration.

2. **Make certain that your monitor is displaying thousands of colors (16 bits) or more. If your monitor is set to 32 bits, don't change it.**

3. **Set your desktop display to a neutral gray using RGB values of 128.**

    If you're not sure how to do these two operations, check with your operating system documentation.

    See "Using a neutral background," earlier in this chapter.

4. **Set the lighting in the room the way you will have it when you are viewing images. Also try and reduce any glare or reflections on the screen.**

5. **Launch the Adobe Gamma utility.**

This program ships with Album, but if you don't have this utility already installed, you can find it on your Photoshop Album installation CD. You can install it by opening the Adobe Gamma folder on the CD and following the simple install instructions in the ReadMe file. Adobe Gamma also ships with Adobe Photoshop, InDesign, and Acrobat, so if you have any of these applications, you may already have it installed.

You can find Adobe Gamma in the Control Panel (Start⇨Settings⇨ Control Panel). If it isn't there, check in your Program Files folder, in the Common Files folder, in the Adobe folder, in the Calibration folder.

6. **You can select either the Step By Step (Wizard) option or the manual Control Panel option, both shown in Figure 10-2. I highly recommend using the Wizard. Then click Next.**

   The Wizard walks you through the calibration process via questions.

7. **Adjust the monitor's contrast and brightness controls, which set the dark point of your monitor. Then click Next.**

8. **Enter the phosphors setting, for example, Trinitron. Then click Next.**

   If you don't know it, check your monitor's documentation.

9. **Choose a gamma (gray or *midtones*) setting by adjusting a slider for red, green, and blue squares on-screen. Then click Next.**

   The default gamma for Windows is 2.2.

10. **Set your white point. Then click Next.**

   The standard for Windows is 6500K (K stands for Kelvin, which measures color temperature).

TECHNICAL STUFF

Taking calibration to the next level

Each of us perceives color a little differently, so your visual perception could affect the way you profile your monitor. If you have a big budget and you really want to do a great calibration job, you might consider purchasing a self-calibrating monitor. These monitors constantly measure their own color and create a profile that is very precise. The technology comes with a price, however. These monitors are obviously more expensive than the average monitor.

If your budget isn't quite so hefty, consider a combination hardware/software calibration package that you can use with your existing monitor. You can get a pretty good package from several manufacturers, such as Pantone/Color Vision, which costs around $300. The package includes software that displays color swatches on your screen. Then you attach a photoelectric device, called a *colorimeter,* to your monitor with a suction cup. The sensors in the colorimeter measure the color, brightness, and other characteristics of the monitor. The software takes the data, adjusts your monitor to its optimum state, and then creates a profile from it. Very *Invasion of the Body Snatchers.* Very high tech.

You can start with the default settings, but they may need a little adjusting depending on what you see. When you're done, Adobe Gamma creates a profile of your monitor so your graphic programs know how your monitor is displaying color.

If you use the Wizard, Adobe Gamma allows you to see a before and after view of your screen. If Adobe Gamma has done its job properly, you won't see any funky color cast, and your monitor won't be too dark or overly bright. If everything looks good, you can click Finish. If not, you can go back and adjust.

Figure 10-2:
Adobe
Gamma is a
simple utility
to help
visually
calibrate
your
monitor.

Using another calibration utility

If you don't have Adobe Gamma, no problem. Quite a few Web sites offer similar calibration utilities. Check out

- www.viewsonic.com/support/calibration.htm
- www.easyrgb.com/calibrate.php
- www.risingphotography.com/calibration
- www.praxisoft.com (a free version wiziWYG XP)

All of the sites listed here offer tools similar or even better than Adobe Gamma. You also can search around the Web and find a utility that I didn't mention here.

Photographer Norman Koren has a great tutorial on monitor and printer calibration at www.normankoren.com, but be warned that while informative and comprehensive, it may be too technical for some folks.

Chapter 11

Making Quick Fixes

*H*ave you ever gotten home from a vacation or special event and anxiously imported your photos only to find that quite a few of them could use a *little* help? Maybe one image is too dark, and another image has a distracting background? Maybe the color is washed out, or the image is blurry? Don't delete your so-so pictures; they can be saved!

Thankfully, Photoshop Album comes equipped with a batch of editing tools to help correct those images and make them worthy of sharing or printing. What's even better is that Album has conveniently put all those editing tools in one handy location called the Fix Photo dialog box.

If you haven't already, be sure to read Chapter 10 so that you can get your work area and monitor ready for some editing magic.

Improving Images with Fix Photo

The Fix Photo dialog box is makeover central for your digital images. It's easy to use and provides several controls for improving their appearance. There are fixes that require a single click of a button and others that need a little more intervention on your part.

Choosing a viewing option

The first step is getting your image into the Fix Photo dialog box. Here's how:

1. **Select the image you want to edit in the Photo Well.**

   If you're not sure how to select a photo, check out Chapter 2.

   You can bring only one photo into the Fix Photo dialog box at a time.

2. **Choose Edit⇨Fix Photo.**

   You also can click the Fix button in the Shortcuts bar, shown in Figure 11-1. Or you also can right-click and choose Fix Photo from the context-sensitive menu. And if those aren't enough ways to get into Fix Photo, you also can just double-click the photo to enlarge it to a Single Photo view and then double-click it again.

   You're prompted with a warning, shown in Figure 11-2, that says you are about to edit an original photo, but that the original file won't be changed. It also specifies where the edited photo will be saved.

   If you've sufficiently digested the meaning of this message, and don't want to see this warning every time you access the Fix Photo dialog box, go ahead and check the Don't Show Again option.

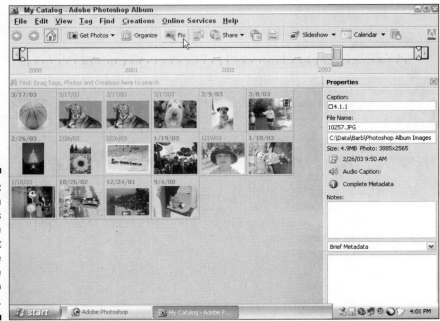

Figure 11-1: Album provides multiple ways to get an image into the Fix Photo dialog box.

3. Click OK.

The warning disappears.

If you are fixing a previously edited photo, the warning will be a little different. It will say you are going to edit a previously edited photo, and your changes will be written to that file. And if you're editing a Photoshop file with multiple layers, you will get an additional warning that the edited photo will be *flattened* (a technical term that means smushed into a single layer called a Background). Again, your original image is still tucked away unaltered.

Figure 11-2: Album warns you that your original file won't be edited.

After you click OK, the Fix Photo dialog box appears, as shown in Figure 11-3.

You can resize the Fix Photo dialog box. Place your cursor in the bottom right corner of the dialog box until your cursor appears as diagonal double headed arrow. Drag to size. I recommend clicking the Maximize button in the upper-right corner to bring the dialog box to its max size. That way your image is as large as possible for your editing session.

4. Select a viewing option from the tabs in the upper-left corner.

Album provides you with four viewing options, as follows:

- **Original:** Shows your image appeared when you first imported it into Album. After you edit the image, the original view is the only place you can view the original, unedited photo (unless you undo your edits, which I describe later in this section).

  After editing, the original photo is stored on your computer, but doesn't display in the Photo Well. The only version you can see in the Photo Well is the edited version.

- **Before:** Displays the photo as it looked when you launched the Fix Photo dialog box. This tab appears only if the photo has been previously edited.

Tabs

Editing options

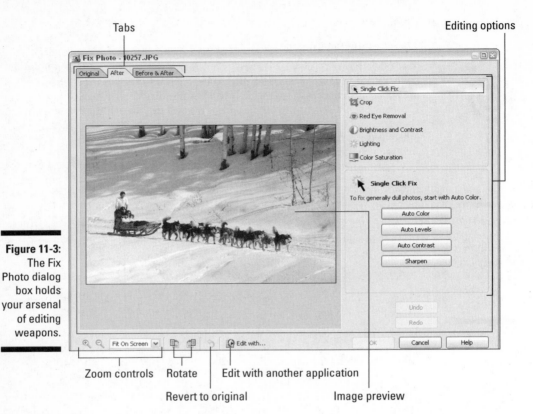

Figure 11-3:
The Fix
Photo dialog
box holds
your arsenal
of editing
weapons.

Zoom controls   Rotate   Edit with another application

Revert to original   Image preview

- **After:** Displays the photo with all of the current edits that you've made since launching Fix Photo.

- **Before & After:** Shows both the Original (or Before) image and the After version. This is a great view for a side-by-side comparison.

When you've found a viewing option that satisfies you, move on to the following section, "Introducing editing tools."

Introducing editing tools

After you're in the Fix Photo dialog box and have chosen your viewing option, you're ready to start editing. Here are a couple of options you'll find in the dialog box to help you along the way:

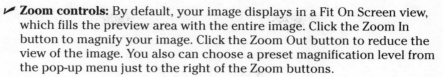

✔ **Zoom controls:** By default, your image displays in a Fit On Screen view, which fills the preview area with the entire image. Click the Zoom In button to magnify your image. Click the Zoom Out button to reduce the view of the image. You also can choose a preset magnification level from the pop-up menu just to the right of the Zoom buttons.

You can use the handy keyboard shortcuts. Press Ctrl+Plus sign to zoom in. To zoom out press (surprise) Ctrl+Minus sign. To view your image at 100 percent, press Ctrl+Alt+0. To see your image in a Fit On Screen view, press Ctrl+0.

✔ **Scroll bars:** To view portions of the image that aren't visible within the preview window, drag the scroll bars on the right and bottom of the window. You only see the scroll bars if the entire image doesn't fit within the preview window.

✔ **Undo:** If you make a mistake, you can easily undo it by clicking the Undo button in the bottom right of the dialog box. And if you really didn't mean to undo, you can click the Redo button to bring your action back.

Feel free to use the standard keyboard shortcuts of Ctrl+X and Ctrl+Y, too.

✔ **Cancel:** Click Cancel (or press the Esc button) to leave the Fix Photo dialog box without accepting any adjustments.

✔ **Revert to Original:** Click the curved blue arrow at the bottom of the dialog box to revert to the original image as it looked when you first imported it into Album.

This option wipes out all previously edited versions of the file, and reverts only to the original.

✔ **Help:** If you're lost and need assistance, click the Help button in the bottom-right corner of the dialog box. The online Help file launches in your browser. For more on using Help, see Chapter 2.

All you ever wanted to know about reverting

Here are a few other points to keep in mind about reverting to previous incarnations of your edited images:

✔ All edits are made to a copy of your image, which is saved as a file called "*filename*_edited" and placed in the same folder as the original photo. The original photo is left untouched. After you edit a photo, it is the only version that displays in the Photo Well.

✔ If later on, you decide the edited version just isn't cutting it, you can choose Edit➪Revert to Original.

> ✔ If you feel the edited version is just so much better than the original ever was and you don't want to waste disk space saving the original, choose Edit➪Replace Original with Edited. That command will overwrite the original and leave you with only the edited file.

For more on managing your images, see Chapter 7.

Quick and Dirty Edits with Single Click Fixes

The quickest and easiest edits to make in the Fix Photo dialog box are what are called Single Click Fixes. These are automatic edits, meaning you really have no say-so in how Album applies them.

You click the Fix you want to apply, and an algorithm (or mathematical formula) churns. Then, boom, the edit is applied.

With Single Click Fixes, you're putting your trust in Album's hands. Often, the quality of your images is improved.

In image editing, there is no right or wrong. The most important factor in whether an edit is *good* is what your eye perceives and likes or dislikes. The contrast and color may look great to you and downright lousy to someone else. If you're editing images to please yourself, that's all that matters. If you're editing images to please someone else, well, maybe the two of you can reach a happy compromise.

One thing to keep in mind. Although your image may benefit nicely from using one of the automatic fixes (Auto Color, Auto Levels, or Auto Contrast), using more than one probably won't make the image look any better. In fact, it may make it look worse. Feel free to go ahead and experiment. That's why the Undo button is in close proximity.

Here are the steps to apply a Single Click Fix:

1. **If your photo isn't already displayed in the Fix Photo dialog box, select it in the Photo Well. Then choose Edit➪Fix Photo.**

   Or simply double-click the image once to enlarge the view and double-click again to bring it into the Fix Photo dialog box.

2. **Select the Single Click Fix option in the top right of the Fix Photo dialog box.**

3. Choose one of the following options:

- **Auto Color:** This option fixes two problems. First it removes color casts and adjusts the color balance of an image. Your image has a color cast if its image looks too red, as in Figure 11-4 or too blue, as shown in Color Plate 11-1 of the color insert. It also corrects oversaturated (neon like) or washed out colors, as shown in Figure 11-4. The black-and-white figures just don't do this editing command any justice.

- **Auto Levels:** This command lightens the highlights and darkens the shadows in a photo. In other words, it automatically improves the contrast of an image, shown in Figure 11-5. This algorithm works by defining the lightest pixels as white, the darkest pixels as black, and redistributing the gray, or *midtone,* pixels in between.

Figure 11-4: An image with a nasty red color cast (top) gets improved with Auto Color (bottom).

Beware that although adjusting Auto Levels may vastly improve the contrast quality, it can sometimes also produce an undesirable color cast.

- **Auto Contrast:** This option also lightens the highlights and darkens the shadows of an image. It does so by converting the lightest pixels white, and the darkest pixels black. This option may not be quite as effective in improving the contrast, but it also preserves the color balance of an image and doesn't cause any unsightly color casts. It works especially well with hazy images like the New York City skyline shown in Figure 11-6. To see the Auto Contrast fix work its magic on a color image, check out Color Plate 11-2.

Try using Auto Levels first, and if it causes a color cast, click Undo and apply Auto Contrast instead.

Figure 11-5:
Auto Levels can improve the contrast of an image, but can sometimes produce an unwanted color cast.

Figure 11-6:
Auto
Contrast
also
improves
the contrast
of an image,
but keeps
the color
balance
intact.

- **Sharpen:** This command adds clarity to an image by sharpening the edges of objects in the photo, as shown in Figure 11-7. Sharpening is a technique that increases the contrast between pixels to give the illusion of improved focus. Try applying the Sharpen fix more than once to further improve a fuzzy picture.

Don't get too carried away, however. It can't take a photo that was shot out of focus and make it look like it was taken on a tripod. In fact, you can oversharpen an image. If it starts looking grainy, you know you've gone too far. So hurry and click Undo.

4. **Choose the Before and After tab in the top left of the dialog box and compare the original unedited image with the edited version.**

5. **If the image looks better, click OK to exit the Fix Photo dialog box, unless you have more editing to do.**

The edited image replaces the original image in the Photo Well.

Original

Sharpened   Oversharpened

Figure 11-7: Sharpening increases the contrast between pixels on the edges of objects to give the illusion of better focus, but be sure not to over-sharpen.

If any of the Single Click Fixes you choose do not produce a satisfactory result, click the Undo button. That particular fix may be unsuitable for the particular correction needed, or it may just be beyond its capability. Instead, try one of the manual adjustments described in the next section, "Using Manual Fixes." Manual fixes take a little more effort on your part but may just provide the enhancement you need.

Using Manual Fixes

If you applied a Single Click Fix and it didn't work out (or maybe it did, but your image still needs a little more help), you can enter the world of manual image fixes. I must say, that there isn't a whole lot of manual labor involved, unless you consider moving a handle or slider a strenuous or tedious maneuver.

Manual fixes give you more control in the editing process by allowing you to set the amount of adjustment necessary. Don't be afraid to experiment and see what happens. As I mentioned earlier, that's what the Undo, or if necessary the Cancel, buttons are there for — to bail you out in times of editing gone bad.

Rotating images

When importing your images in Album, you may find that a number of them need to be rotated. Maybe you turned your camera to fit your subject in the viewfinder or you scanned your image sideways in order to get it to fit on the scanning bed. Well, no worries. One of the easiest and most common editing functions is rotating.

In the Fix Photo dialog box

To rotate your image in the Fix Photo dialog box:

1. **Select the photo in the Photo Well and choose Edit⇨Fix Photo.**

   You also can double-click the photo twice to bring it into the Fix Photo dialog box.

   For the remaining discussion on manual adjustments, I assume your image is in the Fix Photo dialog box and ready to go.

2. **Click the Rotate Left or Rotate Right button located in the bottom, shown in Figure 11-8.**

   You may have to click more than once to get your photo oriented correctly.

3. **After you rotate the image to your liking, simply click OK to exit the Fix Photo dialog box.**

   Album saves an edited (in this case rotated) copy of your original image.

 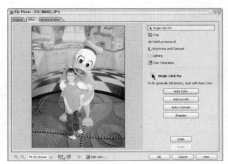

Figure 11-8: Rotating images is the simplest and most popular edit.

In the Photo Well

You also can rotate a photo right in the Photo Well. This option is actually better if you have several photos that need rotating because you can select and rotate multiple photos all at the same time.

One important difference between rotating images in the Photo Well as opposed to using the Fix Photo dialog box: If you rotate the photos in the Photo Well, the rotation is done and *saved over the original file.* A new edited file is not created as it is in the Fix Photo dialog box.

Here's how to rotate images using the Photo Well:

1. **Select one or more photos.**

2. **Click the Rotate Left or Rotate Right button in the Options bar.**

   For a refresher on the Options bar, see Chapter 2.

Like many other commands in Album, there is more than one way to do the same thing. You also can right-click the image and choose Rotate Right or Rotate Left from the context-sensitive menu. Alternatively, you can choose Edit⇨Rotate Right or Edit⇨Rotate Left. If you have selected multiple photos, the command appears as Edit⇨Rotate Selected Photos Right or Edit⇨Rotate Selected Photos Left.

Cropping photos

The second-most popular editing command is *cropping* — selectively getting rid of part of the image. Sigh. How many times have I captured way too much distracting background in a photograph?

One of the cardinal rules of good composition is to get close to your subject. Sometimes when shooting the image you may feel you need to get everything in the shot, only to find later that when the image is cropped, it's so much stronger. It is always best to try and frame your subject when you take the photo, but if that doesn't happen, you also can crop it in Album.

Here are the steps to crop a photo in the Fix Photo dialog box:

1. **Select Crop from the list of editing options in the top right.**

   A cropping rectangle appears on your image. Don't worry, you'll have ample opportunity to adjust the handles so that the rectangle surrounds the part of the image that you want to retain.

2. **To maintain a desired ratio between the height and width of the cropped image, choose one of several options from the Select Aspect Ratio pop-up menu.**

   Choosing an Aspect Ratio isn't the same thing as choosing an actual size. *Aspect ratio* refers to the proportional relationship between height and width. For example, a 4 x 6 aspect ratio is the same as a 2 x 3 aspect ratio.

Choosing No Restriction allows total freedom in moving your cropping handles. Selecting Use Photo Ratio keeps the aspect ratio to the standard rectangular snapshot format no matter what the actual size is.

3. **Position your cursor on one of the handles of the cropping rectangle. Drag that handle, and any others, to frame the portion of the photo you want to retain.**

4. **To move the entire cropping rectangle, position your cursor inside the cropping rectangle. When your cursor changes from an arrow to a hand, drag the rectangle to your desired location on the image, as shown in Figure 11-9.**

Figure 11-9:
Adjust the cropping rectangle to frame your image.

Press the Plus sign key or the Minus sign key to make the cropping rectangle larger or smaller. You also can press the arrows keys to move the rectangle 1 pixel in any direction. Press Shift with an arrow key to move the rectangle 10 pixels in any direction. Luckily, these keyboard shortcuts also work with the red eye rectangle, described in "Removing the dreaded red eye" later in this chapter.

5. **When you've framed the image satisfactorily, click the Apply Crop button.**

   You also can press Enter on your keyboard or double-click inside the rectangle.

6. **Click OK to exit the Fix Photo dialog box.**

   The cropped image appears, as shown in Figure 11-10.

Figure 11-10:
The photo
on the top is
fine, but the
cropped
image
(bottom)
really
shines.

If you accidentally chop off someone's body part, you can always click the Undo button. And if you click the Crop button and decide you don't want to crop after all, simply click the Single Click Fix button. The cropping rectangle disappears, and you'll be back at square one.

When you crop an image in any computer program, you are making the image smaller because you are eliminating pixels. Make sure you have sufficient resolution to print the image at the size you want, or else you may not be happy with the quality. For more on resolution, see Chapter 3.

Removing the dreaded red eye

Digital photographers adore the ability to remove nasty red eye from pictures. *Red eye* occurs when light from a camera's flash bounces off the back of the retina of the eye and back into the camera's lens. It often occurs in low lighting situations and/or when the flash is too close to the lens of the camera, as is often the case with digital and point-and-shoot cameras.

At the source, you can prevent red eye by making sure your camera is set to no red eye mode. Check your documentation to see if your camera has the capability. You also can ask your subjects to look away from the camera. If you are shooting indoors, turn on all the lights in the room. This will help shrink the pupils of the eye. You also can ensure that the flash of your camera is mounted above or to the side of the lens. If you can't move (or remove) the flash (at least not without duct tape), Album offers an easy solution after the fact. Enter the Fix Photo dialog box.

To remove red eye, follow these simple steps in the Fix Photo dialog box:

1. **Using the Zoom In button and the scroll bars, navigate to the offending red eyes.**

2. **Click the Red Eye Removal button in the Editing Options list in the upper-right side of the Fix Photo dialog box.**

   A rectangle appears on the image preview, as shown in Figure 11-11.

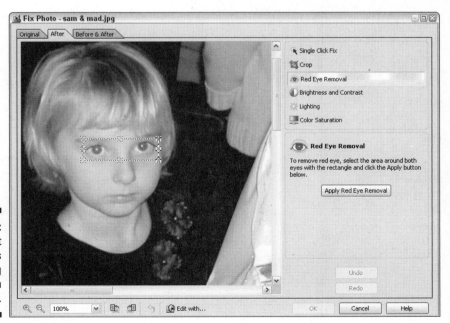

Figure 11-11: Pinpoint the red eyes by using the Zoom controls.

3. **Adjust the rectangle by placing your cursor (which appears as a double-headed arrow) and dragging the handles to size the rectangle.**

   You can place your cursor inside the rectangle and drag with the hand icon to move it. Frame the offending eyes fairly tightly.

4. **When you have adjusted the rectangle, click the Red Eye Removal button again. Like cropping, you also can press the Enter key or double-click inside the rectangle.**

   If you're lucky, the red eyes have been replaced with black pupils once again, as seen in Figure 11-12.

To really see the great red eye removal effort of Album, check out Color Plate 11-4 in the color insert. Album not only got rid of the little girl's red eyes, but also fixed the eyes on the Siamese kitten.

   If your eyes are still looking a tad eerie, first try repeating the steps. On some images, I found that I had to do it two or three times before I completely got rid of the red. If it still doesn't work, you may require the extra strength editing power of Photoshop Elements or Photoshop. See more on editing in these two programs in Chapter 12.

5. **Click OK to exit the Fix Photo dialog box.**

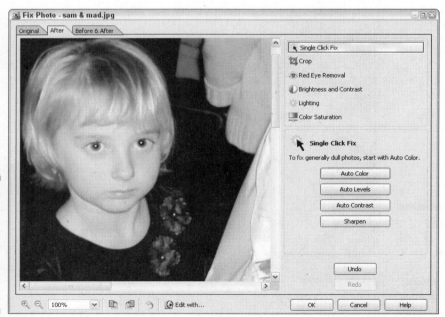

Figure 11-12:
Red-eye removal can make a demon child angelic once more.

Improving contrast with Brightness and Contrast

If you tried the Single Click Fixes to adjust contrast and it didn't quite cut the mustard, you may need a little manual adjusting with the Brightness and Contrast controls.

When I talk about *brightness,* I'm referring to the lightness or darkness of a photo. *Contrast,* on the other hand, refers to the relationship between the light and dark areas of a photo. In some instances you may want to play with these adjustments to get a special mood or effect, but most often you should use this tool to correct the exposure of the photo. A photo with too little contrast looks flat and dull. A photo with too much contrast lacks details in the highlights and shadows.

If you are making brightness and contrast adjustments on a photo that will ultimately be printed, be sure and run some test prints before saving the edits. Often an image may look fine on-screen, only to find it looks darker when printed.

You may also find that adjusting the brightness and contrast settings doesn't really improve your image much after all. That may be partly due to the fact that brightness and contrast makes uniform adjustments to your overall image. It makes no discretion to particular problem areas of the image. If you experience this problem, try canceling the adjustments and using the Lighting editing option instead. You may find that lightening just the shadows and darkening just the overexposed areas are better remedies.

Here are the steps to manually adjust the brightness and contrast:

1. **Select the Brightness and Contrast editing option from the list in the top right of the Fix Photo dialog box, shown in Figure 11-13.**

2. **Drag the brightness slider to the right to lighten the photo or to the left to darken the photo.**

   You also can enter a value between –100 and 100. In my image, I moved the Brightness slider to the left to –20 to darken it.

3. **Drag the contrast slider to the right to increase the contrast in the photo or to the left to decrease it.**

   Again, you also can enter a value between –100 and 100. In my example (shown in Figure 11-14), I moved the contrast slider to the right to 15 to give it more contrast.

4. **Click OK to exit the Fix Photo dialog box.**

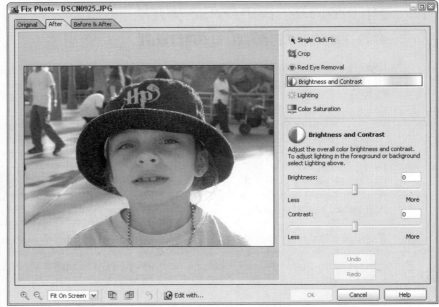

Figure 11-13:
This image is in dire need of brightness and contrast adjustments.

Figure 11-14:
The same image, newly improved with Brightness and Contrast.

Fixing shadows and highlights with the Lighting option

You can use the Lighting option in the Fix Photo dialog box to fix highlights and shadows in your images.

Lightening shadows

In photos taken in bright light, such as at the beach or in the snow on a sunny day, shadows often lose any sign of detail. At the source, you can lighten these shadows by using the Fill Flash mode on your camera. This mode activates the flash on your camera regardless of the available light, providing additional light in those shadowy areas and preserving some detail.

After the fact, you can use the Fill Flash setting on Album's Lighting option.

To lighten shadows using the Fill Flash setting, follow these steps:

1. **Select the Lighting editing option from the list in the top right of the Fix Photo dialog box.**

2. **Drag the Fill Flash slider from Darker to Lighter. You also can enter a value between 0 and 100.**

   Drag the slider until you see detail in the shadows, shown in Figure 11-15, but not so much that your shadows all turn gray. Also check out the Fill Flash in action in Color Plate 11-3.

3. **Click OK to exit the Fix Photo dialog box.**

Adjusting the backlighting

Photos that have been shot with backlighting can be especially dramatic. *Backlighting* means that the light source is behind your subject. Think of a silhouette of a person walking on the beach at sunset. But if the light source is strong, such as midday, and you're trying to capture detail in all areas of the photo, backlighting can cause two problems:

✔ The area surrounding the subject gets overexposed (too light).

✔ Your subject gets underexposed (too dark).

Either way, you're losing detail somewhere. You can correct this problem at the source easily by either moving yourself or your subject so the light source isn't directly behind the subject. Or you can try using a flash. (For the flash to be effective, you will probably need to be fairly close to your subject, though.) For close-up shots, you also can use a white reflector card (like poster board) to reflect light onto your subject.

Figure 11-15:
Adjusting
with the Fill
Flash option
brings out
detail in the
shadow
areas.

After the fact, you can use the Backlighting setting in Album to help darken those overexposed areas, as shown in Figure 11-16. Use the Fill Flash option described above to lighten the underexposed portions of the same image.

To adjust the backlighting in an image, follow these steps:

1. **Select the Lighting editing option from the list at the upper-right corner of the Fix Photo dialog box.**

2. **Drag the Backlighting slider from Lighter to Darker. You also can enter a value between 0 and 100.**

3. **Click OK to exit the Fix Photo dialog box.**

Intensifying with Color Saturation

Saturation refers to the intensity of the color in an image. When colors look washed out, they are undersaturated. If the colors are oversaturated, they appear almost neon like. A happy medium between the two is the ideal.

An easy way to turn a color image into a black-and-white (or *grayscale*) photo is to adjust the saturation. Drag the saturation slider all the way to the left until the color has been removed. Check out Color Plate 11-7 to see this technique in action. Read the following steps for more details.

Figure 11-16:
The Backlighting option helps bring back detail in the overexposed areas of a backlit image.

To manually adjust the color saturation, follow these steps:

1. **Select Color Saturation from the editing options list in the top-right side of the Fix Photo dialog box.**

2. **Drag the Saturation slider to the right to increase the saturation of colors in the photo or to the left to decrease it.**

   You also can enter a value between –100 and 100. In my example, I moved the slider to 45 to increase the saturation.

3. **If your image is improved, as shown in Figure 11-17, click OK to exit the Fix Photo dialog box.**

   The grayscale images shown here make it hard to illicit the oohs and aahs that are so nice to hear when demonstrating a color technique. Open an image in your catalog that needs some saturation help and see for yourself.

Figure 11-17:
Adjusting
the color
saturation in
an image
can bring it
back to life.

Chapter 12

Extra-Strength Editing

- -

- -

Album is spectacular. It enables you to organize your pictures, stay organized, become more productive, and even create some fun and useful projects.

If I have any criticism, it's that the editing tools in Album don't always do the trick if my images are particularly problematic. Don't get me wrong; for the most part, Album is great for getting rid of red eye or improving the contrast of a photo. But if you have an image that you really need to overhaul, you may require the editing horsepower of a full-fledged image-editing program.

Comparing Photoshop Elements and Photoshop

If you're interested in purchasing an external digital-imaging application, I highly recommend either Photoshop Elements or Photoshop, depending on your needs and budget. Trust me; I'm not being paid to endorse these products. It's just that if you use either of these Adobe products you'll have the benefit of seamless integration with Album. You can purchase Elements for about $90. Photoshop will set you back a hefty $600 or so. (Ouch.) If you're not sure whether you want to make the investment, download a 30-day, fully-functioning trial version of either program from www.adobe.com.

If you're not familiar with either of these programs, you may wonder which one is appropriate for your needs and why there is such a vast difference between one program that runs about the cost of two dinners out and another that is about the cost of two car payments.

Elements

Elements is Adobe's amateur photographer-level imaging program. Elements has a large toolbox, as shown in Figure 12-1, filled with selection, color correction, and retouching tools. Here are a few other things you can do with Elements:

- ✔ Size your images.

- ✔ Change color modes. Color modes define the color values used to display an image and affect the number of colors shown, the size of the files, and other characteristics.

- ✔ Apply color, shapes, and stylized text to your images.

- ✔ Merge photos and construct photo collages using layering techniques.

- ✔ Add bevels, shadows, glows, and other special effects and filters to jazz up your images.

It's actually quite amazing that a program with a price of $90 can do all this and more. Check out Color Plate 12-5 to see this program in action.

Figure 12-1:
Adobe Elements has tools and commands to make the most marginal images ready for a gallery.

Photoshop

Photoshop is Adobe's professional photographer/graphic designer–level image editor. It can do everything that Elements can, of course, plus more. Much, more. In fact, Photoshop stops just short of brewing and serving you a latte.

Photoshop has more tools and commands for selecting, color correction, and retouching. The program also includes ImageReady, which is Adobe's Web graphics program. With ImageReady, you can easily construct animations, slices, rollovers, and image maps. All this power comes with a price, however. Not just the price tag, but also the learning curve.

Elements gives you a palette with Hints and Recipes (instructions to perform certain techniques), but Photoshop leaves you to your own devices. This program isn't for a once-a-month hobbyist.

Specifying an External Image Editor in Album

If you have another digital-imaging application installed on your computer, you can jump to that application directly from Album to edit your images. But what if you're lucky enough to have more than one image editor installed on your system? Well, you can instruct Album to choose one over the other by setting it as the default editor in the Preferences file. Here's how:

1. **Choose Edit⇨Preferences.**

2. **Select the Editing category on the left side of the Preferences dialog box, shown in Figure 12-2.**

3. **If you have an Adobe image-editing program, choose either Photoshop Elements 2.0 or later or Photoshop 6.0 or later.**

   If you have another image-editing program, you have two choices:

   • **Default Application for File Type:** This option launches the image-editing program associated with the type of file you have selected. During the installation of programs like Elements and Photoshop, you have the option of associating the particular application with various file types. For example, if you are in Windows Explorer or at the desktop whenever you double-click a TIFF or JPEG, you can specify that Elements is launched. Similarly, if you are working in Album and want to externally edit a TIFF or JPEG, Album will automatically launch Elements.

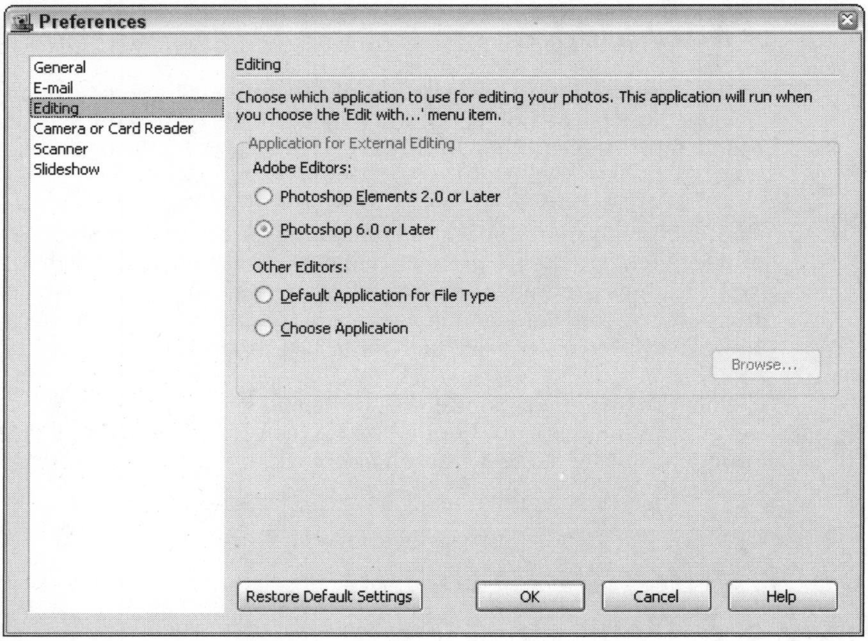

Figure 12-2:
You can
choose your
default
external
image editor
in the
Preferences
dialog box.

• **Choose Application:** Click the Browse button and select the image editor you want Album to launch.

4. **Click OK to close the Preferences dialog box.**

Fixing a Photo in an External Image Editor

After you've established which image editor you want Album to jump to (as described in the preceding section), you're ready to, well, jump. You can fix a photo in an external image editor a couple of ways — either directly from the Photo Well or via the Fix Photo dialog box.

Editing in Elements or Photoshop

Here are the steps for launching either Photoshop Elements or Photoshop:

1. **Select a photo in the Photo Well.**

2. **Choose one of these methods to launch the editor:**

- Choose Edit➪Edit with (your designated image editor). The name that appears in the menu depends on whether you chose Elements or Photoshop as your editor in the Preferences dialog box (as described in "Specifying an External Image Editor in Album" earlier in this chapter).

- Click the Fix Photo button in the Options bar. Then click the Edit With button at the bottom of the Fix Photo dialog box, as shown in Figure 12-3.

A warning message appears telling you that you're editing a copy of the image and not the original.

3. Click OK to get rid of this warning.

Album launches the editor, and your image is opened and ready to be improved. Meanwhile, in Album, a red lock icon with a label that says, "Edit in Progress" appears on the image thumbnail (shown in Figure 12-4) while you're editing the photo in your external editor. This lock remains on the image until you close it in your editor.

4. Edit the photo in either Elements or Photoshop.

If you got here accidentally or you've changed your mind and want to cancel your external editing session, return to Album and choose Edit➪Cancel External Edit.

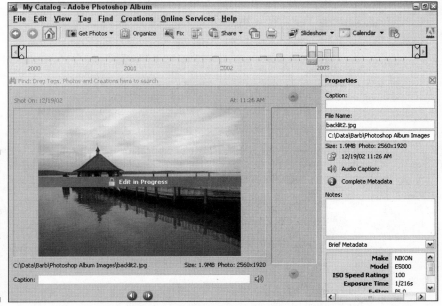

Figure 12-3: You can easily jump to an external image editor from the Fix Photo dialog box.

Although you can jump to Image Ready from Photoshop, you can't use Image Ready on an image you opened from Album.

5. **Choose File➪Save and close the photo in your image editor.**

   In either Elements or Photoshop, you also can choose the File➪ Save As command and rename the edited photo (for example "*filename_ edited.jpg*"). If you use this option, when you return to Album you have the choice of saving the edited photo as (see Figure 12-5)

   • An edited copy of the original

   • A new photo

   If you rename the file in Photoshop, rather than Elements, when you return to Album you have the additional choice of saving the edited photo as (see Figure 12-6):

   • A copy of the original in its original file format

   • A copy of the original as a Photoshop (PSD) file

   • A new Photoshop (PSD) file with a new name

   • Nothing — not saving it at all

6. **Return to Album.**

   The red lock icon goes away, and the fixed photo is automatically updated in Album.

If you don't want to keep the edits you made, choose Edit⇨Undo External Edit.

New Edited File

You have created a new file while editing the original file 'DSCN0925.JPG' in Photoshop or Elements. This is a result of saving the file with a new format.

What would you like to do?

New File Options

○ Save the edited file using the format of the original file. The new file name will be 'kylie.jpg'.

○ Save this file as the edited copy of the original file. The edited file name will be 'kylie.jpg'.

○ Import this file as a new file in your catalog. The new file name will be 'kylie.jpg'.

☐ Always use this choice, and don't show this dialog again.

[OK]   [Cancel]

Edited File from Photoshop

You have finished editing the original file 'snowgirl.jpg' in Photoshop.

What would you like to do?

Edited File Options

○ Save the edited file using the format of the original file. The new file name will be 'snowgirl_edited.jpg'.

○ Save the edited file as a Photoshop file. The new file name will be 'snowgirl_edited.psd'.

○ Import the edited file as a new Photoshop file in your catalog. The new file name will be 'snowgirl.psd'.

○ Do not save the edited file, just close the editing session in Photoshop.

☐ Always use this choice, and don't show this dialog again.

[OK]   [Cancel]

Editing in an application other than Elements or Photoshop

If you have an external image editor other than Elements or Photoshop, such as CorelPAINT, you can jump to that application from Album. All of the steps are identical except that when it comes to saving the file in the external image editor. Here are the steps to follow:

1. **Select a photo in the Photo Well.**

2. **Choose one of these methods to launch the editor:**

   • Choose Edit⇨Edit with Editor (where Editor represents your designated image editor). The name that appears in the menu depends on what editor you chose in the Preferences dialog box (as described in "Specifying an External Image Editor in Album" earlier in this chapter).

   • Click the Fix Photo button in the Options bar. Then click the Edit With button at the bottom of the Fix Photo dialog box (refer to Figure 12-4).

   A warning message appears, telling you that you're editing a copy of the image and not the original.

3. **Click OK to rid yourself of this warning.**

   Album then launches the editor, and your image is opened and ready to be improved.

4. **Perform your editing voodoo.**

5. **Choose File⇨Save in the external image editor.**

   You must save the edited photo without changing the filename in any way. Don't even add the word "edited" after the name. If you save the file with a different name, Album will not be able to find the photo automatically. You will have to look for the photo using the Get Photos command (for more details on getting photos, see Chapter 4).

6. **Return to Album.**

7. **Choose Edit⇨Finish External Edit.**

   By doing so, you complete the external editing process, and the changed photo appears in the Photo Well in Album.

   You also can select the photo in the Photo Well; right-click the image and choose Finish External Edit from the context-sensitive menu.

If you don't want to retain the edits, you can choose Edit⇨Undo External Edit. You also can cancel the process midstream by choosing Edit⇨Cancel External Edit in Album.

Bringing Photos into Other Applications

When your photos are all coiffed and ready to be used, you may want to bring them into another application. Maybe you want to insert the image into a Word memo or a PowerPoint presentation. Or maybe you want to use the photo in a collage in Elements. Of course you can always go the traditional route and either insert or open the image in the destination program. But you also can copy and paste, export, or drag and drop between Album and many applications.

Album won't keep track of any changes you make to the images in other applications unless you reimport them to Album. If you need to make changes to the images before using them, be sure to read the previous section. It gives you all the necessary know-how to do so properly.

Copying and pasting to other applications

Here are the short and simple steps to copy photos to other applications:

1. **In Album, select one or more photos in the Photo Well.**

   Note that you also can select video clips.

2. **Choose Edit⇔Copy in Album.**

3. **Go to your destination application and choose Edit⇔Paste into an open file, shown in Figure 12-7.**

Figure 12-7: Album allows you to copy and paste images into a variety of programs, including Corel PHOTO-PAINT.

Exporting images

I feel that using the Export command is better than copying and pasting if you want to get an image ready for use in another program. When you export photos, you can control file formats, size, and quality, depending on how you plan to use the image. For more on the characteristics of each file format and associated options, see Chapter 3.

You can only export *photos* using the Export command. It doesn't apply to creations. For more on creating and saving creations, see Chapter 17.

Here are the steps you need to export an image:

1. **Select the images you want to export.**

   You can select more than one image at a time.

2. **Choose File➪Export.**

   The Export Selected Items dialog box appears, as shown in Figure 12-8.

3. **Select your desired file format in the File Type area.**

   You have a choice between Original Format, JPEG, PNG, TIFF and PSD. For everything you've ever wanted to know about file formats, check out Chapter 3.

4. **Choose a Size for your image.**

   The Photo Size option keeps your image at its original dimensions. You can choose from a number of preset sizes, as well. Choose Custom to enter in a specific height and width in pixels.

   Although Album lets you enter any custom size you want, it retains the original proportions of the image. As a result, you may get either your desired height or width, but not both. For example, if you enter a custom size of 200 x 200 pixels and your original photo is rectangular, you may end up with a size of 200 x 132 pixels.

5. **If you selected JPEG in Step 3, drag the Quality slider to your desired quality setting.**

   The Quality slider offers 13 compression settings. The JPEG compression is a trade-off between file size and quality. Drag to the left to export a smaller, lower-quality image. Drag to the right to export a larger, higher-quality photo.

   The compression scheme used by JPEGs is *lossy,* which means that it compresses images by deleting image data, which it later remanufactures. Use the setting with the highest quality that you possibly can get away with so that you have less loss of detail in your image.

6. **In the Location area of the dialog box, either accept the path listed or click the Browse button to navigate to the location on your computer where you want to store the image(s).**

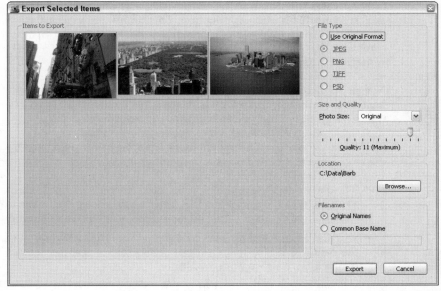

Figure 12-8:
The Export
dialog box
offers
options for
file format,
size, and
quality.

7. In the Filenames area of the dialog box, click Original Names or Common Base Name.

If you choose Common Base Name, type the name you want in the field. Album then adds sequential numbers to your base name for all exported photos. For example, if you are exporting a bunch of photos from the latest Alpaca shearing show, you may want to give the base name of Alpacas. Each photo you export will then be named `Alpacas-1.jpg`, `Alpacas-2.jpg`, and so on.

8. When you have established your options, click the Export button.

A progress bar shows the saving process. After a couple seconds, a message appears saying you have successfully exported your images.

9. Click OK.

You're transported back to the Photo Well.

Dragging and dropping into other applications

If copying and pasting or using the Export command is too tedious for you, you can always drag and drop images from Album's Photo Well into other applications.

Simply select the photo in the Photo Well, and drag the image from the Photo Well to your destination application. This technique works if you want to drag and drop an image into an image editor (like Elements), a page layout program (like Adobe InDesign), a word processor (such as Word), or a presentation program (such as PowerPoint).

Not all applications support the drag-and-drop method, however. If you see a nasty No symbol (a circle with a slashed line) when you try to drag and drop, that's a sign that what you're trying to do won't work.

By the way, you also can drag an image from the Photo Well directly onto your desktop. Here are a few points to remember about dragging and dropping:

✔ If you are dragging and dropping into Elements or Photoshop, you don't even need to have an open file. You can just drag the image directly into the application itself, and the file opens automatically in a new window.

✔ You don't have any options in the size, quality, or format of the exported file. So drag and drop an image only if you are planning on using the image in its current state in Album.

✔ You also can drag photos from the desktop into the Photo Well in Album. When you drag and drop the photo, the Getting Photos dialog box appears with a preview of the photo. Album then creates a new file with the image data, which appears in the Photo Well.

Part IV

Sharing and Printing Photos

The 5th Wave   By Rich Tennant

IMAGE editor   PHOTO MAKER   GRAPH Accent   CAMERA SOFT   PICTURE CLICK   PHOTO

"...and here's me with Cindy Crawford. And this is me with Madonna and Celine Dion..."

In this part...

It's never been easier to share your photos, so whatever you do, don't keep them to yourself — spread the love. In Part IV, you see how simple it is to e-mail your photos as images or slideshows. You also find out how to share your images online by posting them on a photo sharing Web site. Chapter 14 tells you what you need to know about getting high quality prints on your home printer. Discover how to print single images, contact sheets, and portrait studio-like picture packages. And for those of you who are time challenged, or want to leave the details for someone else to take care of, Chapter 15 shows how to order prints, photo books, and calendars via your friendly online service providers.

Chapter 13

Spreading Photographic Joy Electronically

Album makes it easy for you to share your files in many fun and high-tech ways. You can create albums, snazzy slide shows, calendars, or share your files online with at Shutterfly.com. If your recipients just want the images unadorned so that they can let their own creative juices flow and make their own masterpieces, sending the files as plain, old e-mail attachments fits the bill.

Album walks you through the process of preparing and e-mailing your files, making it quick, simple, and fool-proof. So share those photos you've been hoarding.

Sharing Photos Via E-Mail

About the only thing Album doesn't do in e-mailing your files is read your mind and type the e-mail message. It creates the attachments, sets up your desired recipients, and launches your e-mail client.

The most important things to keep in mind when e-mailing photos are file size and the Internet connection speed of your recipient. You want the file size to be small enough that your recipient can download it fairly quickly, without using your name in vain, especially if the recipient has a dial-up connection.

Avoiding Web-based e-mail problems

Many Web-based e-mail providers limit the space on their Web servers for storing and sending messages. Some Web servers limit the size of files you can send, as well. For example, Yahoo! Mail has a 6MB limit for individual mailboxes. Yahoo! Mail users can send and receive attachments up to 3MB in size. Send two e-mail messages, each with a big picture attached, and you can pat yourself on the back — you have officially flooded your buddy's inbox, and all other incoming messages will bounce back to the sender. Good job.

Many ISPs don't have any limits on incoming and outgoing messages — as long as you're using an e-mail client such as Outlook to accept messages. However, if you check e-mail from the Web (say, while you're traveling), your mailbox has a limited capacity.

On the other hand, you want a large enough pixel dimension in the photo so that the image displays with good quality, and it doesn't leave your sister in Duluth scratching her head saying, "Was that a photo of Aunt Mabel or Duke the wonder dog?" Therefore, be sure to check out Chapter 3 to learn the vitals about pixel dimension and resolution. Also, if you need to send high-quality images (which translates to high-resolution, large files) to family and friends, you also can try uploading them to a Web photo-sharing site like Shutterfly.com. Sure, it might take your friends and family members awhile to download the image, but at least you won't bog down their e-mail accounts.

If your recipient is lucky enough to have a high-speed connection, like a DSL, cable, or T1 line, you can get away with e-mailing larger files. Of course, make sure your connection is high-speed as well.

Setting Up Album for E-Mail

Before you can start e-mailing photos and even creations (see Chapter 18), you need to establish your e-mail preferences and set up your contact book with your recipients.

Setting your preferences

Follow these steps to establish your e-mail preferences:

1. **Choose Edit⇨Preferences.**

2. **Select E-mail from the list on the left side of the dialog box, as shown in Figure 13-1.**

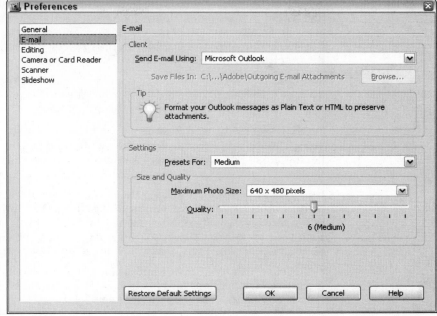

Figure 13-1:
Set up your
e-mail
preferences
before
sharing your
photos via
e-mail.

3. **Choose your default e-mail client from the Send E-mail Using pop-up menu.**

   If you use America Online (AOL), see the sidebar "Psst . . . Confidential for AOL users" later in this chapter for special instructions. Album can create e-mail messages with AOL, Eudora, Hotmail, Outlook, and Outlook Express. If you use another e-mail client, or if Album has problems generating the e-mail message, select Other from the Client pop-up menu, and your attachment will be saved to your hard drive. Then you can open the saved file directly from your e-mail client.

   You won't need to change this setting again unless you want to choose a different e-mail client.

4. **Select a preset size from the Presets For pop-up menu. Here are your options:**

   • **Big:** This option creates high-quality photos with good resolutions. The recipient can view large images on-screen with all the details crisp and all the colors intact.

   Quality comes with a down side — the file size will be large. Make sure that your recipients can handle big files before choosing this option. Give them a call and ask if they are capable of receiving a file of a specific size. Consider this nicety a matter of simple "netiquette."

When you choose a Preset size, the Maximum Photo Size (width and height in pixel dimensions) and Quality settings display in the Size and Quality section of the dialog box. This dialog box tells you the size and quality associated with the Presets; you can change these settings if you desire. See Step 5.

- **Medium:** This setting provides a good quality photo. You get an average file size and decent detail in the image. This is Album's default setting and works fine for most attachments.

- **Small:** If you really need to squeeze the file size down to the minimum, choose this size. File sizes will be tiny, and the quality won't be that great. But what the heck — the files will download in a flash.

- **Leave As Is:** If you want to keep the photo's original settings, this is the option for you. If you choose this setting, the Maximum Photo Size and Quality options are not available. If you want to send your recipient a high-resolution image that will be used for optimum quality printing, make sure and select this option.

In this case, it is *really, really* important that the recipient has a high-speed connection. Also make sure that your file size doesn't exceed any limits placed by the recipient's ISP.

5. **If you want to alter the default size associated with the Presets, choose your desired pixel dimension from the Maximum Photo Size pop-up menu.**

   Don't worry; these size settings aren't written in stone. Even though the preference settings become the defaults, you can change the size settings for individual e-mail attachments as you send them.

6. **You also can adjust the default Quality setting. Drag the Quality slider to the left to export a smaller file with lower quality and detail. Drag to the right for a larger file with higher quality and detail.**

   The Quality slider determines how much compression is applied to the image. The more compression, the smaller the file, but the poorer the quality — and vice-versa. For more details on quality and compression, see Chapter 3.

7. **Click OK to save the settings and exit the Preferences dialog box.**

   You can now barrage your family and friends with photo attached e-mails.

Creating your contact book

Your *contact book* is just like your little black book of friends who like pictures. You should include everyone and anyone you plan on sending files to.

When you enter e-mail addresses in the book, you can easily send e-mail messages to those people. Note that this contact book is unique to Album. You cannot exchange it with other applications, including your e-mail client.

Album keeps a record of who you've e-mailed photos and even what images were sent. You can actually search for files based on who you have e-mailed them to. For details on finding photos, see Chapter 8.

If you often e-mail files to the same group of people, you can set up a group in the contact book to make your e-mailing process even more productive.

Here are the steps to create your contact book:

1. **Choose View⇨Contact Book.**

   The Contact Book dialog box appears, as shown in Figure 13-2.

2. **To add a person, click the New Contact button.**

   The New Contact dialog box appears.

3. **Enter the person's name and e-mail address, as shown in Figure 13-3. Click the Address tab to add a mailing address and phone number, if desired.**

   Repeat Step 3 to add all the people you want to include.

Figure 13-2:
Enter the names and e-mail addresses of people with whom you plan on sharing your photos in your Contact Book.

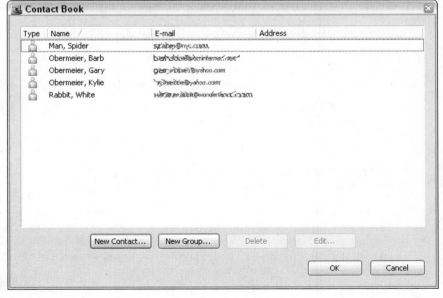

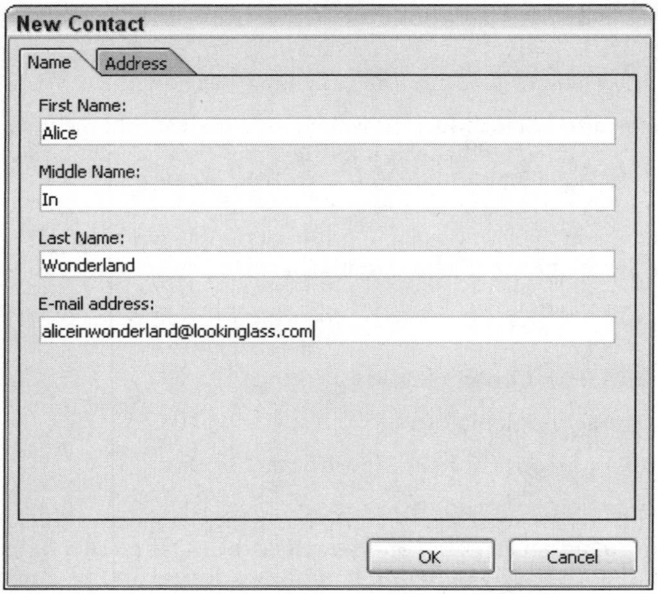

New Contact

Name \ Address

First Name:
Alice

Middle Name:
In

Last Name:
Wonderland

E-mail address:
aliceinwonderland@lookinglass.com

OK   Cancel

Figure 13-3:
Type the
name and
e-mail
address in
the New
Contact
dialog box.

4. **Click OK when you're done.**

   Here are a few other Contact Book tidbits:

   • **To create a group:** Click the New Group button and type a name
     for the group. Select the contacts you want in the group and click
     the Add button to move it to the Members list. Click OK when
     you're done.

   • **To edit an entry:** Select the entry in the list, click the Edit button,
     and make your changes. Click OK when you're done.

   • **To delete an entry:** Select the entry in the list and click the Delete
     button.

E-Mailing Photos and Creations

After you've established your e-mail preferences, you're ready to prepare
your attachments and send the messages. The only thing left to decide is
which of your great images, video clips, audio clips, and creations you want
to share. The following steps help you with the mechanics of sending your
e-mail — the attachment choices are up to you:

1. **Select one or more items in the Photo Well.**

   You can send photos, video clips, audio clips, and creations, but remember audio and especially video clips can be quite gargantuan in size.

2. **Choose File➪Attach to E-mail.**

   You can use either of these methods, as well:

   • Click the Share button in the Shortcuts bar, and choose E-mail from the drop-down menu.

   • If you're in the Workspace, choose E-mail from the Options pop-up menu, shown in Figure 13-4. For details on the using the Workspace, see Chapter 16.

   If you haven't set your e-mail preferences or if this is the first time you've e-mailed using Album, a dialog box appears so you can confirm your desired e-mail client.

3. **Choose your client and click OK.**

   The Attach Selected Items to E-mail dialog box appears, as shown in Figure 13-5. A thumbnail preview of the attachment appears on the left side of the dialog box.

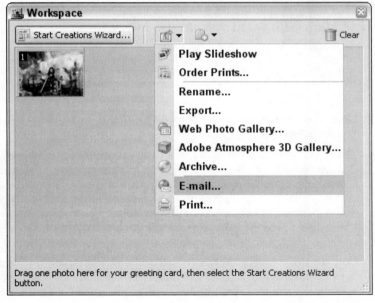

Figure 13-4: You can e-mail from the Workspace, as well as the Photo Well.

Psst . . . Confidential to Hotmail users

If you are a Hotmail user, you may encounter a problem if you try and attach multiple individual attachments. Try combining all of your individual photos into a PDF slide show. Also, if you are using Hotmail to e-mail an attachment for the first time, you may be asked to download and install the Hotmail Attachments Control. By all means, say Yes and get this file installed.

Figure 13-5:
Choose your recipients and prepare your attachment in the Attach Selected Items to E-mail dialog box.

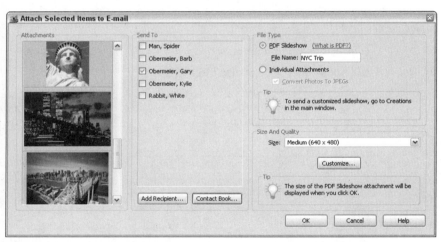

4. **Choose your recipients by selecting a name, or names, in the Send To list.**

   The names in the Send To list are from your contact book (see the preceding section for more on setting up a contact book). If you need to add a recipient, click the Add Recipient button and enter the name and e-mail address of your new recipient, as shown in Figure 13-6. If you want to add the person to your contact book, select the Add to Contact Book check box. Click OK. The new recipient shows up in the Send To list.

   You can access your Contact Book by clicking the (no surprise here) Contact Book button. You also can add a new recipient by clicking the New Contact button. Enter the name, e-mail address, and, if you want, address, of the recipient. Click OK. The person then shows up in the Send To list.

Figure 13-6:
It's easy to add new recipients to your e-mail list.

5. **In the File Type area, choose a file format for the attachment:**

   • **PDF slide show:** This option creates a PDF document in which your selected images are combined into a single slide show. This is a great way to e-mail multiple photos because they're bundled in one neat little package. It is also handy if you, or your recipient, use Web mail and there are limits to the number of attachments you can send or receive.

   This is a toned-down version of other slide show capabilities offered by Album. You won't be able to add all the bells and whistles (styles, music, captions, and so on) that you can when making a slide show using the Creations Wizard. For more on creations, see Chapter 18. Enter a name for your PDF file.

   PDF (Portable Document Format) is a universal file format that can be read on any computer platform, without the need for any special programs except Adobe Acrobat Reader. Acrobat Reader is free and can be downloaded from www.adobe.com. For details on the PDF format, see Chapter 3.

   • **Individual Attachments:** Select this option to send each photo as a separate attachment. By default, the file formats of all attachments are converted to the JPEG format (if they aren't JPEGs already). If you want to keep your photos in their original file formats, deselect the Convert Photos to JPEGs check box. For more on file formats, see Chapter 3.

   If you're attaching a creation, you don't get to choose between PDF and an individual attachment. It is what it is. You can provide a name for the file, though. If you're attaching an audio clip, you can send the file only as an individual attachment, not as a PDF.

Psst . . . Confidential to AOL users

If you're one of the million America Online users, you need to make sure and set Association preferences in AOL so that AOL is the default e-mail client Album uses. If you neglect to do so, you will get an error message when you try to e-mail attachments. To change your Association preferences, simply log on to AOL. Then check the preferences under Associations. If you need more assistance, check AOL's Help database.

---

6. **Choose a size for your attachment or leave the default setting as is.**

   If you have already set up your e-mail preferences, your default setting is displayed in the Size field. If you want to choose a different setting for this attachment, select the setting from the Size pop-up menu (described in "Setting your preferences," earlier in this chapter). Click the Customize button to open the E-mail Preferences dialog box, in which you can change your default preferences.

   If you're attaching a creation, you have the choice between optimizing your file for viewing on-screen, optimizing your file for printing, or using full resolution. For details on each option, see Chapter 18.

   If you're attaching an audio or video clip, you don't have any size and quality options.

7. **Click OK.**

   Album proceeds to prepare the attachment. A dialog box with your attachment's size and modem download time appears, as shown in Figure 13-7.

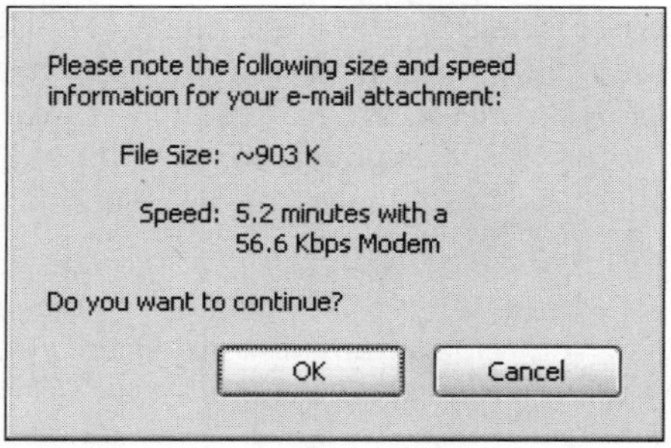

Figure 13-7:
After preparing your attachment, Album displays its size and download time.

Please note the following size and speed information for your e-mail attachment:

> File Size: ~903 K
>
> Speed: 5.2 minutes with a 56.6 Kbps Modem

Do you want to continue?

[OK]   [Cancel]

8. Click OK to continue.

If your attachment is larger than 1MB, Album prompts you with an Attachment Warning, asking you whether you want to continue.

Album launches your e-mail client.

9. Enter your message, as shown in Figure 13-8, and click Send.

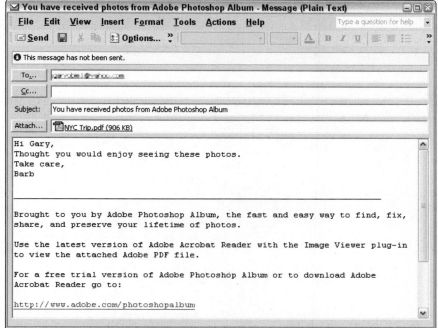

Figure 13-8:
Album automatically launches your default e-mail client.

Chapter 14

Getting Your Images on Paper

• •

In This Chapter

▶ Getting to know your printer

▶ Establishing your print options

▶ Printing single photos, picture packages, and contact sheets

▶ Printing creations

▶ Getting better prints

• •

For some reason, printing in general seems be a thorn in the side of most computer users. Either your print doesn't match what you see on-screen, the quality of the print is marginal, or worse, the print simply doesn't want to emerge from the printer. This chapter helps you avoid these unhappy scenarios. This chapter helps you get a handle on these and other ways of improving your prints, demystifying the printing process along the way.

Basics on Getting High-Quality Prints

Here's a preview of what you can do to ensure that you get quality prints every time:

✔ **Get friendly with your printer.** Learn everything you can about it.

✔ **Be sure you follow the directions and establish the correct printing options to get your prints.** Know what options are best for different formats — single prints, contact sheets, cards, calendars, and so on.

✔ **Make absolutely certain you have the best source material possible.** If your image is of lousy quality, you're not going to get a great print, no matter what you do. You need to make sure your images have sufficient resolution, are saved in the correct file format, and are cleaned up and fixed of any flaws.

✔ **Make sure you use good quality equipment and materials.** This includes everything from your printer to your paper to ink.

What you see is not always what you get

Although you can do many things to improve the quality of your prints, you can't translate all the colors, nor their vivid brightness from screen to paper. Here are a few factors that influence this disparity:

✔ **Color models:** Monitors and printers use two different color models. Your monitor displays colors in RGB (red, green, and blue), while printers print in CMYK (cyan, yellow, magenta, and black). The RGB color *gamut* (or range) is 16.7 million colors, and the CMYK gamut is around 55,000 colors. There's a big difference between those two numbers, so a lot of what you see on-screen cannot be physically output onto paper. (See Chapter 3 for more on color.)

✔ **Quality and calibration of your monitor:** You can do a basic calibration of your monitor by following the steps in Chapter 10.

✔ **Whether or not you use a color management system for all your devices:** For example, a color management system based on using ICC (International Color Consortium) profiles can help you control your color across all of your devices. Unfortunately, color management is way beyond the scope of this book. But if you are bound and determined to try and get your monitor to match your printed output, I would suggest buying a book solely devoted to this topic.

Getting Intimate with Your Printer

If you print your photos on your home printer, Album provides several options. For example, you can print single prints, picture packages, or creations. But before you can get to the fun stuff, you really have to get to know your printer:

✔ **Read the manual.** If you've been using your printer for awhile, you may have a good handle on its strengths and shortcomings, but have you really put the printer through the paces? To really understand your printer, you should — please don't slam the book shut — read your manual. I know, it can be tedious and not very enjoyable, but you never know what good info and recommendations you may glean from it.

✔ **Test, test, and test some more.** I don't mean, stick a piece of paper in the printer and see whether something is printed on it when it comes out the other end. I mean really make your printer jump through some hoops. Try each and every print setting. Try different combinations of options. Try different kinds of papers. Label each print with the settings, options and kind of paper and compare the results. What setting works best with photos? What setting is best for glossy paper? Is there a difference between a print at 1440 dpi and another at 2880 dpi? Only when testing can you discover your printer's proclivities. For example, some printers have a tendency to print a certain color cast (some printers tend to create bluer or greener output, for example).

Testing is a very time-consuming process, but one that will reap rewards. You will know what works and what doesn't. Only when you've got your printer's personality down to a science can you can sit back and print anything and everything without worrying about the quality of the output.

Setting Print Options

Before you run off on a printing frenzy, you need to give Album some basic info about your print job — little details like the size and orientation of your paper, the width of the margins, and so on. These options are found in the Page Setup dialog box. Keep in mind that if your computer is connected to multiple printers, you need to set your print options each time you change printers.

Here's how to set your print options:

1. **Choose File↪Page Setup.**

   The Page Setup dialog box appears, as shown in Figure 14-1.

2. **Set the following options:**

   • **Size:** Choose the size of your paper from the pop-up menu.

   • **Source:** Specify the tray or feeder that provides the paper to your printer. Also be sure to select the appropriate paper in your printer settings if you're using a photo-quality or specialty paper.

   • **Orientation:** Choose your desired page orientation, either Portrait or Landscape.

   • **Margins:** If available, set your margins on all sides.

   The preview at the top of the dialog box changes according to your settings.

3. **If you have multiple printers and want to change the printer, click the Printer button. Choose a printer from the Name pop-up menu, or click the Network button to choose a printer from your network.**

4. **Click the Properties button to specify additional options. When you're done setting options, click OK.**

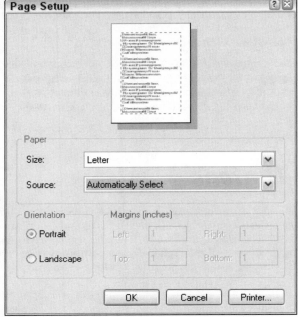

Figure 14-1:
Set
your print
options
in the
Page Setup
dialog box.

The options in this dialog box are determined by your printer, not Album, so be sure and check your printer manual for more information if you're unfamiliar with the settings. You'll find options such as printer resolution, color adjustments, and so on.

5. **Click OK in the main Page Setup dialog box.**

Printing Your Images

After you've set your print options (see the preceding section), you're ready to start printing your images. Album gives you several options for printing, as discussed in the following sections.

Printing individual photos

If you want individual prints, all you have to do is choose a print size, and Album combines as many photos as will fit on a single sheet of paper.

Choose a print size that is appropriate for the resolution of the image. If you need more details on working with resolution, see Chapter 3 and also the "Tips for Getting Better Prints" section at the end of this chapter.

If you choose a size that causes the print to be printed at less than 150 dpi, Album issues a stern alert, shown in Figure 14-2, so you can adjust the print size smaller.

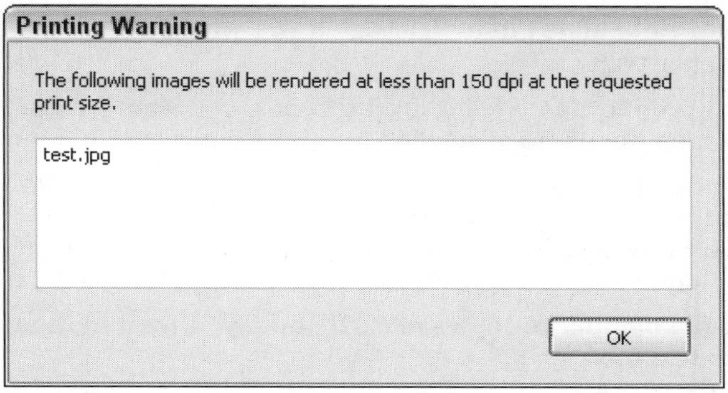

Figure 14-2:
Album slaps
your wrist if
you try to
print an
image at a
size that will
render at
less than
150 dpi.

> **Printing Warning**
>
> The following images will be rendered at less than 150 dpi at the requested print size.
>
> test.jpg
>
> [OK]

Make sure your printer is turned and the ready light is on, and then follow these steps to print individual photos:

1. **From the Photo Well, select one or more photos. Then choose File⇨Print or click the Print button in the Shortcuts bar.**

   You can print a video clip — sort of. Only the first frame will be printed.

   In the Print Selected Photos dialog box, shown in Figure 14-3, the left side of the dialog box shows the selected photo(s).

2. **In the Layout area of the dialog box, select Individual Prints (if it's not already selected).**

3. **In the Individual Print Format area of the dialog box, choose one of these options:**

   • **Select a preset size from the list.** If more than one copy of the photo(s) fits on the page, the preview shows the layout of the photos. If only one print will fit on a page, you can scroll through the pages using the Backward and Forward buttons.

   • **Choose Fit on Page to scale the image to fill the page.** If the photo is small or has a low resolution, and it is scaled to fit the page, the quality may be unsatisfactory.

- **Choose Custom Size.** When you select this option a second dialog box appears to allow you to enter your desired dimensions.

The right side of the dialog box shows the preview of how the images will be printed on the page. If you change a print option, Album updates the preview.

Being the ever-so-frugal program that it is, Album may automatically rotate your images in order to maximize the number of prints that it can fit on a page.

4. **Select Print Single Photo Per page if you would rather print only one photo per page.**

5. **Select Crop to Match Print Proportions if you want Album to automatically crop the photo as needed to fill the entire space.**

I'd be careful of using this option because vital parts of your image may be cut off. If you're having problems getting your images at a specific size, try cropping the photo before you print it. For more on cropping, see Chapter 11.

6. **Type the number of copies of each photo you want in the Use each Photo text box.**

You also can click the up and down arrows to specify the quantity.

7. **If you have multiple pages, click the Forward and Backward buttons to preview each page of the print job.**

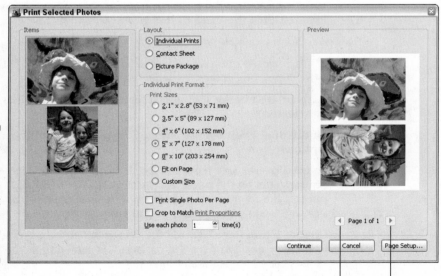

Figure 14-3:
Specify the size of your prints in the Print Selected Photos dialog box.

Backward   Forward

Refer to Figure 14-3. To access the Page Setup dialog box from here, click Page Setup.

8. When you're done with the settings, click Continue.

The Print dialog box (as shown in Figure 14-4) appears, displays your current printer settings.

9. Click the Preferences button to specify settings specific to your particular printer, as shown in Figure 14-5. Click OK when you're done.

The options displayed in this dialog box are determined by your printer, not by Album. If you need more help with these options, check your printer manual.

10. Click Print to print your images.

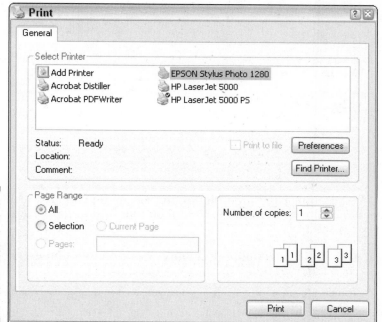

Figure 14-4:
Choose your printer and select other options in the Print dialog box.

Printing a picture package

Besides individual photos, you also can print picture packages. A *picture package* lays out and prints each photo in a variety of sizes, similar to various-sized portraits that you can purchase from a photography studio. You dictate the layout style, and Album arranges the photos on the page. If you select more than one photo, each photo is printed in various sizes on its own page.

Figure 14-5:
Specify your
printer's
settings in
the Printing
Preferences
dialog box.

Unfortunately, you can't mix photos on a single page. You can view each page by clicking the Forward and Backward buttons. Follow these steps to print a picture package:

1. **From the Photo Well, select one or more photos. Choose File⇨Print or click the Print button in the Shortcuts bar.**

   You can print a video clip, if you want to call it that. Only the first frame will be printed.

   In the Print Selected Photos dialog box, shown in Figure 14-6, the left side of the dialog box shows the selected photo(s).

2. **Select a picture package format from the Layout pop-up menu.**

   The layout options that appear are the only ones that will fit on your selected paper size.

   You can change your paper size in the Page Setup dialog box. For details, see the earlier section on setting print options.

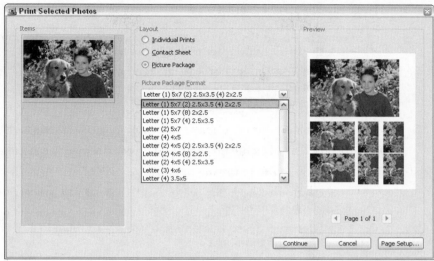

Figure 14-6:
Print a
picture
package
to get
printouts of
a photo in
various
sizes, just
like you
would
get at a
photography
studio.

3. **Each photo is arranged on its own page. To preview each page, click the Forward and Backward buttons.**

    It may take Album a few seconds to update the preview. Be patient, please.

4. **After you have specified your settings to your satisfaction, click Continue.**

    When you click the Continue button, the Print dialog box appears (refer to Figure 14-4), and shows your current printer settings.

5. **Click the Preferences button to specify settings specific to your particular printer, shown back in Figure 14-5. Click OK when you're done.**

    Don't forget that the options displayed in this dialog box are determined by your printer, not by Album. Consult your printer manual if you need assistance.

6. **Click Print to print your images.**

Printing a contact sheet

Album gives you the ability to print a contact sheet that shows thumbnails of each of your selected photos. You can print the sheet with captions, filenames, dates, and page numbers. Contact sheets are great because they give you a concise printed inventory of your entire catalog.

Here's how to print a contact sheet:

1. **From the Photo Well, select one or more photos. Choose File⇨Print or click the Print button in the Shortcuts bar.**

   In the Print Selected Photos dialog box, shown in Figure 14-7, the left side of the dialog box shows the selected photo(s).

2. **Under Layout, select Contact Sheet.**

3. **Type the number of columns you want in the Columns text box.**

   You also can click the up and down arrows to specify the number.

4. **Select any of the following options:**

   • **Captions:** Select this option, and Album prints any captions that you have attached to the images.

   • **Filename:** Select this option if you want Album to add filenames under the thumbnails.

   • **Date:** Select this option if you want Album to print the date the photo was taken or imported.

5. **Select the Show Page Numbers option to print page numbers at the bottom of each page.**

   This option is available only if your contact sheet is more than one page.

Figure 14-7: Printing a contact sheet provides you with a printed inventory of your catalog.

6. **Click the Forward or Backward buttons to preview each page.**

7. **Click Continue.**

   The Print dialog box appears and shows your current printer settings (refer to Figure 14-4).

8. **Click the Preferences button to specify settings. Click OK when you're done.**

   Refer to Figure 14-5, and check your printer manual if you need assistance.

9. **Click Print to print your images.**

Printing creations

Album allows you to make a variety of projects it calls *creations*. A couple of these creations, such as greeting cards and calendars, are specifically designed to be printed on your home printer. For specifics on making creations, see Chapters 17 and 18. I'll just give you the rundown on printing them here.

When you have completed and previewed your creation in the Creation Wizard (described in detail in Chapter 17), you arrive at Step 5, the printing stage. From here, you can print the creation by following these steps:

1. **In the Output Options section of the Creations Wizard window, shown in Figure 14-8, click the Print button.**

   The Print dialog box appears and shows your current printer settings.

2. **Click the Preferences button to specify your settings. Click OK when you're finished.**

   Check with your printer manual if you need help with these settings.

3. **Click Print to print your images.**

Here are a few specifics in regards to each type of printed creation.

✔ **Greeting cards:** After the page is printed, you need to fold the page in half and then fold it again. Some types of photo paper can crack when folded, so be careful. It helps to score the card with a paper clip or thin-tipped burnishing tool before folding.

✔ **Calendars:** After you print the pages of your calendar, you can either bind them yourself or take them to your local copy shop for binding.

Ask for a clear acetate cover and vinyl backing to give further polish to your custom calendar. After you create and preview your calendar, you have the option to have it printed via an online service for $19.95. Simply click the Order Online button in Step 5 of the Creations Wizard. See more about ordering online in Chapter 15.

✔ **Albums:** As with calendars, after you print your album, you can take it to a copy shop to have it bound with a front and back cover. Or you can simply place the pages in your leather-bound photo album or scrapbook.

If you choose to print creations that do not have sufficient resolution, Album presents you with a warning dialog box, shown in Figure 14-9. At this point, you have a couple options:

✔ Use another image, with higher resolution, for the creation.

✔ Try to print the image anyway, using the individual print method described earlier in this chapter, at a smaller size. You won't get the image in the cool creation form, but at least you may be able to get some kind of print.

✔ Send the creation to recipients to view on-screen. Make an eCard instead of a greeting card, or send friends and family that calendar as a PDF to view on-screen. What the heck — you'll save a few trees, too.

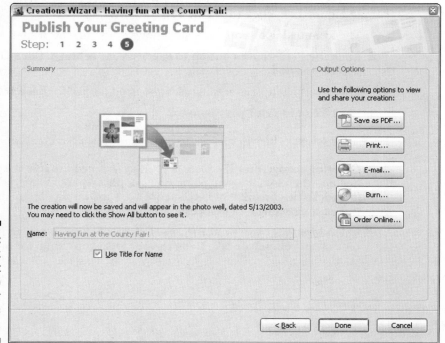

Figure 14-8: Click the Print button to put your creations on paper.

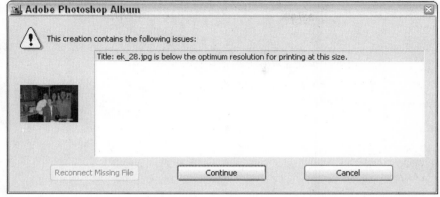

Figure 14-9:
Album
warns you
if your
images do
not have
sufficient
resolution
to print.

Finding Images You've Previously Printed

Album allows you to locate images by their *history*. Part of an image's history is whether or not it has been printed. If you need to locate images that you have previously printed, follow these steps:

1. **Choose Find⇨By History⇨Items Printed On.**

   A list of the photos you have printed, and the dates they were printed, will appear.

2. **Double-click an item in the list.**

   The image appears alone in the Photo Well, which can be helpful if you are being bombarded for requests for prints from the last family reunion, and you can't remember which ones you have already printed and handed out.

You also can locate images for which you have ordered prints online:

1. **Choose Find⇨By History⇨Items Ordered Online.**

   A list of all photos for which you have ordered online prints and the dates you ordered them appears, as shown in Figure 14-10.

2. **Double-click an item in the list.**

   Those images will appear in the Photo Well.

For more on finding photos, see Chapter 8.

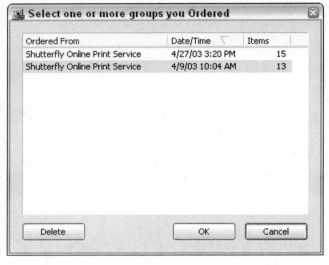

Figure 14-10:
Album
lets you
find images
you have
printed
or ordered
online
prints of.

Tips for Getting Better Prints

If there is one complaint I hear constantly from my graphic students it's that their prints look so much better on-screen. Often printing problems are a result of operator error, and the problem can be easily solved. But I have to admit, there have a few times I myself wondered whether it was going to take a voodoo ritual to get my print to come out correctly. You may need to do a few voodoo rituals along the way, but if you consistently follow a few rules, you're likely to be ahead of the game and will have great printed output more often.

Check your resolution

The most basic thing to keep in mind is that you have a good chance of getting a high-quality print if you start with a high-quality image. And one of the keys to a high-quality image is to make sure the resolution of your images is high enough to accommodate high-quality printed output, as shown in Figure 14-11.

Images from a digital camera

If you are capturing images with a digital camera, do not set your camera to low-resolution capture mode. Always use the maximum megapixel size of your camera.

Other ways to print your photos

If your printer is of marginal quality or is acting contrary, you can always get your images printed by ordering them via an online service. See Chapter 15 for details. Another option is to use the Kodak Picture Maker. I'm sure you have seen the walk-up kiosks at your local mall or drugstore. Simply insert your memory card, CD, or even a diskette into the appropriate slot, and the machine at the kiosk scans the images for you.

You can even insert slides and negatives. Using a touch-screen monitor, select the photos you want to print. You can get rid of red eye, crop your images, and add borders and small amounts of text to the pictures. Choose the print size, and in a few minutes you have a finished print for a very reasonable price. The kiosk even lets you print stickers and cards.

The maximum print size you will be able to achieve depends on the image resolution. If you have a camera that is only capable of capturing 1 to 2 megapixels, you're not going to be able to get high-quality large-size prints.

Table 14-1 gives a few approximate guidelines on print sizes in relationship to the camera's resolution.

Figure 14-11: A high-resolution image provides a great quality print, while a low-resolution one leaves a lot to be desired.

3.5 x 4.5 inches, 300 dpi, 4MB file size   3.5 x 4.5 inches, 72 dpi, 231KB file size

Table 14-1	Camera Resolutions and Quality Prints
Camera Setting	*Produces*
1 megapixel	Good 4 x 6 prints and fair 5 x 7 prints
2 megapixels	Good 5 x 7 prints and fair 8 x 10 prints
3 megapixels	Fine 8 x 10 prints and fair 11 x 14 prints
4 or 5 megapixels	Excellent 8 x 10 prints and good 11 x 14 prints
5 or 6 megapixels	Good 11 x 14 prints and fair 20 x 30 prints

Scanned images

If you're scanning hard-copy prints to import into Album for editing or inclusion in a creation such as a photo book or calendar, be sure that you set your scanning resolution high enough to ensure good-quality prints. In terms of scans, here are a few guidelines:

- Images that are 4MB are suitable for 4 x 6 prints.
- An 8 x 10 print requires at around a 9 or 10MB file. If you want top-notch quality for an 8 x 10 print, you'll need to have a file that is around 16 to 20MB.
- In terms of pixels per inch, use the general rule of thumb of 300 ppi at 100 percent scale of the image size for a very high-quality print.

Be aware that your image will be extremely large, so be sure and have adequate hard drive storage. Working with an image of this monstrous magnitude will also eat up your available RAM like nobody's business, so be sure you're locked and loaded with plenty of memory.

If you plan on making a large print, I recommend making a small 4 x 6 print first. Proof it and see if it requires any adjustments before you incur the expense and time of making a larger print.

Watch your file format

Although some people may disagree, my recommendation is to capture your digital images in TIFF format, if your camera allows it. TIFF images do not utilize the lossy compression scheme that the JPEG file format does and therefore produce a higher-quality image.

There are downsides to capturing your images as TIFFs:

- ✔ The file size is much larger and will therefore fill up your camera's memory card faster.
- ✔ It takes a little longer to record the image to your camera after you capture it, so your camera may be hung up for as little as a second or two to as long as 30 seconds.

If your cameras can only capture images in JPEG format, then select the highest-quality JPEG setting possible (such as High, Fine, or Large). The result will be the lowest amount of compression and therefore a higher-quality image.

Even if you decide to capture your image as a JPEG, if you feel that you are going to be opening, editing, and resaving the image, be sure and save the file on your hard drive or external media as a TIFF.

 You can apply LZW compression, which is a lossless compression scheme, to your TIFF image, which makes your file size a bit smaller without deleting image data.

Nothing beats running a test. Shoot the same subject using TIFF and JPEG modes (of various quality settings). Print out prints of varying sizes and check the results. You may find that for your specific needs, a high-quality JPEG will be sufficient in most cases, except where you need a very large-size print.

 If you are scanning prints to bring into Album for editing or inclusion into a creation, be sure and save them as TIFFs as well.

See more details on resolution and file formats in Chapter 3.

 Calibrating your monitor is essential to having the best editing environment possible. You should also set up your work environment and desktop so that you have no distractions when you edit your photos. For all you need to know about calibrating your monitor and optimizing your editing environment, see Chapter 10.

Crop and clean up

If you didn't capture quite the image you wanted, you have the opportunity to digitally edit those images. Album gives you tools to rotate, crop, sharpen and fix red eye, contrast and color. See Chapters 11 and 12 for information about the tools at your disposal, all of which are quick and easy to use.

Remember that your print can only be as good as your original image. If the original image is flawed, so will be the print, as shown in Figure 14-12.

If you are scanning your images, you may want to especially consider sharpening the image. Flatbed scanners are notorious for producing soft images, and a little sharpening may be just the ticket.

Always make sure that sharpening is the last edit you make on your image. Album automatically saves your edited image as a new file, which is a wise move. That way you can always go back to the original if the need arises.

Use a good printer

Just as the source of the print is important, so is the final destination. If your printer is old or on the low end of the printer quality totem pole, you may be disappointed with your prints, no matter how great the image looks on-screen. High-quality photo printers are so reasonably priced now that it would be a shame not to have one if you are serious about home printing.

Shop around and request some sample prints. Some companies or retail outlets even let you print your file. Make sure the printer's specs say that the printer provides photo-quality printouts and can handle all of the paper types and sizes you need. After you acquire a good printer, get to know it. Run it through a gamut of tests. For more on this topic, see the first section in this chapter.

Keep your inkjet printer clean. Use the cleaning utility to unclog or align the heads. You may find that if you haven't used your printer in awhile, you may need to clean the nozzles. And aligning the heads when you change ink cartridges may be necessary. Refer to your owner's manual for details.

Print resolution

Many printers are capable of printing at various resolutions, such as 360 dpi, 720 dpi, 1440 dpi and 2880 dpi. How do you know which to use? It depends on the intended use. For example:

- ✔ Is it for a flyer for your child's school? If so, maybe 360 to 720 dpi is fine.
- ✔ Is it for an exhibit at the local coffeehouse? Better crank it up to 1440 to 2880 dpi.

Run sample prints to see the differences between the various print settings. The higher the printer resolution, the longer the print time and the more ink is consumed.

Figure 14-12:
Performing a few fixes on your image can transform a mediocre photo into a very good image.

Alternatives to the inkjet

There are a couple of other types of photo printers to consider besides inkjet:

- ✔ **Dye-sublimation printers:** These printers, which are becoming more affordable, use a heating element to melt pigment from a colored ribbon onto the paper. Dye-sublimation printers print much faster than inkjet prints and provide excellent quality prints, but are more expensive to purchase than the average inkjet printer. The printers in the Fujifilm PG series are the most expensive, but can produce prints that rival traditional photographic prints.

- ✔ **Direct-print printers:** These printers allow you to bypass the computer completely. Instead, you cable your digital camera to the printer or insert your memory card into a slot on the printer. You can print everything from contact sheets to regular-size prints. The downside, of course, is that aside from a couple of brightness and color adjustments on some models, you cannot repair or fix your images before you print them.

Use good paper

Don't make that penny squeak when it comes to buying paper. Plain paper absorbs ink like a sponge and makes the colors appear dull and muddy. Invest in premium photo-quality paper that is designed for inkjet printers. Paper comes in a variety of finishes, from glossy to matte to luster, depending on your preference. Here are a few things to look for when choosing paper:

- ✔ **Whiteness:** Look for paper that has a bright whiteness. The whiteness of the paper will play a part in how vibrant the print looks. Bright white paper also gives the widest range of colors. Try to find paper that has a brightness of 90 percent or higher.

- ✔ **Weight:** Also consider the weight of the paper. Lightweight paper won't hold up when saturated with ink and is more prone to damage. Look for a weight of 65 lbs. or more per ream, or 10 mil. or more in thickness per sheet. These weights are similar to the weight of traditional photographic paper. Go online to see if manufacturers are offering free sample packs.

I have owned four models of Epson printers and have tried dozens of brands of paper. I always end up going back to Epson paper. It's expensive, but it gives me the best results. Epson obviously formulates the paper to work exceptionally well with the printer and Epson brand inks. I never use third-party inks, by the way. They may work great for you, but I have had very bad luck using them.

Also, even though their durability has improved, prints from inkjet printers are not as resistance to water, smudging, direct sunlight and fading as traditional prints. Traditional photographic prints last around 12 years, but prints from inkjet printers may survive just 2 months (most last for 2 years).

Some manufacturers claim to offer longer-life prints. Epson, however, says that its inks are designed to last around 12 years if used with certain Epson papers. And the company claims that prints will last 40 years if you use its Matte Paper Heavyweight. Epson provides a great paper and ink guidebook that you can request for free. Visit the Epson Web site (www.epson.com) for more information.

You may want to look into archival papers and archival inks or UV coatings to protect your prints. Service bureaus can apply UV coatings to your images, or you can purchase sprays. Just make sure that whatever UV coatings you add to prints are compatible with the type of paper you are using.

You aren't limited to just the standard size sheets of paper. You also can purchase inkjet paper in the form of precut and scored greeting cards, postcards, sticker, transparencies, banners, iron-on transfer paper, and more.

Chapter 15

Using Online Services to Share and Print Photos

In This Chapter

▶ Adding online services

▶ Checking for new online services

▶ Sharing photos online

▶ Ordering prints online

▶ Ordering creations online

▶ Downloading templates

*H*ave you ever put a small plant in a really big pot, knowing full well that in time, that puny plant would flourish and grow to accommodate the currently oversized container? That's the feeling I got when I started poking around Album's Online Services feature. At press time, there are only a few services to take advantage of. But Album has set itself up nicely to accommodate more in the future.

The Online Services feature allows you to send images directly from Album to service providers online. You can share images online with family and friends. You can order prints of all sizes. And you can even order a professionally printed and bound book of your images. The procedure is pretty seamless, easy to use, and so far, reasonably priced. Because the Online Services feature is in its infancy, be sure and update the list periodically to see whether there are any new services or providers. Read on to find out how.

Signing Up for Online Services

If want to explore using an online service, you first have to register with one and create an account. This process takes just a few mouse clicks. Here are the short steps:

1. **Choose Online Services➪Manage Accounts.**

   The Create or Modify Online Service Accounts dialog box appears, as shown in Figure 15-1.

2. **Make sure All Service Types is selected in the pop-up menu.**

   This action ensures that all types of services, from print to share, are visible.

3. **Choose the name of the service provider you want to sign up with.**

   You can share your photos online or order professional-quality prints from Shutterfly.com. Another company, MyPublisher, prints and binds photo books (find out more about this type of Album creation in Chapter 17).

4. **Click the Select button.**

   The Online Services Wizard appears.

5. **Follow the instructions using the Wizard to register and create an account.**

You also can go to www.shutterfly.com and www.mypublisher.com to sign up for their services.

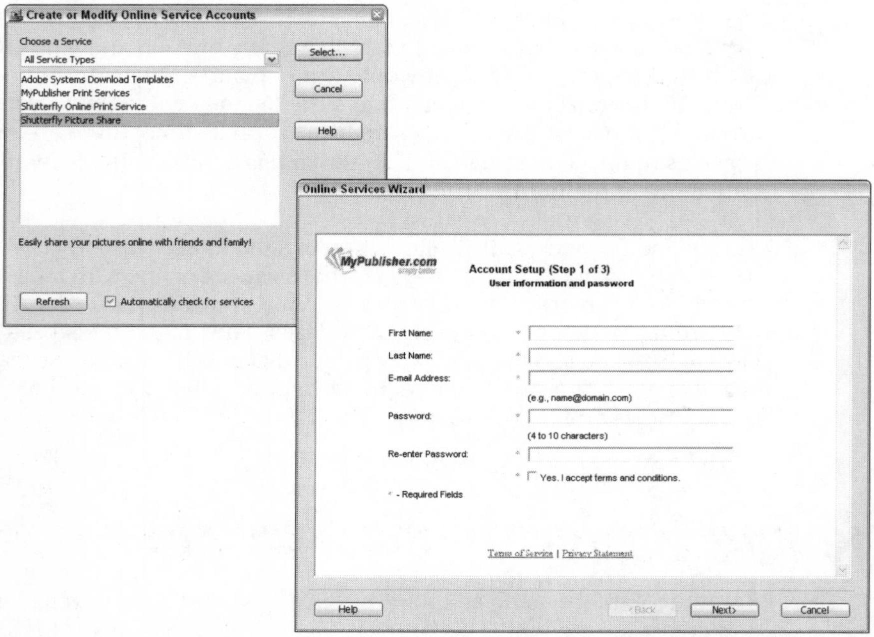

Figure 15-1:
Before using any online service, you must first register and set up an account.

Checking for New Online Services

Although Album has only a few online service providers to date, it's almost certain that new providers will be added over time. So be sure and check for new providers every so often. You never know what cool service could be around the corner.

To check for new online services, choose Online Services⇨Check for New Services. Album checks for any changes in services and installs them on your system. If there are no new services, a dialog box appears telling you that your services are up-to-date.

Sharing Photos Using Online Services

Some services, like Shutterfly, let you post images to a Web site so that you can easily share your photos with others. This is a great alternative to e-mailing photos as attachments, especially for those without a broadband Internet connection.

What's great is that you don't even have to leave Album. You don't have to launch your Web browser or use FTP (file transfer protocol) software. If you are using a dialup connection, you will have to open your connection first, however. If you already have registered and received an account with an online service like Shutterfly, you are ready to start sharing. If you haven't registered be sure and check out the earlier section, "Signing Up for Online Services."

Follow these steps to share your photos using an online service:

1. **Select your desired photos in the Photo Well.**

2. **Choose Online Services⇨Share Services. Choose a service from the submenu.**

   Or you can click the Share button in the Shortcuts bar. Choose Share Online from the pop-up menu.

   I chose the only available option at this time, which is Shutterfly Picture Share. Outside of Album, you can use your Internet browser to go directly to Web sites such as Microsoft's Internet Photo Site at `http://photos.msn.com`, Kodak at `www.kodak.com` or PhotoFun at `www.photofun.com`.

   Here are the advantages of using Album as your vehicle to online sharing and printing:

   - Convenience
   - Ease of use
   - A handy record of who you shared with or what and where you ordered services from (details are covered in Chapter 8).

If this is the first time you are using an online service provider, a dialog box filled with legalese that explains that Adobe isn't responsible for anything you do with third-party vendors (so no scanning and printing money, okay?) appears. Click OK if you agree to the terms.

The Share Items Using Online Service dialog box appears next, as shown in Figure 15-2.

3. **Select the recipients you wish to share your images with.**

The recipients will receive an e-mail from Shutterfly giving them a link to a Web site that will display your images.

If your desired recipients are not in the list, click the Contact Book button. Click the New Contact button and enter the person's name and e-mail address. Click OK. The person now appears in the list of Recipients.

You also can choose your desired online service from this dialog box.

4. **Click OK to close the dialog box.**

The Online Services Wizard window appears.

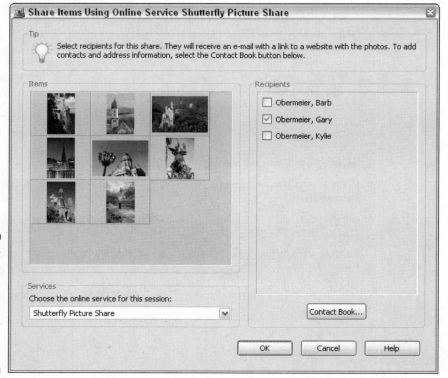

Figure 15-2:
Check the people with whom you would like to share your photos with online.

5. **If you're a member, enter the e-mail address and password you established during the registration process. Then click the Next button. If you aren't a member, click the Sign Up button and register now.**

6. **In the Online Services Wizard window, check the e-mail addresses of your desired recipients. Click Choose From Address Book to select or add recipients. Enter a Subject and Message for your e-mail if you so desire. Click the Next button.**

Shutterfly transfers the photos from Album to its Web site. If your images are large, this process may take some time.

Shutterfly then confirms that your photos have been transferred and provides you with the Web link used in the e-mail to your recipients. You also can e-mail the link to others you forgot to initially share with or post the link to a personal Web site as a picture gallery.

When your recipients receive the e-mail and click the Web link, they are taken to the Shutterfly site, where they can view your images as a slide show, shown in Figure 15-3. They also can order prints of those images.

If you need help sharing your images using the Shutterfly service, contact Shutterfly's customer service department at (510) 266-8333 or send an e-mail message to ols_support@shutterfly.com.

Figure 15-3: Shutterfly makes it so easy to share your photos online with family and friends. And what's great is that it is free!

126858300360000000_218.jpg

Ordering Prints from Online Services

If you perused Chapter 14, you're probably a pro, or at least a seasoned amateur, at getting your images on paper in some form or another. But maybe you're time challenged, or perhaps you prefer the convenience of ordering prints online.

Ordering prints online is easy to do, and the results are very reasonably priced. For example a 4 x 6-inch snapshot is less than 50 cents, and an 8 x 10-inch print is less than $4. You even can have prints shipped directly to friends and family, saving you a trip to the post office.

Many online printing services also offer additional goodies. For example, Shutterfly offers online tools that enable you to add decorative borders or color effects to an image before you order your prints, as shown in Figure 15-4. You also can order additional photo products, such as cards, calendars, and printed albums.

The most critical preparation you must make before ordering prints online is to make sure that the resolution of the digital images is high enough to ensure quality results. Even if your images look beautiful on-screen, printing them is a whole other ballgame; you don't want to waste money on low-resolution, low-quality prints. If you're unsure how to determine the resolution of your pictures, check out Chapters 3 and 14.

Figure 15-4:
Shutterfly offers print services and extras such as online tools to add borders and effects.

Here's the scoop on ordering prints online:

1. **Select your desired photos in the Photo Well.**

2. **Choose Online Services⇨Order Prints. Choose a service from the sub-menu.**

   You also can click the Order Prints and Books from Online Services button in the Shortcuts bar.

   The Online Services Wizard appears.

   At press date, there are only two available services from which to order prints directly through Album. One is Shutterfly and is located in California. The other is Dixons and is located in the United Kingdom. This isn't to say you can't find other places to order prints. For example, Microsoft's MSN Photos (`http://photos.msn.com`) and Kodak (`www.kodak.com`) are popular photographic sharing and printing Web sites. But again, working through Album is easy, convenient and provides a record of all images you have used with an online service.

3. **If you're a member, enter the e-mail address and password you established during the registration process. Then click the Next button. If you aren't a member, click the Sign Up button and register now.**

   If this is the first time using a service provider, an End User License Agreement dialog box may appear. Click OK if you agree with the terms.

4. **Select your desired sizes and quantities in the dialog box and click Next when you're done.**

   A great bonus in ordering prints from Shutterfly is that you can print a message (up to 80 characters) on the back of each print. With this handy feature, even your hard-copy prints will be identified and organized.

5. **Select a recipient for your prints. Click Next.**

6. **Review your order and click Next.**

7. **Enter your credit card number, billing address, and shipping address. Then click Next.**

   When you first sign up with Shutterfly, you get 15 free prints. Take advantage! You can check out the service for nothing.

8. **Review your billing info and click Next.**

   Shutterfly uploads your photos to its Web site. If your images are large, this process may take a few minutes. Go and grab an icy beverage. You deserve it.

   After uploading is complete, a dialog box confirming your order appears.

9. **If all is okay, click the Finish button and await your gorgeous prints in the mail. Otherwise, click Cancel to cancel your order.**

   My photos came in three days and were sent first class via the U.S. Postal Service. Of course, you can choose from a variety of shipping methods that range from cheap (er, *inexpensive*) to pricey.

Ordering Creations from Online Services

Prints aren't the only items you can order online. Photoshop Album also allows you to send your creations, such as Albums or Photo Books, directly to online services. Currently, MyPublisher is the only online service that provides printed Photo Books. These printed Photo Books are coffee-table quality, 8½ x 11 inches, printed on archival paper, and bound with linen or leather covers. Prices start at $29.95 for a 10-page book, with each additional page costing $2.95 apiece.

Follow these steps to order a creation from an online service:

1. **Select your creation in the Photo Well.**

2. **Choose Online Services⇨Order Creations. Choose the service from the sub-menu.**

   You also can click the Order Prints and Books from Online Services button in the Shortcuts bar.

   At press time, only MyPublisher Print Services is available for creations.

3. **Select a service from the list in the Print Items Using Online Service dialog box. Click OK.**

   Album chunks along, publishing your PDF.

   If this is your first time using this online provider, a Create or Modify Online Service Accounts dialog box appears.

   If you see this dialog box, select your desired service from the list, select the Automatically Check for Services option (shown in Figure 15-5), and then click OK.

   The Online Services Wizard appears asking you for your e-mail address and password, if you're a member.

4. **Enter both and click Log In.**

   If you're not a member, you can register and set up an account at this point. Once you've established an account, Album starts publishing your PDF.

   Another dialog box appears, asking again for your e-mail and password.

Create or Modify Online Service Accounts

Choose a Service

Order Creations Services ▾

MyPublisher Print Services

Print Services

[Select...] [Cancel] [Help]

[Refresh] ☑ Automatically check for services

5. **Click Log In.**

6. **Follow the on-screen instructions at the Web site to choose options for your Photo Book.**

   Depending on your chosen method of shipment, you should receive your printed and bound Photo Book in two to seven days. If you don't like the book, send it back. MyPublisher offers 100 percent satisfaction or 100 percent refund. You can't beat that.

You can order online services when making creations using the Creations Wizard. For more details, see Chapter 18.

You can locate photos using an image's history. In fact, one of the search criteria if you're looking for files based on history includes if and who you shared the pictures with online and also what items you ordered online. For more on finding files, see Chapter 8.

Downloading Templates from Online Services

Adobe and its third-party partners plan on making downloadable templates for you to use in your creations. Templates are the preset creation types that you can choose from, such as albums, eCards, and so on, as shown in Figure 15-6. Each template offers several styles to choose from.

At press time, there aren't any new templates to download, but I have no doubt that they will be forthcoming. Album has made it easy for you to download these templates once they arrive and here's how:

1. **Choose Online Services⇨Download. Select the item you wish to download from the sub-menu.**

   If you're in the Creations Wizard, you can click the Download New Templates button, shown in Figure 15-6. For more on creations, see Chapter 18.

   If this is your first time using this service provider, you may see the End User License Agreement dialog box.

2. **Click OK if you agree to the terms.**

   The Online Service Wizard dialog box appears.

3. **Click OK.**

   The Online Services Wizard dialog box appears (refer to Figure 15-6).

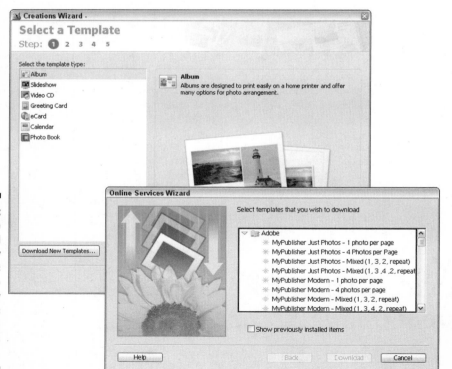

Figure 15-6: Click the Download New Templates button to get new templates from Adobe and its partners.

4. **Select the items you want to download and click the Download button.**

   If you want to see items you've downloaded previously, select the Show Previously Installed Items check box.

   After you click the Download button, a dialog box displays the status of your downloads.

5. **Click the Finish button to close the Online Services Wizard dialog box.**

Part V

Creating Larger Projects with Photos

The 5th Wave   By Rich Tennant

"Hey - let's put scanned photos of ourselves through a ripple filter and see if we can make ourselves look weird."

In this part. . .

If you check out the three chapters in this part, you may never need to buy another greeting card or prefab calendar again. Chapters 16, 17, and 18 show you how to use the Workspace and the Creations Wizard to crank out custom albums, cards, calendars, slideshows, and photo books. You also discover how to make online photo galleries to post on the Web. Your friends and family will be so awestruck by the wonderful personalized gifts they're receiving that they'll think you secretly went to photography or art school. Be careful, though, you may be inundated with requests to create everything from wedding invitations to baby announcements to Great Uncle Artie's retirement party.

Chapter 16

Using the Workspace

*W*hether you've thumbed right to this chapter after cracking the seal on the book or you've dutifully perused the preceding 15 chapters first, you have imported all of your photos and video clips into your catalog. I say this because getting familiar with the Workspace is a kind of warm up for the making of creations. And to make a creation, you have to have some source material to use.

In addition to making creations, you can execute other operations from the Workspace, such as e-mailing, printing, viewing a slide show, and so on. These operations also require files to use. So if you're staring at an empty Photo Well, you may want to go back and revisit Chapter 4, which describes what you need to know about importing files. If, on the other hand, you have a bustling, robust Photo Well full of files, you're in the right place.

Getting Cozy with the Workspace

You can think of the Workspace as a kind of light table within Album. Although you can do just about everything *without* using the Workspace, the Workspace makes tasks easier because you can view all your selected items in a neat little window. (By the way, you *must* use the Workspace in order to make creations.)

The Workspace is especially convenient if you have a large catalog, and you need to do a lot of scrolling to pick and choose your files. You can see only a few images at one time if you look at them in the Photo Well. The Workspace, on the other hand, provides a compact viewing arena.

Follow these steps to add items to the Workspace:

1. **Choose View➪Workspace.**

   You also can click the Show or Hide Workspace button in the Options bar or click the Create button on the Shortcuts bar. Figure 16-1 shows the locations of these three commands.

   The Workspace window appears. Now add your desired items.

2. **Select one or more photos or video clips in the Photo Well and choose Edit➪Add Selected Items to Workspace.**

   Or you can use any of the following methods:

   • Click the Create button in the Shortcuts bar.

   • Drag the items into the Workspace window.

   • Right-click one of the selected items and choose Add Selected Items to the Workspace from the context-sensitive menu.

   Your items are copied into the Workspace and numbered accordingly, as shown in Figure 16-2.

Figure 16-1: You can access the Workspace several ways.

Create

Show or hide Workspace

Select command   Attach tags   Clear

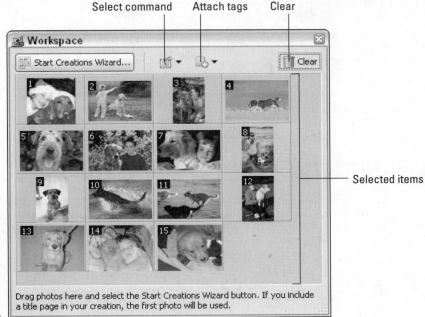

Selected items

Figure 16-2:
Bring your
desired
images and
video clips
into the
Workspace.

You also can select items before you access the Workspace. Select your files and then use one of the methods described in Step 1. Your images appear when you open the Workspace.

Here are some additional tips for using the Workspace:

✔ **Moving or resizing the Workspace window:** To move the window, drag it by the title bar. To resize, move your mouse over a side or corner of the window. Drag when the pointer changes to a double-headed arrow.

✔ **Changing the order of the files in the Workspace:** Select and drag the item to a different position. A yellow line appears where the item will be placed when you release the mouse. The files will automatically renumber themselves.

Once you are in the Workspace, if you want to add files, don't click the Create button on the Shortcuts bar. If you do, Album will clear your currently selected items and replace them with your new additions. Instead, use one of the other methods described in Step 2 to add more files to the Workspace.

✔ **Removing an item from the Workspace:** Use one of the following methods to remove an item:

- Drag the item to the Clear button in the Workspace window.

- Right-click an item and choose Remove from Workspace from the context-sensitive menu.

- To remove all items, click the Clear button in the Workspace window.

Working with Workspace Items

When you're happy with the selection and order of the photos in your Workspace, you can get to work. You can execute a ton of tasks from the Workspace. For example, you can add tags, create a slide show, share files online, e-mail photos, and print images from the Workspace.

Adding tags to Workspace items

You can attach tags to items in your Workspace. To add a tag in the Workspace, simply click the Attach Tag to All Items button at the top of the window, and choose your desired tag from the drop-down menu, as shown in Figure 16-3. For example, if you're assembling a group of vacation photos because you want to have Shutterfly.com create prints for you, you could create a tag called Vacation Print Order #1.

All items are tagged. You can't attach tags to individual items. Tags can be attached to individual files only in the Photo Well. For the lowdown on tags, see Chapter 5.

It isn't wise to use the Workspace as a temporary storage area because whenever you start to work on a new creation the Workspace clears out all the files that were placed there before. Do what you need to do with the files, but don't forget about them.

Creating a slide show from Workspace items

If you want to create an instant slide show from the items in your Workspace, click the Select Command to Apply to All Items in the Workspace button at the top of the window, and choose Play Slideshow from the drop-down menu. Album displays each image in full-screen preview mode. The images are shown in the order in which they appear in the Workspace.

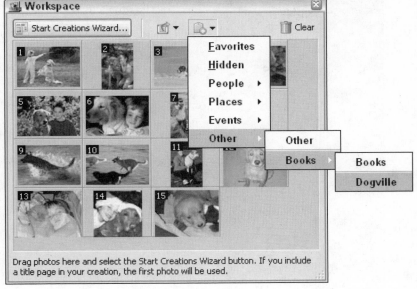

Figure 16-3:
You can
apply a tag
to all items
in your
Workspace
for better
identifi-
cation.

Use the on-screen controls in the top-right corner to control the slide show, as shown in Figure 16-4. Click the Close button or press Esc to end the slide show and return to the Workspace. For details on instant slide shows, see Chapter 9.

Sharing, exporting, e-mailing, and printing items from the Workspace

You can execute several other commands from the Workspace window. Click the Select Command to Apply to All Items in the Workspace button at the top of the Workspace, and choose one of the following commands from the drop-down menu:

- **Order Prints:** See Chapter 15.

- **Export:** See Chapter 12.

- **Web Photo Gallery:** The Web Photo Gallery with Workspace Items dialog box displays, as shown in Figure 16-5. When it's done churning, your gallery displays in your Web Photo Gallery browser, shown in Figure 16-6. For details on creating Web Photo Galleries, see Chapter 18.

Figure 16-4:
You can
create an
instant slide
show from
the items
in your
Workspace.

Figure 16-5:
Specify your
file type,
size, quality,
and location
before
exporting
your
Workspace
items.

Figure 16-6:
Your Web
Photo
Gallery
displays in
the browser.

- ✔ **Adobe Atmosphere 3D Gallery:** Choose your gallery style, destination, and other settings. You can even add music to your gallery. Click OK. When done processing, your gallery displays in your 3D Gallery browser, shown in Figure 16-7. For details on creating an Adobe Atmosphere 3D Gallery, see Chapter 18.

- ✔ **Archive:** You can archive the items in your Workspace and burn them onto a CD or DVD. You can create archives to use as backups or you can choose to move high-resolution files from your hard drive if you are low on storage space. A low-resolution proxy file remains in your catalog. For details on archiving, see Chapter 7.

- ✔ **E-mail:** You can choose to e-mail all your Workspace items. Specify your recipients and the settings for your e-mail in the Attach Workspace Items to e-mail dialog box and click OK. Album preps the attachment and launches your e-mail client. For information on e-mailing your files, see Chapter 13.

✔ **Print:** The Print Workspace Photos dialog box appears (see Figure 16-8). From here, follow these steps:

    1. **Choose individual prints, contact sheets, or picture packages. You also can specify sizes.**

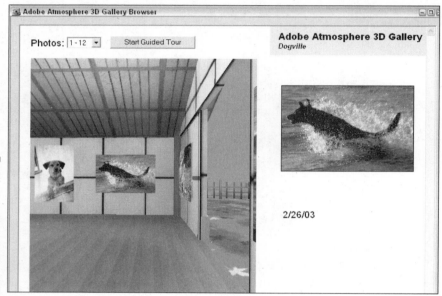

Figure 16-7:
You can create an Atmosphere 3D Gallery from your Workspace items.

Figure 16-8:
Album enables you to print individual prints, picture packages, or contact sheets from your Workspace.

2. **When you're done, click the Continue button.**

    The Print dialog box appears.

3. **Specify your print settings and click OK.**

Printing is covered in more detail in Chapter 14.

Making creations from the Workspace

Although you can perform are all sorts of operations in the Workspace, you usually find yourself there because you want to make a creation. After you have your desired items arranged in the Workspace, click the Start Creations Wizard button and follow the steps. In no time you're off to making great things like albums, photo books, and eCards. See Chapters 17 and 18 for more on using the Creations Wizard and making creations.

Finding photos from the Workspace

If you need to find a Workspace item in your Photo Well, you can

- ✔ Double-click the thumbnail in the Workspace.

- ✔ Right-click the thumbnail in the Workspace and choose Find in Photo Well from the context-sensitive menu.

The Photo Well scrolls to locate the image and places a yellow border around the item.

Conversely, you can have the files you used in a creation appear in the Workspace. Select a creation in the Photo Well, right-click, and choose Show Photos in Workspace from the context-sensitive menu. The photos used in your creation appear in the Workspace window.

Chapter 17

Creating Projects

This chapter touts the merits of creations. Album does a fantastic job in giving you a variety of ways to share your photos, video and audio clips with family and friends. These ways range from the usual e-mailing of attachments or making prints to the more creative making of albums, eCards, Web galleries, or photo books. The results are so good, people will think you slaved for hours to create these personalized projects. Little will they know it took longer to boot up your computer and was just as simple.

In Chapter 16, I introduce you to the Workspace, which is an integral component in making creations.

Making Creations with the Creations Wizard

With the Creations Wizard, you choose from a variety of projects, or what Album calls *templates*. Each template offers various design styles you can choose from. Depending on the project you choose, you can add various details and options. You can make albums, slide shows, video CDs, greeting cards, eCards, calendars, and photo books.

Web Photo and Adobe Atmosphere 3D galleries are not created with the Creations Wizard. For details on these creations, see those sections later in this chapter.

To make a creation, follow these steps:

1. **From the Photo Well, select the photos and video clips you want to use in the creation. Then choose Creations⇨New.**

   You also can use one of these methods:

   • Click the Create button in the Shortcuts bar.

   • Right-click a file and choose Add Selected Items to the Workspace from the context-sensitive menu.

   If you need to add another file to the Workspace, drag the file from the Photo Well into the Workspace. Don't select the files and then click the Create button on the Shortcuts bar or Album will delete *all* the files currently in the Workspace and replace them with the new files.

   You can choose Creations from the Menu bar, and then choose your desired type of creation directly from the menu. If you do so, the Creations Wizard skips the first step of choosing the type of creation (Step 4).

2. **In the Workspace, shown in Figure 17-1, arrange the photos in your desired order.**

   To add additional files, drag and drop them into the Workspace. See Chapter 16 for the lowdown on the Workspace.

   Don't select the files and click the Create button on the Shortcuts bar. Your newly added files will delete the ones currently in the Workspace.

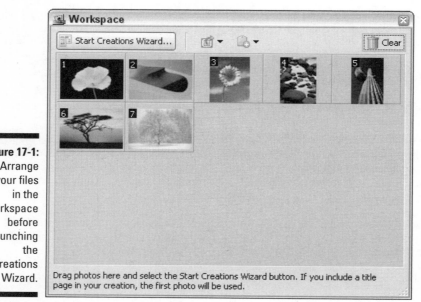

Figure 17-1: Arrange your files in the Workspace before launching the Creations Wizard.

3. **Click the Start Creations Wizard button.**

   Step 1 of the Creations Wizard appears.

4. **Choose the type of creation you would like to make from the list of templates, shown in Figure 17-2. Then click Next.**

   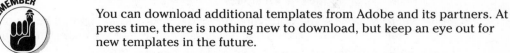

   You can download additional templates from Adobe and its partners. At press time, there is nothing new to download, but keep an eye out for new templates in the future.

5. **Follow the remaining few steps using the Creations Wizard. For details on each kind of creation, see the sections that follow.**

Creating albums

If you're like me, you have tons of snapshots languishing in boxes, drawers, and baskets. Drumming up the time and enthusiasm to put them into albums and with titles and captions just never seems to happen. But in Album, creating, er, albums is quick, easy, and fun. After you create an album, you can e-mail it as an attachment or print it and have the pages bound at a copy center. Here are a few album ideas:

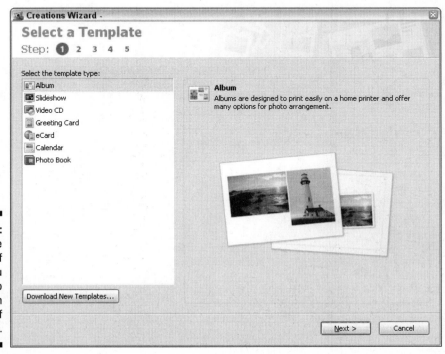

Figure 17-2: Choose the type of creation you want to make from the list of templates.

✔ **Events:** At the next wedding or family reunion, take a lot of candid snap-shots or solicit photos from other attendees. Make a personalized album and e-mail it to everyone.

✔ **Themes:** You can center your album on a theme, such as a particular person, project, pet, or vacation.

✔ **Records:** Maybe you want your album to take a chronological approach to recording events over a longer period of time. For example, you could create a scrapbook that records a child's year at school or a baby's first year of life.

✔ **Locations:** Your album can focus on a special location, such as your recent one-year trek through the Himalayas. Okay, if your locale isn't that exotic, you can focus on your hometown.

To make an album, follow these steps:

1. **Start your creation by following the steps in the section "Making Creations with the Creations Wizard," earlier in this chapter.**

   Step 2 in the Creations Wizard appears, as shown in Figure 17-3.

Figure 17-3:
In Step 2 of the Creations Wizard, choose your template's style.

2. **Choose the style of template you want to use and then click Next.**

   For albums, you have the choice of several categories, from full photo to simple, from decorative to seasonal. A description and preview of each style appears in the window.

3. **In Step 3 of the Creations Wizard, customize your album by using the following options, shown in Figure 17-4. Click Next when you're done.**

   - **Title:** If you want your album to have a title page, enter the text you want to use in the Title text box. The first photo of your album will be used for the title page. No caption appears on the title page.

   - **Photos Per Page:** From this pop-up menu, select the number of photos you want to display on each page.

   - **Include Captions:** Select this option if you want your captions to appear below each photo (except for the title photo).

     You should add captions to your photos before you make a creation (for details on captions see Chapter 6).

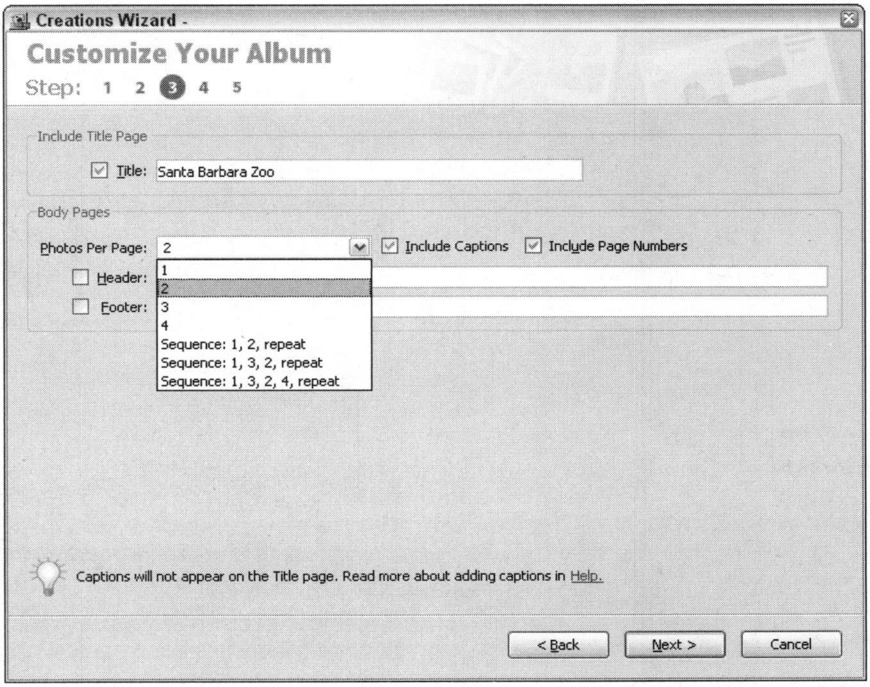

Figure 17-4: Customize your album with various options.

- **Include Page Numbers:** Select this option if you want your album to display page numbers.

- **Header and Footer:** Select either or both of these two options, and type the text in the box to add headers and footers. Headers and footers are small lines of text that appear at the top or bottom of each page.

4. **Here's your chance to preview your album. When you're happy with it, click the Next button. If you are not happy, you can edit your creation. Click the Back button to return to a previous step.**

   Use the navigation buttons, shown in Figure 17-5, to scroll through the pages. Click the Full Screen Preview button to see your album at full-screen size, as shown in Figure 17-6. Press Esc to get out of full-screen mode and return to the Wizard.

First page   Last page

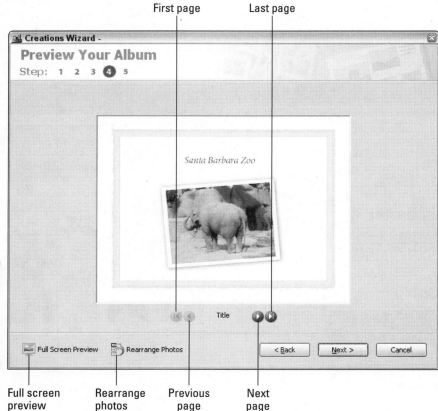

Figure 17-5:
Step 4 is where you get to preview your album.

Full screen preview   Rearrange photos   Previous page   Next page

5. **To publish your album, select one of the Output Options. If you don't want to publish your album right now, skip this step.**

   Table 17-1 gives cross-references to the chapters where you can find more information about these output options.

6. **Click Done to save your creation.**

   Album saves the creation, and it is selected at the top of your Photo Well.

You can access your album, as well as any creation, to apply edits or publish it at any time by simply double-clicking the thumbnail in the Photo Well. It opens in Step 4, the preview stage. Click the Back button to go back and make changes if necessary.

The saved album, like all creations in the Photo Well, has references, or _links,_ to your photos. The photos you use are not embedded in the creation, but are low-resolution copies that are linked to the full-resolution originals. The links are to the latest versions of your photos. So if you edit or remove a photo after the creation has been saved, the creation is updated accordingly.

Figure 17-6: To really see the details, view your album in full-screen preview mode.

Table 17-1	Finding More Information on Output Options
Output Option	*Where to Find More Information*
Save As PDF	Chapter 3
Print	Chapter 14
E-mail	Chapter 13
Burn	Chapter 7
Order Online	Chapter 15

Creating slide shows

Slide shows are a great way to share photos. They provide such a better viewing experience than simply looking at photos as e-mail attachments. You also can burn slide shows onto CDs and give them to family and friends to play at their leisure, either on their computer or on their TV via a DVD player.

Instant slide shows, described in Chapter 9, are quick-and-dirty slide shows you create with selected photos. While great for previewing your images, you cannot add all the bells and whistles that you can with the regular slide shows described here.

Your collection of photos is saved in a single, compressed file. This is very handy when e-mailing multiple photos to people who have attachment number limits evoked by their Internet provider or e-mail client.

Album allows you to set up the sequence of your images, choose a template style, add captions, music and transitions between slides, such as fades and wipes. Slide shows also include a control panel so that the viewer can control the playback.

Follow these steps to create your own slide show:

1. **Start your creation by following the steps in the section "Making Creations with the Creations Wizard," earlier in this chapter.**

   This takes you to Step 2 in the Creations Wizard.

2. **Choose the style of template you want. Then click Next.**

   You can choose from several categories. For example, you can choose a full photo, a simple style, or something more decorative or seasonal. A description and preview of each style appear in the window.

3. **In Step 3 of the Wizard, customize your slide show by using the following options, shown in Figure 17-7. Click Next when you're done.**

- **Title:** If you want your slide show to have a title screen, select this option. Enter a 30-character or less title in the Title text box. The first photo of your slide show will be used for the title page, as shown in Figure 17-8. No caption will be displayed on the title page.

- **Photos Per Page:** From the pop-up menu, select the number of photos you want to display on each page.

- **Include Captions:** Check this option if you want your captions to appear under each photo, as shown in Figure 17-9.

- **Background Music:** If you want background music to play during the slide show, choose a file from the pop-up menu or click Browse to locate an MP3 or WAV file. Album installs some sample files that you can use if you're short on music.

The pop-up menu lists only music files that have been imported into your catalog. If you browse and select a music file, Album automatically imports it for you. For my Disneyland show, I included a clip of kids laughing. But a kid's tune would have made great background music as well.

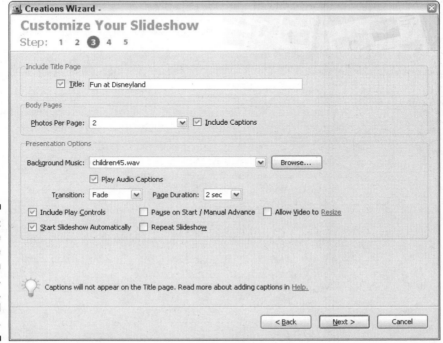

Figure 17-7:
Customize your slide show with music, captions, and transitions.

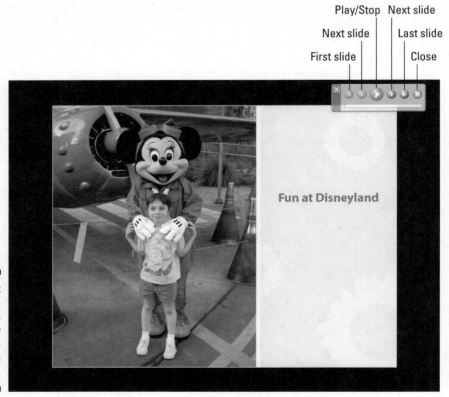

Play/Stop   Next slide
Next slide   Last slide
First slide   Close

Figure 17-8:
Adding a
title page is
a nice way
to introduce
your slide
show.

Fun at Disneyland

When selecting background music for slide shows, use MP3 files whenever possible. When using the other format, WAV files larger than 2MB may not play properly.

- **Play Audio Captions:** Select this option to play audio captions that you have recorded for your photos. For details on creating audio captions, see Chapter 6.

- **Transition:** Select how you want one image to change to the next from the pop-up menu. You have your choice of fades, wipes, dissolves, boxes, random, or none. Fade is my personal favorite.

- **Page Duration:** Choose how long you want each photo to be displayed on-screen. You can choose 2, 4, or 10 seconds from the pop-up menu or you can type a time into the text box. I usually use 2 to 3 seconds, but it is up to you.

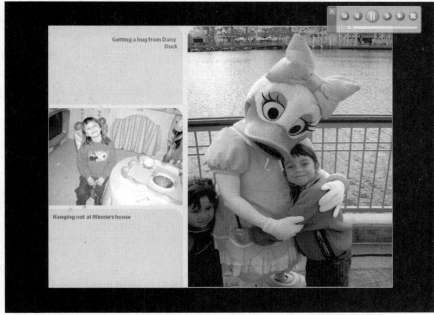

Figure 17-9:
Including
captions
can make
your slide
show more
personal.

- **Include Play Controls:** Select this option to include an on-screen panel of controls for playing and stopping the slide show (refer to Figure 17-8).

- **Pause on Start/Manual Advance:** Choose this option if you don't want your slide show to play automatically. With this setting, only the first page displays. The viewer then clicks the Play controls to advance the next slide.

- **Allow Video to Resize:** If you have a video clip in your slide show, select this option if you want the clip to resize itself to the dimensions of the slide show's window.

  Be careful about resizing video clips. The average video clip doesn't have a high resolution, so making it larger may degrade the image quality significantly. I recommend allowing video clips to display at their original resolution settings. Smaller and sharper are always better attributes than larger and lousier.

- **Start Slide Show Automatically:** Choose this option if you want the slide show to display the first page at full screen and then automatically play the show. If you don't select this option, the slide show opens in Acrobat or Acrobat Reader. The recipient can then choose to either play the slide show or view the pages in the Acrobat or Acrobat Reader window. However, viewers won't be able to hear any audio, view any video, or see any transitions.

- **Repeat Slideshow:** Choose this option if you want the slide show to *loop,* or repeat continuously until you make it stop.

4. **Preview your slide show in Step 4 of the Wizard. If you are satisfied with the slide show, click the Next button.**

   Use the navigation buttons below the preview to scroll through the pages. Click the Full Screen Preview button to see your slide show at full-screen size (refer to Figures 17-8 and 17-9). Press the Esc key to exit from full-screen mode.

5. **If you want to publish your slide show, select an output option. If you don't want to publish your slide show right now, skip to Step 6.**

   Refer to Table 17-1 for a list of cross-references to the chapters where you can find more information about these output options.

6. **Click the Done button.**

   Album saves the creation, and it is selected at the top of the Photo Well.

Creating greeting cards

Ads for well-known card company suggest that you should buy its cards when you care enough to send the very best. Well, I think the very best is making your own personalized greeting cards. No more searching through hundreds of cards for just the right message or image. Using Album, you can create a variety of cards and then print them a couple ways:

- ✔ **Inkjet printer:** Although you can print cards on your inkjet printer, I recommend using card stock.

- ✔ **Copy shop or service bureau:** You can take your file to a copy shop or service bureau when you need larger quantities of prints. Depending on the quantity you order, you can often get your greeting cards at below-retail prices.

The next time you or a family member receives a gift, take a photo of the person using the gift and make it into a thank-you card. How much more personalized can you get than that?

Here's the scoop on creating a greeting card:

1. **Start your creation by following the steps in the section "Making Creations with the Creations Wizard," earlier in this chapter.**

   This takes you to Step 2 in the Creations Wizard.

2. **Choose the style of template you want and then click Next.**

   For a greeting card, you have the choice of several categories, from simple, to decorative to colorful and seasonal.

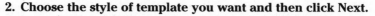

   Because a greeting card creation only uses one photo (always the first one), it ignores any other images you have in the Workspace.

3. **In Step 3 of the wizard, customize your greeting card by using the following options, shown in Figure 17-10. Click Next when you're done.**

   • **Title:** Enter a title in the text box. The title will appear on the front of the card. You can have the title appear next to or below the image, depending on the style you chose in the previous step. Your title is limited to 30 characters.

   • **Greeting:** Enter your greeting in the text box. The greeting will appear in the inside the card along the top. Again, you are limited to 30 characters.

   • **Message:** Type a message in the text box. The message will appear below the greeting on the inside of the card.

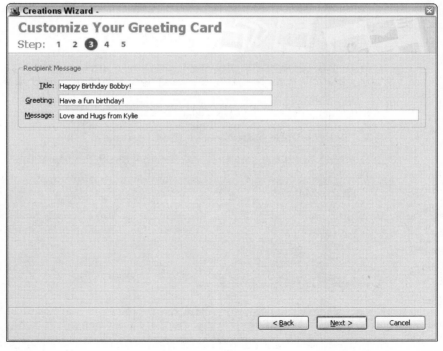

Figure 17-10:
Customize your greeting card with a title, greeting, and message.

4. **Preview your card in Step 4 of the wizard. If you like your card, click the Next button.**

   Use the navigation buttons to preview both the outside and inside of the card. Click the Full Screen Preview button to see your card at full-screen size, which is shown in Figure 17-11.

Figure 17-11: Preview your card in full-screen mode to really see the details.

Have a fun birthday!

Love and Hugs from Kylie

Happy Birthday Bobby!

5. **To print your card, click the Print button in the Output Options list. If you don't want to print your card now, skip to the next step.**

   After your card is printed, fold it in half and then in half again. For details on printing, see Chapter 14.

6. **Click the Done button to exit the Creations Wizard.**

   Album saves the creation, and it's selected at the top of the Photo Well.

   You can access the card at any time by double-clicking it in the Photo Well.

Don't just limit yourself to just greeting cards. You also can make personalized invitations to parties, weddings, graduations, and other events.

Creating eCards

If you feel like being environmentally conscious and don't want to be a gasp, "tree killer," try sending an eCard. Here are a few benefits to sending eCards:

✔ Your recipient gets it quickly.

✔ You save on postage and envelopes.

✔ You don't need a high-resolution image. Because eCards are meant to be viewed on-screen, they are a great option if the image you want to use doesn't have a high enough resolution to print.

✔ You can personalize an eCard. That's more meaningful than the ones you find at online e-greeting Web sites.

If your recipient doesn't have access to e-mail, you also can burn your eCards onto CD if you so desire. See Chapter 7 for more on burning CDs.

Like all creations, Album kindly provides you with a potpourri of template styles and options to choose from. As a final crowning touch, you can add music or an audio caption to your eCard. What family member wouldn't melt when receiving an eCard from their loved one with a personal audio message, like "I love you?"

Here's how to create an eCard:

1. **Start your creation by following the steps in the section "Making Creations with the Creations Wizard," earlier in this chapter.**

   This takes you to Step 2 in the Creations Wizard.

2. **Choose the style of template you want and then click Next.**

   For an eCard, you have the choice of several categories — simple, seasonal, decorative, and colorful. Like a greeting card, an eCard uses only the first photo for the front page of the card. It will ignore any other images you have in the Workspace.

3. **In Step 3 of the wizard, customize your eCard by using the following options, shown in Figure 17-12. Click Next when you're done.**

   • **Title:** Enter a title in the text box. The title will appear on the front of the card next to or under the photo, depending on your template style.

You are limited to 30 characters. for the title, greeting and signature.

   • **Greeting:** Type a greeting for the salutation. It will appear inside of the card at the top.

   • **Message:** Enter a message which will appear inside the card below the greeting.

   • **Signature:** Type a name in the text box for the signature which appears inside the card on the bottom.

   • **Background Music:** Choose an MP3 or WAV file from the pop-up menu or click Browse to locate a file on your computer. When your recipient opens the eCard the music will play.

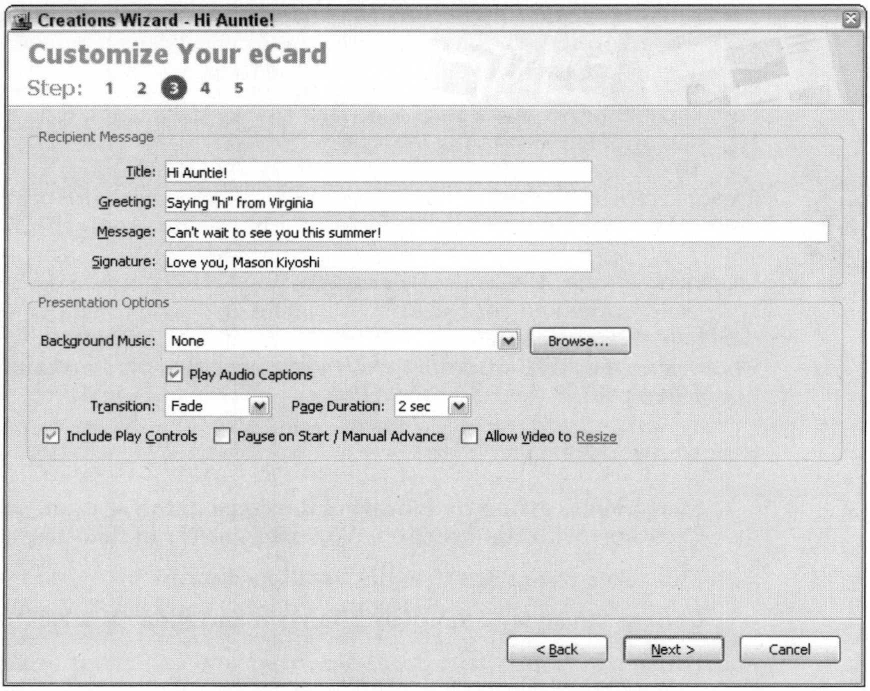

Figure 17-12:
Adding music or a personalized audio caption provides a special touch to an eCard.

- **Play Audio Captions:** Select this option to play an audio caption that you previously recorded for the photo in your eCard. For details on creating audio captions, see Chapter 6.

- **Transition:** Select the way you want the front page to transition to the inside page from the pop-up menu.

- **Page Duration:** From the pop-up menu, choose how long you want each page to display. You also can enter a time in the Page Duration text box.

- **Include Play Controls:** Choose this option to include an on-screen panel of controls for playing and stopping the eCard.

- **Pause on Start/Manual Advance:** Choose this option if you don't want your eCard to play automatically. With this setting, only the first page will display. The viewer then clicks the Play controls to go to the inside page.

- **Allow Video to Resize:** If you have a video clip in your eCard, select this option if you want the clip to resize itself to the dimensions of the eCard.

Be careful about when you size a video clip because you could degrade image quality significantly.

4. Preview your eCard in Step 4 of the Wizard. If you're pleased with your card, click the Next button.

Use the navigation buttons below the preview to view both the outside and inside of the eCard. Click the Full Screen Preview button to see your card at full-screen size, as shown in Figure 17-13.

If you need to edit the image or change the audio caption, see the section on editing creations in Chapter 17.

5. If you want to e-mail the card to your recipient, click the E-mail button in the Output Options list. If you don't want to e-mail your card right now, proceed to the next step.

For all you need to know about e-mailing, see Chapter 13.

6. Click the Done button to exit the Creations Wizard.

Album saves the creation, and it is selected at the top of your Photo Well.

Figure 17-13:
Adding music or a personalized audio caption provides a special touch to an eCard.

To access the eCard, just double-click it in the Photo Well.

Creating calendars

Creating calendars is another perfect way to use your digital images. Create a theme for the calendar or just use your best shots. For example, a calendar featuring grandchildren doing seasonal activities (skiing, swimming, wearing Halloween costumes, and so on) is perfect for grandparents. Give a calendar featuring your favorite vacation shots to a travel buff friend. The themes are endless.

You can print the calendars at home or at your local copy shop or service bureau if your printer isn't up to snuff. Album gives you a choice of several styles, and all you need to do is just enter the range of months you want.

Follow these steps to create a calendar:

1. **Start your creation by following the steps in the section "Making Creations with the Creations Wizard," earlier in this chapter.**

   This takes you to Step 2 in the Creations Wizard.

2. **Choose the style of calendar you want and then click Next.**

3. **In Step 3 of the wizard, specify the following options. Click Next when you're done.**

   • **Title:** Enter a title for your calendar. Your title will appear either next to or below your first photo, depending on the style you selected.

   • **Starting:** Choose the month and year you want your calendar to start.

   • **Ending:** Choose the month and year you want your calendar to end.

   • **Include Captions:** Select this option if you want your captions to appear under each photo. Note that a caption will not appear under the title photo.

4. **Preview your calendar in Step 4 of the Wizard. If you like your calendar, click the Next button.**

   Use the navigation buttons to preview each month. Click the Full Screen Preview button to see your calendar at full-screen size, as is shown in Figure 17-14.

October   2003

Sun Mon Tue Wed Thu Fri Sat

                    1   2   3   4
5   6   7   8   9   10   11
12   13   14   15   16   17   18
19   20   21   22   23   24   25
26   27   28   29   30   31

Waiting for the Great Pumpkin

Figure 17-14:
Calendars
make great
gifts for
family and
friends.

5. **If you want to publish your calendar, choose one of the following output options. If you don't want to publish it as this time, proceed to Step 6.**

    These are your printing options:

    - **Print it on your home printer:** Click the Print button (see Chapter 14 for tips on printing). You can then take the prints and have them bound at your local copy center.

    - **E-mail it:** For e-mail details, see Chapter 13.

    - **Burn it onto CD:** For CD burning advice, see Chapter 7.

    - **Have it professionally printed and bound via an online service:** You can have this done for around $20. To do this, click the Order Online button, which will launch the Online Wizard and take you to MyPublisher.com.

    Shutterfly.com will also print your calendar, but you cannot order the calendar directly from Album using the Online Wizard. Check shutterfly.com for details on how to submit your file. For general details on using an online service, see Chapter 15.

6. **Click the Done button to exit the Creations Wizard.**

   Album saves the creation, and it is selected at the top of your Photo Well.

Creating Video CDs

Not all your recipients may be tech savvy. In other words, what do you do if your family member or friend doesn't own a computer? You can send printed output of course, but then you can't show off your wonderful slide shows and eCards with music, audio captions, and transitions. If they have a DVD player, you can create a video CD (you need to have a CD burner, of course), which is basically a slide show designed for viewing on TV. Recipients also can view video CDs on a computer provided that it is equipped with a DVD drive and DVD player software that is compatible with the video CD format.

Follow these steps to make a video CD:

1. **Start your creation by following the steps in the section "Making Creations with the Creations Wizard," earlier in this chapter.**

   This takes you to Step 2 in the Creations Wizard.

2. **Choose one of the three styles of video CD slide show you want and then click Next.**

3. **In Step 3 of the wizard, specify the following options. Click Next when you're done.**

   - **Title:** Choose this option if you want your video CD to have a title screen. Type a title using a maximum of 20 characters.

   - **Background Music:** Choose a file from the pop-up menu or click Browse to locate an MP3 or WAV file on your computer. The background music will play during the slide show.

   - **Transition:** From the pop-up menu, choose how you want one image to transition to the next.

   - **Page Duration:** Decide how long you want each photo to be displayed on-screen. Choose a time from the pop-up menu or type in your own time.

   - **Allow Video to Resize:** If you are using a video clip, you can choose this option if you want the video clip to resize itself to the dimensions of the video CD template window.

   I would avoid this option and let it play at its original size.

   - **Include Captions:** Select this option if you want your captions to appear under each image. If you don't have any captions, nothing will appear.

4. **Preview your slide show in Step 4 of the Wizard. If everything is fine, click the Next button.**

   Use the navigation buttons to scroll through each image. Click the Full Screen Preview button to see your images at full-screen size, which is shown in Figure 17-15.

5. **To burn the slide show onto a CD, click the Burn button in the Output Options list, shown in Figure 17-16. If you want to publish the CD later, proceed to the next step.**

   For more on burning onto CDs, see Chapter 7.

6. **Click the Done button.**

   Album saves the creation, and it is selected at the top of your Photo Well. You can access the video CD slide show by double-clicking it in the Photo Well.

Creating photo books

When you're looking for that special gift, either for yourself or someone else, photo books can fit the bill. Using Album, you design the book with your photos and text. After you design your book, you access an online service, such as MyPublisher, which I discuss in Chapter 15. Prices start as low as $29.95 for a book with a minimum of 10 pages.

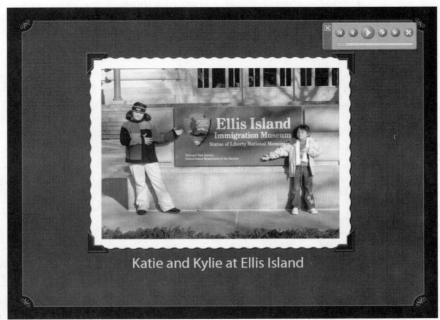

Figure 17-15:
Create a video CD to make slide shows to view with a DVD player and TV.

Katie and Kylie at Ellis Island

Figure 17-16:
Choose
an output
option, like
Burn, to
publish your
creation.

Photo books can be great for preserving the memories of a wedding, reunion, birth, graduation, or other special occasion. They are also perfect gifts for less formal occasions as well. Here are a few situations when a photo book would make an excellent gift:

- ✔ **Classroom or team gift:** Take photos of all the students in a class or on a sports team or club. Let them all create their own message, which you then enter as a caption for their photo. Have the students pitch in a dollar or two toward the price of the book, and you have a wonderful, personal thank-you gift for a teacher or coach.

- ✔ **Gift for the bride and groom:** You could do the same thing for a couple getting married. Take childhood photos of the bride and groom, add photos of their courtship, and finally end with photos of their wedding. Add personalized captions, and I guarantee you've got a gift that will be appreciated much more than a toaster.

Here are the steps to create a photo book:

1. **Start your creation by following the steps in the section "Making Creations with the Creations Wizard," earlier in this chapter.**

   This takes you to Step 2 in the Creations Wizard.

2. **Choose the style of photo book you want and then click Next.**

   If you choose the Just Photos style, you will not have the option of adding captions.

3. **In Step 3 of the wizard, specify the following options. Click Next when you're done.**

   - **Title:** The title will appear on the cover and first page of the photo book.

   - **Subtitle and Author:** The subtitle and author name will also appear on the cover and first page of the photo book.

   - **Header and Footer:** Enter text for the header and footer of the photo book, if you want these items, and if the style you chose allows them to be added.

   - **Include Captions:** Select this option if you want captions to appear under each photo.

   - **Include Page Numbers:** Select this option if you want your photo book to have page numbers.

4. **Preview your photo book in Step 4 of the Wizard. If things look okay, click the Next button.**

   Use the navigation buttons to scroll through each page. Click the Full Screen Preview button to see your photos at full-screen size.

5. **If you want to publish your book, select one of the following printing options. If you want to print it later, skip to the next step.**

   These are your printing options:

   - **Order the book online:** Click the Order Online button to order a hard-bound, printed photo book from MyPublisher.com.

   - **Print it yourself:** If you want to print the book on your own printer, click the Print button in the Output Options list. You can then take it to your local copy shop to have it wire or coil bound.

   See Chapter 15 for details on using online services. For details on printing, see Chapter 14.

6. **Click the Done button to exit the Creations Wizard.**

   Album saves the creation, and it is selected at the top of your Photo Well.

Editing Creations

If, when previewing your creation in Step 4 of the Creations Wizard, you notice that a photo needs cropping, rotating, or other edits, you need to work outside of the Workspace and Creations Wizard to fix the problem. Follow the steps below to find out how:

1. **In the Preview Your Album window of the Creations Wizard, click the Rearrange Photos button.**

   The Workspace window opens.

2. **Double-click the photo in the Workspace to select it in the Photo Well.**

   Move your Workspace window around your screen until you locate the selected image in the Photo Well. It will have a yellow border around it, as shown in Figure 17-17.

3. **Click the Fix button in the Shortcuts bar.**

   The Fix Photo dialog box appears, as shown in Figure 17-18. You can apply edits such as cropping, rotating, sharpening, and red eye removal. You also can adjust or color, contrast, and lighting.

Image selected in Photo Well

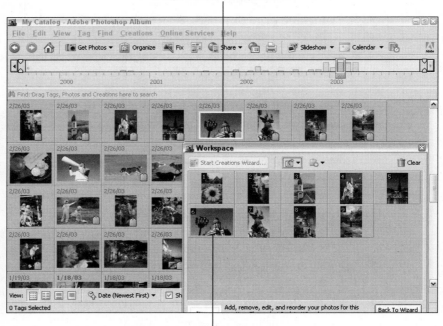

Figure 17-17: To edit an image in your creation, double-click the photo in the Workspace and select it in the Photo Well.

Double-click image in Workspace

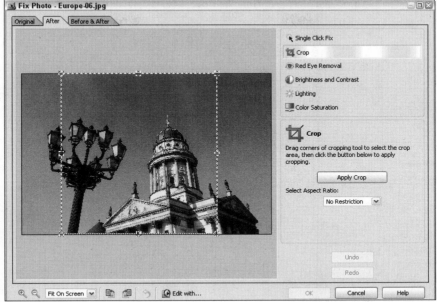

Figure 17-18:
Edit the
image
using the
Fix Photo
dialog box.

4. **Make your desired edits and then click OK.**

   For details on editing images, see Chapter 11.

5. **To edit a caption or audio caption for a photo, open the Properties pane and then type the revised text in the Caption field or record a new audio caption.**

   To open the Properties pane, click the Show or Hide Properties Pane button in the Options bar. For details on working with captions, see Chapter 6.

6. **Click the Back to Wizard button in the Workspace and finish saving and publishing your creation.**

   Your edited image and captions should now appear in the creation.

Opening Saved Creations

Saved creations appear with a Creations icon in the upper-right corner of the thumbnail, as shown in Figure 17-19. You can open saved creations any time to preview, make edits, or publish them.

To open a saved creation, use one of the following methods:

✔ Choose Creations➪Open. In the Open Creation window, shown in Figure 17-20, select the creation and click OK.

✔ Double-click the creation in the Photo Well.

✔ Right-click the creation in the Photo Well and choose Preview, Publish, or Edit from the context-sensitive menu.

Creations icon

Figure 17-19: Creations appear with the Creation icon on the thumbnail in the Photo Well.

Only the descriptive information of the creation is saved in your catalog. You will not find a creation file residing on your hard drive. If you want the physical file, you need to publish the creation as a PDF.

If you need to find your creations in the Photo Well, choose Find➪By Media Type➪Creations. All of your creations appear in the Photo Well.

Creations won't be displayed when the Photo Well is sorted by Import Batch or by Folder Location because there is no physical file on the hard drive, so be sure to sort by date instead. For more on finding files, see Chapter 8.

Figure 17-20: Choose the creation you want to open in the Open Creation window.

Chapter 18

Taking Creations to the Next Level

*I*f you've made enough albums, slide shows, and cards (see Chapter 17) to keep your friends and family happy for awhile, then you may be ready to try your hand at some other types of projects. Web photo galleries and Adobe Atmosphere 3D galleries are great ways to share your images with others. You post the galleries online, and anyone who knows the URL can go and view the images in his or her Web browser. Both galleries offer a variety of creative styles and different options. If online galleries aren't your cup of tea, then check out the section on "Going Beyond Album" later in this chapter. Here you will find lots of ideas on how you can use your inventory of digital images to make your life more productive, more organized, and more fun.

Creating a Web Photo Gallery

Album allows you to share your photos by posting them online in a Web Photo Gallery. Don't worry, you don't need to know HTML (the code used to publish Web pages). If you can push your mouse button, you can create a Web Photo Gallery. Album gives you different gallery styles and various options to customize your gallery to your liking. Follow these steps to create a Web Photo Gallery in a matter of minutes:

1. **In the Photo Well, select the photos and video clips you want to include in your Web Photo Gallery.**

2. **Choose Creations⇨Web Photo Gallery.**

   You also can click the Create button on the Shortcuts bar. Or you can click the Select Command button in the Workspace window and choose Web Photo Gallery from the menu.

Photoshop Album opens the Web Photo Gallery dialog box with your items added. You can now select options and specify text to determine the look of your gallery.

For detailed instructions on selecting an option or determining the look of your gallery, click the Help button in the dialog box. For more information on creating a Web Photo Gallery, click the <u>Creating a photo gallery for the Internet</u> link; advanced users who want to create an Adobe Atmosphere 3D Gallery can click the <u>Creating an Adobe Atmosphere 3D Gallery for the Internet</u> link.

3. **Choose a style from the Gallery Style drop-down menu, shown in Figure 18-1.**

   You have several options, from Vertical Frame to Spotlight to Theater.

   A preview of the splash page for your selected style appears in the top-right corner of the dialog box.

4. **Enter a name in the Site Folder text box for the folder that will contain your gallery files. Use the path listed to save the folder or click Browse to select the folder location on your hard drive.**

   It is a good idea to keep it simple and use lowercase letters and numbers with no space or punctuation when naming your site folder. That way the Web server will be able to easily decipher the name.

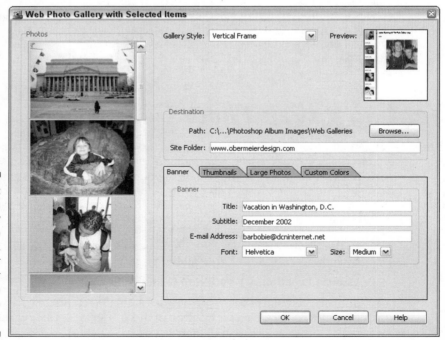

Figure 18-1:
Select a gallery style, photo quality, and other options for your Web Photo Gallery.

Once the Web Photo Gallery is completed, you can copy this folder of gallery files to a Web server.

5. **Click the Banner tab, (refer to Figure 18-1), and specify the following options, which may or may not be available depending on your chosen style:**

    • **Title:** Type a name for the gallery. The title will display on your Web page and in the browser's title bar.

    • **Subtitle:** Type an optional subtitle for your gallery. Depending on which gallery style you chose, the subtitle may appear in the footer, the header, or not at all.

    • **E-mail Address:** Type your e-mail address if you want it to appear in your gallery. Depending on the gallery style you choose, it may or may not be displayed.

    • **Font and Size:** Choose a font style and size.

6. **Click the Thumbnails tab, shown in Figure 18-2, and set the following options:**

    • **Thumbnail Size:** Choose a size option for your thumbnails from the pop-up menu. In my example, I chose Medium.

    • **Font and Size:** Choose a font style and size for the labels of your thumbnails.

    • **Use Filename, Caption, or Date:** You can choose to have the filename, caption, and date appear next to each thumbnail. Note that captions and dates are not available for some gallery styles. For more on adding captions, see Chapter 6.

7. **Click the Large Photos tab, shown in Figure 18-3, and set the following options for your full-size images:**

    • **Resize Photos:** Choose this option if you want the photos to resize and then choose a size from the pop-up menu. If your recipients have fast Internet connections, you can choose X-Large, and your photos will fill up the screen. Stick to smaller sizes if your viewers have slower connections.

If your photos are small and low resolution, resizing them larger than their original size will degrade their quality. Conversely, if your images are large and very high resolution (larger than 1 megapixel), as are mine in the example, they will take a long time to load, and your viewer may have to scroll in all directions to see the entire image.

Because the files in my example are very large, I resized them to Medium. For lots of information on resolution, see Chapter 3.

- **Photo Quality:** Drag the slider bar to specify the quality of your photos. Better quality means a larger file size and longer download times for your viewers.

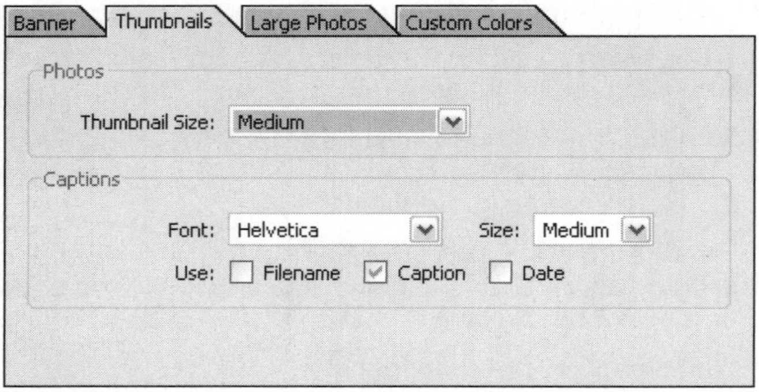

Figure 18-2:
Specify options for the thumbnails in your gallery.

- **Font and Size:** Choose a font style and size for the labels that will appear next to your photos. Note that this option may not be available for all styles.

- **Use Filename, Caption, or Date:** Select any or all of these labels for your photos.

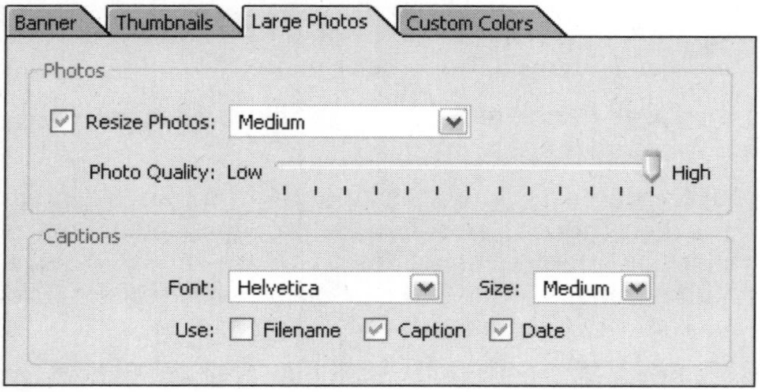

Figure 18-3:
Specify options for the photos in your gallery.

8. **Click the Custom Colors tab (if available) to specify the colors to be used in your gallery. To change the color of a component of your gallery, click its color swatch and select a new color using the Color Picker, shown in Figure 18-4.**

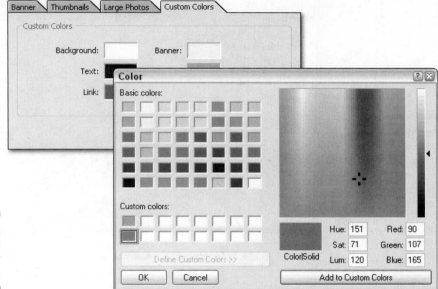

Figure 18-4:
Choose the
colors for
your gallery.

You can choose colors from the Color Picker several ways:

- Choose a color from the Basic colors list.
- Click any color in the large multicolored box (called a *color matrix*) on the right side.
- Enter numeric values in the Hue, Saturation and Lightness or Red, Green and Blue text boxes to define a custom color. Then click the Add to Custom Colors button.

Your chosen color appears in the Customs Color list.

9. **Click OK to create the gallery and preview it in the Web Photo Gallery Browser window, shown in Figure 18-5. When you are doing previewing, click the Close button.**

Album creates and saves the following HTML and JPEG files in your destination folder (which you specified in Step 4):

- JPEG images inside the Images subfolder
- HTML pages inside the Pages subfolder
- JPEG thumbnail images inside the Thumbnails subfolder
- Index HTML file for the splash (or home) page of your Web Photo Gallery

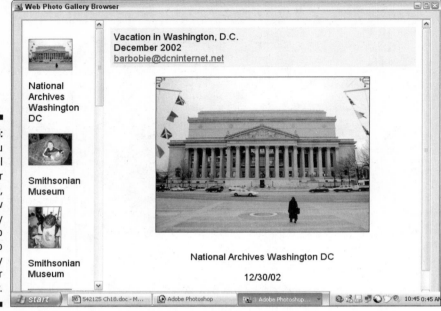

Figure 18-5:
After you
choose all
of your
options,
preview
your gallery
in the Web
Photo
Gallery
browser
window.

10. **Upload the files in your destination folder to a Web server.**

    Contact your Internet service provider (ISP) to find how and where to transfer the files. Don't worry; almost all ISPs will walk you through the process.

You also can post your images online by using a photo sharing Web site, like Shutterfly.com. Posting images online is even easier than creating a Web Photo Gallery and allows you to add fun decorative borders around images and other goodies. See Chapter 15 for details.

Creating an Adobe Atmosphere 3D Gallery

Feel like making something really funky? Try creating an Adobe Atmosphere 3D Gallery. This gallery type takes your photos and puts them on the walls of a 3D virtual building that viewers can walk through (virtually, that is). You can then post this gallery on the Web. You also have a chat option that enables multiple visitors to walk around the gallery at the same time and chat online about the experience.

Making a 3D Gallery

Follow these steps to create your Adobe Atmosphere 3D Gallery:

1. **From the Photo Well, select the photos you want to include in your 3D Gallery.**

2. **Choose Creations⇨Adobe Atmosphere 3D Gallery.**

3. **Choose a style from the Gallery Style pop-up menu, shown in Figure 18-6.**

   A preview of the style you chose appears in the top right of the dialog box.

   A music track will accompany the gallery. The type of music depends on the style of gallery chosen. Refer to the left of the preview window for details on the type of music for each gallery style.

4. **Choose the Enable Chat option if you want to let multiple visitors view your gallery at the same time.**

   Here's more information on this option:

   • Each visitor will be displayed in the gallery by a human figure called an *avatar*. The avatars walk around, representing the visitors' navigation through the gallery.

   • If you select this option, when viewing your completed gallery, a check box appears, enabling users to show or hide the chat area. If the chat area is showing, a field is available for visitors to type their comments. In turn, visitors can see the comments of all of the other visitors.

   • The chat/multiple visitors option only works if you upload your 3D Gallery to a Web server. Contact your Internet service provider to find out how and where to upload your files.

   Web pages are available to anyone who has an Internet connection. If you choose the Enable Chat option, your gallery may be visited by people you don't know. If you want to keep the gallery private, do not select the Enable Chat option. Or consider password-protecting the gallery Web page when you upload it to the Web server. Your Internet service provider can show you how to password-protect the Web page containing your gallery.

5. **Enter a name in the Site Folder text box for the folder that will contain your gallery files. Use the path listed to save the folder or click Browse to select the folder location on your hard drive.**

   When you've completed the 3D Gallery, you can copy this folder of gallery files to a Web server.

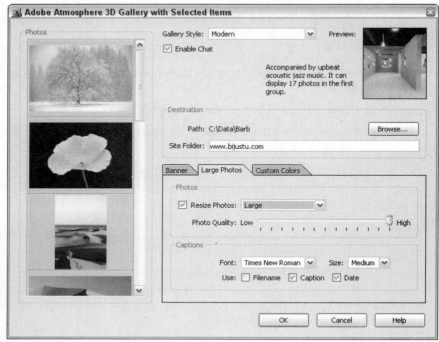

Figure 18-6:
Choose the
style of 3D
Gallery you
want from
the menu.

6. **Click the Banner tab and set the following options:**

   - **Title:** Type a title for your gallery that will display on your Web page and in the browser's title bar.

   - **Subtitle:** Type an optional subtitle for your gallery.

   - **E-mail Address:** Leave this field blank if you don't want your e-mail address to appear in your gallery.

   - **Font and Size:** Choose a font style and size.

7. **Click the Large Photos tab and set the following options:**

   - **Resize Photos:** Choose this option if you want the photos to resize and then choose a size from the pop-up menu. For more on this option, see Step 6 in the preceding section.

   - **Photo Quality:** Drag the slider bar to specify the quality of your photos. Remember that better quality means a larger file size.

   - **Font and Size:** Choose a font style and size for the labels of your photos.

- **Use Filename, Caption, or Date:** You can choose to have the filename, caption, and date appear next to each full-size gallery image. For more on adding captions, see Chapter 6.

8. **Click the Custom Colors tab to specify the colors of all the gallery components. To change the color of a particular component, click its color swatch, and then select a new color from the Color Picker.**

9. **Click OK to create the Adobe Atmosphere 3D Gallery.**

   Album launches the 3D Photo Gallery Browser, shown in Figure 18-7, so that you can preview your gallery and creates and saves the following HTML and JPEG files in your destination folder:

   - A splash, or home, page for your gallery named `index.html`. You can open this file in any Web browser to preview your Adobe Atmosphere 3D Gallery.

   - JPEG images inside the Images subfolder.

   - HTML pages inside the Pages subfolder.

   - Additional resource files inside the Gallery subfolder.

   - A Thumbnails subfolder and a ThumbnailFrame HTML file.

10. **Click the Close button to leave the Gallery Browser.**

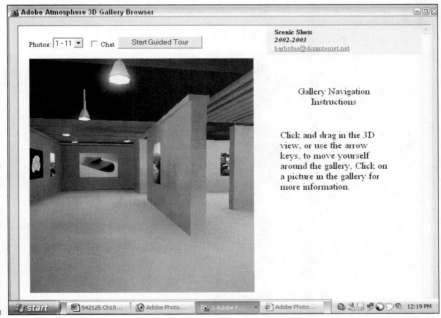

Figure 18-7:
Your completed 3D Gallery appears in a browser window for you to preview.

11. **All that's left is to upload the files in the destination folder to a Web server.**

    Contact your ISP for the directions on how to do this.

    Read the next section to find out all you need to know to navigate around the 3D Gallery.

You can replace any gallery style, or what Adobe calls *worlds,* that shipped with Album with your own designed world by placing the new gallery AER file into one of the template folders in `Program Files/Adobe/Photoshop Album/Shared Assets/AtmosphereWebGallery`. And, if you have Atmosphere Builder software program, you can open up any of the template gallery AER world files and edit them as you see fit.

Viewing and navigating the Adobe Atmosphere 3D Gallery

After you upload your Adobe Atmosphere 3D Gallery to a Web server, it is accessible for visiting. When your visitors go to your Web page and view your gallery in the Web browser, they can walk around it in various ways.

An Adobe Atmosphere 3D Gallery can only be viewed with Internet Explorer Version 5.0.1 or greater. No other Web browsers are supported at this time.

Here's the lowdown on navigating around the gallery:

- ✔ **Click the Start Guided Tour button to move through the gallery.** You view the photos along the walls. To stop the tour, click in the 3D view or click the Stop Guided Tour button.

- ✔ **Drag the mouse in the 3D view to move through the gallery.** Drag left and right to rotate the direction of view. Drag up and down to move forward and backward. To change the view up and down, hold down the Ctrl key while dragging up and down.

- ✔ **Use the arrow keys to navigate through the gallery.** Press the left- and right-arrow keys to turn left and right. Press the up- and down-arrow keys to move forward and backward. Again, hold down the Ctrl key, and the up and down arrows move the view direction up and down.

- ✔ **Click any photo in the gallery to see a larger view.** This view also includes the caption or other labels you chose during the creation process, as shown in Figure 18-8.

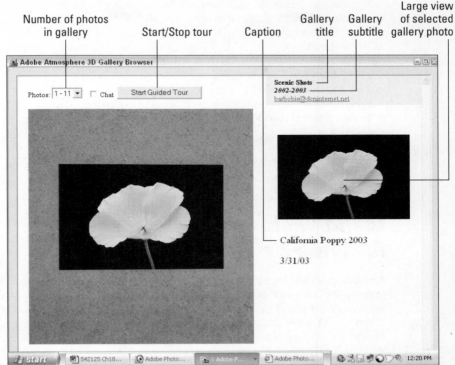

Figure 18-8:
You can get a larger view of images in your gallery.

Using Your Photos on Your Desktop

If you want to enjoy your photos while you're working at your computer, set your favorite image as desktop wallpaper or use several images to create a screen saver.

Using photos as desktop wallpaper

If you want to use one of your photos for the background of your computer, also known as desktop *wallpaper,* you can do so very easily. And you don't have to settle for one image. Switch it monthly, weekly, or even more frequently if you really want to.

As I mention in Chapter 10, if you are serious about image editing, you really should have a neutral gray background. I know this is oh, so boring, but a neutral and unbiased editing environment ensures that your color corrections are as accurate as possible. Still, you gotta have *some* fun. As long as your wallpaper isn't showing while you do your image editing, then feel free to go crazy.

Follow the simple two-step procedure below to use a photo for wallpaper.

1. **From the Photo Well, select the photo you want to use.**

2. **Choose Edit⇔Set as Desktop Wallpaper.**

   That's all there is to it! Your photo is now desktop wallpaper, as shown in Figure 18-9.

Using photos as a screen saver in Windows XP

You can take two or more photos to create a Windows XP screen saver. That way, when you walk away from your computer you can have your gorgeous photos display and protect your monitor at the same time. If you're not using Windows XP, check the Help file of your particular operating system to find out how to create a screen saver.

Figure 18-9:
Turn your photo into desktop wallpaper with a single command.

To create a Windows XP screen saver, follow these steps:

1. **From the Photo Well, select the photo(s) you want to use.**

2. **Choose File➪Export.**

3. **Choose JPEG for your file type, select your photo size, and choose a quality setting.**

   I recommend using a photo size that matches the resolution setting you're using for your monitor. I recommend using a quality setting between 8 and 12.

   For details on these exporting options, see Chapter 12,

4. **Click the Browse button. Click the Make a new folder button, and save the photos as JPEGs to a new folder. Name the folder "screen saver."**

5. **Click your Windows XP Start button in the bottom-left corner of your screen. Click Control Panel, and then double-click the Display button.**

6. **Click the Screen Saver tab and under Screen saver, choose My Pictures Slideshow from the pop-up menu, shown in Figure 18-10.**

7. **Click Settings and choose the Screen Saver folder containing your photos. Define the photo size and specify all of your other options.**

Figure 18-10: Create a slide show screen saver using your personal photos.

8. **Click Preview to see how it will appear on your monitor.**

   Move your mouse or press a key to end the preview.

9. **Click Apply and then OK to close the Display window.**

Going Beyond Album

If you have gone through this chapter from the beginning, then you've uncovered all the great things Album can create. But why stop there? There are so many other ways of using your photos. In this section, I give you a few ideas, but in no way does this list represent everything you can do. There are virtually no limits. Before you know it, there won't be an element left in your life that doesn't include your photos.

Getting your images onto stuff

Many local copy shops, retail shops, and Web sites enable you to add photos to T-shirts, mugs, buttons, tote bags, ties, mousepads, plates, and even cakes and lollipops! If you can think of it, they can put a photo on it. You can even do a lot of this stuff yourself, as described in the following sections.

T-shirts

Buy plain white T-shirts at your local discount department store or plain aprons and tote bags at your neighborhood craft or fabric store. Then buy special transfer paper at your office supply or computer store. Print your photos on the transfer paper, iron the print onto the fabric, and you've got yourself a personalized gift for very little cash outlay.

I've known a couple of really ambitious people who transferred photos onto patches of fabric and created gorgeous memory quilts. What grandparent wouldn't love a quilt with photos of their children and grandchildren? If you're not crafty, maybe you could trade your photographic skills with someone who can sew?

Posters

You can get poster-size prints at some copy shops and service bureaus. Call and talk to a knowledgeable rep at your copy shop or service bureau so you know exactly how you need to prep your file. Here are a few questions to ask:

✔ What file format and resolution should the file be?

✔ What size prints do you offer?

✔ Do you provide mounting and lamination services? Many service bureaus offer great-looking oversized prints that they then mount on foam core or a sturdier material called gator board. These service bureaus also can laminate prints to protect them from scratches and UV rays. The edges of these posters are finished and clean, and the print is ready to hang on the wall.

Documenting projects

Another great use for photos is to document your projects from beginning to end. Whether it is a project involving home improvement, auto repair, furniture building, crafts, or cooking, take photos at each stage to document the project both for the preservation of memories and for more practical reasons.

Photos can be great as a teaching tool when showing others how to do something. Import the photos into Album and create notes on each step of the project. Here are a few examples of projects you may want to document:

✔ **Your garden:** Take pictures of your garden each month or each season. That way you can create a journal of how your garden looks during the year. It is also fun to see how that little twig of a tree goes to maturity over the years. Import the images into Album and create notes on what and when you planted, what worked, and what didn't.

✔ **Classes and workshops:** If the instructors don't mind, you also can take your camera to your next class or workshop. Whether it is a new yoga, pottery, or flower-arranging class, documenting the positions or steps of a class will help you to practice or recreate it on your own later.

Photo Potpourri

Before I leave you to take your photos to the next dimension, here a few extra ideas:

✔ **Use photos to show off your work.** That's right. Photographers and artists aren't the only people who benefit from portfolios. Think of caterers, florists, carpenters, landscape architects, interior designers, tailors and seamstresses, jewelry designers — the list is endless.

✔ **Use pictures if you're selling something.** Pictures speak louder than words. Whether its real estate or puppies, attaching a photo to an ad adds some sales punch. Post those photos for online auction sites like eBay.

✔ **Have your kids incorporate photos into their school reports and projects.** In fact, buying your children their own inexpensive point-and-shoot cameras may give them a little more enthusiasm for school work.

✔ **If you're having a dinner party, make fun placecards for your guests.** Then when they leave, give your guests recipe cards with a photo of the wonderful meal on the front of the card.

✔ **Make CD labels and jewel case covers with your photos.** If you are burning a CD of images or of a creation, why not also create a custom label and cover that features a photo or two? It gives the CD a more polished appearance and looks much better than writing the title with a magic marker. There are many inexpensive CD labeling packages that come equipped with templates to use with a variety of programs.

✔ **If you have storage boxes or drawers that are hard to reach or access, take photos of the contents, print them out, and attach them to the outsides of boxes or drawers to show what is inside.** I recently saw a TV show on homes of the stars, where an actress took Polaroids of her shoes and pasted them to the outside of the boxes so she could see at a glance what shoes were inside what box. At first, I thought this was frivolous and only for the rich and famous, but in retrospect I think it can come in handy. You can even laminate the cards at home or at a copy shop. It will make searching through storage containers a lot less aggravating.

Part VI

The Part of Tens

The 5th Wave   By Rich Tennant

"I'VE GOT SOME IMAGE EDITING SOFTWARE, SO I TOOK THE LIBERTY OF ERASING SOME OF THE SMUDGES THAT KEPT SHOWING UP AROUND THE CLOUDS. NO NEED TO THANK ME."

In this part. . .

Welcome to the Part of Tens. Why ten? Because I give you ten (maybe more, maybe less) "things" in each chapter. Don't worry; they're useful "things." For example, do people politely excuse themselves, or worse, run the other way when you offer to show them your latest photos? Then, look at the tips on better composition in Chapter 19. And if you've really gotten the digicam fever, glance at Chapter 20. There I give you ten camera accessories you may be interested in — from the essential category to the nonessential-but-nice category. Be warned that reading this chapter may cause you to run out and spend cash. And finally, Chapter 21, you can skip altogether, especially if your Album experience is going well. If you run into a problem, though, check out this chapter for a list of cures.

Chapter 19

Ten Tips for Composing Better Photos

*E*ven if you have no aspirations to be the next Ansel Adams or Edward Weston, you'll want to take photographs that are interesting and well composed. Keeping a few simple concepts in mind, you can vastly improve the quality of your photos — both in production quality and conceptual or creative quality.

Don't worry. You won't have to memorize all these tips. Employing just one or two will make a huge difference in your photos.

Establishing a Focal Point

The single most important compositional tool is to establish a *focal point* — a main point of interest. A viewer should be able to immediately identify the subject of your photo. If there are too many elements competing for attention, then the focal point is probably not obvious. The eye needs to be drawn to a subject.

One of the biggest mistakes amateur photographers make is not having a clearly defined focal point. Make sure that your pictures don't include too much insignificant background clutter like furniture, walls, tables with food, and so forth. What you really want to capture are the smiles and surprised expressions of your family and friends.

Here are some tips on establishing a clearly defined focal point:

- ✔ Move closer to your subject.
- ✔ Include a point of interest in scenic shots.

  One sunset pretty much looks like the rest. But throw a fisherman casting his line or a child finishing up the final touches on a sand castle, and your image is elevated to a higher level.

- ✔ Include elements in the foreground to add depth and a sense of scale.

  It is even better if you place that foreground element off center.

- ✔ Use foreground elements to frame your subject. You can use elements like tree branches, windows, archways, and doorways to frame a wide shot and add depth.

Using the Rule of Thirds

One of the primary concepts of good composition is based on geometry. The *Rule of Thirds* says that if you mentally divide an image into a grid of nine equal segments, as shown in Figure 19-1, the elements most appealing to the eye and most likely to be noticed first are those that fall on or close to the intersections between the sections, on the dividing lines. Therefore, when framing your shot, try mentally dividing your frame into vertical and horizontal thirds and position the main focal point, your most important visual element, of the shot at any one intersection of the dividing lines. Check out the image of the buffalo in Color Plate 19-8 to see this rule in action.

For portraits, try putting the face or eyes of a person at one of those intersecting points, as shown in Figure 19-1.

Moving from Center

If you follow the Rule of Thirds (described in the preceding section), you will naturally move things away from the center of the frame. But if the Rule of Thirds is too hard for you to remember or employ, when you look through the viewfinder, just repeat this mantra, "move from center." We have been told since we were toddlers to always color within the lines. So naturally, we have a tendency to want to center everything. Get it nice and orderly. But centered subjects are often static and boring. Asymmetry often gives us more dynamic and interesting images, as shown in Figure 19-2.

Figure 19-1:
The Rule of
Thirds says
to place
your focal
point close
to an
intersecting
point on
the grid.

Here are a few tips to get you moving from center:

- ✔ Either move your subject off center or move your viewfinder and place the focal point off center.

- ✔ In landscapes, avoid placing a horizon line dead center. It makes your images look like they're cut in half. Instead, position the horizon one-third or two-thirds of the way up. A low horizon creates a dreamy and spacious feeling, while a high horizon gives an earthy and intimate feeling.

If you have an autofocus camera, make sure that you lock the focus when moving from center. If you have an autofocus camera, you'll need to lock the focus when moving from center because the autofocus sensor will lock onto whatever is in the center of the viewfinder — not on your desired subject. Autofocus can also be problematic when trying to do something as simple as photographing two people (in this case you may want the two people in the center), and your camera keeps focusing on the space in the distance between them. Here is how to lock the focus:

Figure 19-2: Asymmetrical composition can make an image more dynamic and impactful.

Getting Close to Your Subject

Many people worry about photographers cutting their heads off when they get their photos taken from an amateur photographer. But in actuality, more often than not, most photographers tend to capture too much. Too much boring or distracting background, that is. Although you can always crop your image later, either at the photo lab or on the computer, it is better to try and get your subject to fill the frame when you take the photo. Not only is the composition usually stronger that way, but it always ensures you have enough pixel information to enlarge the photo if necessary. See Chapter 3 for more on pixels and resolution.

Getting closer provides intimacy, especially with people, as shown in Figure 19-3. Long shots create distance and distraction. Look through the viewfinder and fill the frame with your subject. Only include what complements your main subject.

Figure 19-3:
Getting
close to
your
subjects
gives an
image
intimacy.

Don't get too close, or your image may turn out blurry. If you're less than three feet away from your subject, the chances are good that you will end up with blurry images.

Cleaning Up Your Background

I bet you have at least one or two photos that have a telephone pole, branches, or some other inanimate object sticking out of your loved one's head (I know I have torn up a few such pictures in my day).

Here are some tips on ways you can clean up your background:

- ✔ **Shoot at a different angle.** Sometimes a vertical shot helps to eliminate unproductive space on the sides of the subject.

- ✔ **Move around your subject, even go above or below it, if possible.** Moving around may help eliminate unwanted clutter.

- ✔ **Move your subject, if it is a person or small object, to try and get the optimum background.** An optimum background is usually free from distracting elements like furniture, tree branches, poles, wires, chain link fences, signs, bright lights, lots of loud colors, busy wallpaper, and so on.

If the background doesn't enhance the subject, rethink including it in the photo. A plain background places the focus on the subject.

- ✔ **Use background elements to enhance, not distract.** This is not to say that your background has to be a totally blank slate. That can be boring. You can use landmarks, props and even use decorations in background to give context to images, as shown in Figure 19-4, and help to define an important event. Just don't give the background first priority.

Figure 19-4:
Use background elements, like decorations, to add context to an image and help define an event.

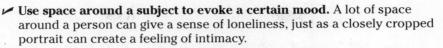

✔ **Use space around a subject to evoke a certain mood.** A lot of space around a person can give a sense of loneliness, just as a closely cropped portrait can create a feeling of intimacy.

✔ **If you're stuck with a distracting background, you can try blurring it by using a wider aperture (like f/4 instead of f/11 or f/16) on your camera.** This will make the *depth of field* (areas of sharpness in relation to your focal point) shallower so your subject is in focus, but the background isn't.

Because consumer digital cameras use image sensors that are typically one-third of the size of a 35mm frame, the lens is very close to the sensor, which really increases the depth of field. This can make it hard to blur the background. Not a problem, if you can't do this on your camera, you also can do it digitally, using a program like Photoshop or Photoshop Elements.

Lighting Your Subject

Lighting is one of the most important elements to consider when taking photos. When we think of lighting in regards to photography, the first thing that comes to mind are all those photos that we've taken in the past that are either overexposed (too dark) or underexposed (too light). With lighting you have to not only consider whether there isn't enough or there's too much, but also consider these factors:

✔ The direction of the light

✔ The intensity of the light

✔ The color of the light

✔ Whether you're shooting in natural light (outdoors) or artificial light (indoors)

✔ How to use lighting creatively to lead the eye and create a certain mood

A lot of these factors are interrelated. I bet you never thought that light could be so darn complex. Well, don't go anywhere because it's all broken down concisely below.

If the light isn't right for your shot, you have quite a few choices — hurry up and wait, move yourself, move the subject, add more light with a flash, or diffuse light. Of course, which you choose depends on the circumstances around the shot and what's convenient or most productive. Here are a few tips to remember about light:

✔ **The best light for photographs is in the early morning and later afternoon.** The light is softer, and the shadows are less harsh.

✔ **Avoid taking portraits at midday.** The overhead sun causes ugly shadows and makes people squint.

✔ **If you must shoot in midday sun, use a reflector to block some of the sunlight or fill in the shadow areas.** Or you can use a scrim to diffuse the light. See Chapter 20 for more on both items.

✔ **Cloudy or overcast days are great for photo taking, especially portraits.** The light is soft and diffused, and flatters the face.

✔ **Shooting subjects with backlighting (where the lighting is coming from the back) can produce very dramatic results.** Figure 19-5 shows an example. Subjects have a soft halo around them. If you want to see the details of the subject, and not just their silhouette, use a fill flash to lighten the shadow areas.

✔ **Watch that the brightest light source isn't directed right into the lens.** This will cause *lens flare,* those funky light circles that appear in the final image.

Figure 19-5:
Backlighting
can yield
dramatic
images.

If you're up for it and it's a bright, sunny, cloudless day, you can try the *Sunny f/16 rule.* This rule helps prevent the camera from automatically *underexposing* (making too light) your subject because of all the bright light. Put your camera on manual mode. Then set the aperture to f/16

(if the subject is being lit from the front) and the shutter speed to the nearest reciprocal of the ISO of your film. For example, if your film is ISO 200, set the shutter speed to 1/200. For side-lit subjects, use f/11. For backlit subjects, use f/8.

✔ **Take into account the color of the light.** The light at noon is white, the light at sunset is orange, and the light at twilight is blue See Color Plate 19-9 to see how the color of the light can make an image feel warm or cool.

✔ **Use a flash when necessary.** Use a flash in low-light conditions. If your built-in flash isn't cutting the mustard, you may want to invest in an accessory flash (see Chapter 20). Use a fill flash with a backlit subject or in midday sun to help lighten harsh, shadowy areas.

Getting Creative with Light

Even though I tout the merits of certain kinds of light, you can actually find good things to shoot in all lighting conditions. Look for those unique compositions created by the interplay between light and shadow areas or how the light illuminates a particular subject.

Lighting by itself can make or break a certain mood or emotion. Think of a simple beam of light coming through the roof of an old barn. Or a thin shaft of light that streaks across an otherwise shadowed face. Even in the lousiest weather, the most beautifully lit images can emerge. Think of how dramatic a backdrop is with dark, stormy clouds. When wet objects are lit, they seem to shimmer, as shown in Figure 19-6. Remember the wise old proverb about everything being beautiful? It is up to you to see it.

Using an Unexpected Angle

For photos of people, using direct eye contact is a good thing. It provides a sense of realism and makes the image more intimate and warm, pulling you into the photo. But for some subjects, using a front or eye level angle may not be the best. More of an extreme angle may provide a more interesting image.

Experiment by taking a photo from above (bird's eye view) or below (worm's eye view) the subject. Try changing your perspective on how you normally would look at the subject. Here are a few ways this can change the photograph:

✔ **Unexpected angles can exaggerate the size of the subject.** The subject may appear either larger or smaller than normal, as shown in Figure 19-7. Try this technique with scenic shots, which can tend to be rather static or even plain boring.

Figure 19-6:
Lighting
can create
drama.

✔ **Changing your viewpoint can change the mood of the image.** If the shot of this cactus had been taken from a directly front angle, it would have been pretty dull. Taking from below, looking up, exaggerates the height and makes for a stronger and more exciting composition, making the cactus seem like nature's skyscraper.

Remember that children are not at the same eye level as adults. We so often shoot down at them, making them appear smaller than they really are. Try kneeling, or sitting on the floor and getting down to their level. Do the same for pets and other small creatures. You will also find that you get less distracting background in the frame, and the lighting from your flash will more evenly cover the face.

Figure 19-7:
Shooting
subjects
from
extreme
angles can
exaggerate
size,
resulting
in a more
interesting
shot.

Keeping It Sharp

With the great digital imaging programs we have today, it's amazing the number of flaws that can be fixed. Red eyes, color casts, and flat contrast all can be repaired with a click of a few buttons. One flaw that isn't so easily reversed is out-of-focus or blurry images. You can apply sharpening filters in Elements and Photoshop, but even those applications do a marginal job and often make the image appear overly grainy.

It's better to capture an image sharply and in focus rather than to try and salvage it later. The following sections give you some tips on how to capture sharp images.

Using a tripod

Using a tripod or monopod will give you the sharpest image, especially in low-light conditions. It will also allow you to shoot a slower shutter speed without the risk of incurring blurriness. If you don't have a tripod or monopod, use the roof a car, a fence post, a tree branch or any other handy and fixed ledge. See Chapter 20 for more on tripods.

Using a tripod along with the self-timer on your camera will let you get some shots of yourself, too!

Catching fast-moving subjects

Using slower shutter speeds creates colorful blurs of moving lights or sparks. Faster shutter speeds freeze the image and capture it as-is. For sports shots or any shots where there is movement, you have a couple options:

- ✔ **Prefocus on an area where you anticipate the next action will be.**

- ✔ **Pan the action.** Set the shutter speed to ⅟₃₀th of a second or slower and move the camera to follow the motion of the subject. In other words, keep the subject in the same spot in the viewfinder. This technique keeps the subject sharp and blurs the background, enhancing the feeling of motion.

Understanding Digital Camera Focus Issues

There are some specific focus issues that are unique to digital cameras:

- ✔ **Image sensors:** It is especially important to keep digital cameras steady because the image sensors these cameras use are a third smaller than 35mm film. This means a digital image will be three times larger than a 35mm image. Consequently, any movement will make the digital image three times as blurry.

- ✔ **LCD monitors:** If you consistently have blurry images, try using the camera's viewfinder, not the LCD monitor, for taking your photos. When you use the LCD monitor, you hold the camera away from your body and, therefore, probably won't hold it as still. Hold your camera with both hands, keep your arms close to your body and stand with your feet firmly planted.

- ✔ **Shutter lag:** You probably noticed there is a lapse from the time you press the shutter release button and when the exposure is complete. This is referred to as *shutter lag* and may be the cause of a blurry image.

Or even worse, your subject may even move out of the photo during that lag, as shown in Figure 19-8. It goes without saying that you want to try not to move the camera after you press the shutter release button.

Get used to the lag of your camera so you can anticipate it. If your camera has a burst mode or best shot mode, try it.

Check your camera documentation to see what features are offered.

Digital cameras are great because they give you instant feedback on your photos. Check the photo in the LCD monitor immediately after taking it, make the necessary adjustments you need and reshoot, if possible.

Figure 19-8:
Watch the
shutter lag
on your
camera.
Your subject
may move
before the
exposure is
complete!
Reshoot if
you're using
a digital
camera.

Giving Direction

When you look at those magazines that feature the year's best photos, they all appear spontaneous and a matter of pure serendipity. Sometimes that's the case, but more often than not, the photographer arranged the shot or waited for the right light.

As an amateur photographer, you also shouldn't be afraid to play photo stylist:

- ✔ Give directions on where you want people to stand, how to stand, and so on. For example, tell people to touch each other, putting their arms around each other, as shown in Figure 19-9, or bringing their heads in toward each other.

Figure 19-9: Provide direction to the people you're photographing, while also trying to capture their spirits.

✔ Designate the location.

✔ Use props, such as trees or cars, to arrange people around.

✔ Use a variety of poses. Have some people sit and others stand.

✔ If it is a large group of people or you are dealing with unruly kids or wild pets, get someone to help direct. Just make sure that the parties being photographed pay attention and look at you, the camera.

✔ Try and get people to relax. While spontaneity can yield great images, you can still get good photos from posed subjects if they aren't hating the experience.

Getting Vertical

Sometimes it's hard to fight comfort. Most photos are horizontal just for the mere fact that it is easier to hold the camera that way. That's fine for a lot of shots (such as the ubiquitous group photo and many landscape shots). But other subjects — portraits of one person, buildings, trees, waterfalls, mountain peaks, flowers, giraffes, Shaquille O'Neal, and so forth — lend themselves to a vertical format, as shown in Figure 19-10.

Figure 19-10: Turn that camera! You may find that your composition is stronger in a vertical format.

 Turn the camera and look through the viewfinder to check if a vertical orientation lends itself to a stronger composition. Often, vertical images are more impactful because vertical lines by nature create a feeling of action, whereas horizontal lines create a feeling of harmony or tranquility. Vertical shots often help to fill the frame and either reduce useless space to the left and right of the subject or eliminate distracting background elements.

Using Leading Lines

Leading lines are lines that, either by the actual elements in the image or by the composition of those elements, lead the eye into the picture and often to a point of interest. These lines add dimension, depth and perspective by carrying the eye through the photo:

- ✔ Diagonal lines are dynamic and evoke movement.
- ✔ Curves are graceful and harmonious.
- ✔ Horizontal lines are peaceful and give a feeling of balance.
- ✔ Vertical lines are direct and active.

There are many elements that provide natural leading lines, especially in scenic or landscape photos such as roads, walls, fences, rivers, shadows, skyscrapers, bridges and so on. The image of the Great Wall in China in Figure 19-11 is an example of curved leading lines. Check out Color Plate 19-8 to see another example of leading lines.

Telling a Story

This last tip can't really be quantified in technical terms. You just know it when you see it. When you look at an image and it evokes an emotional response from you, you will end up with a memorable photo. Maybe the image tells an immediate story or maybe the image is more mysterious. It draws you in and makes you yearn to know more. The bottom line is you want an image that carries a message.

Figure 19-11: You don't have to trek to China to find leading lines, although you may not find a longer unbroken curve than the Great Wall.

So often people snap away capturing the obligatory "record" shots. I'm not suggesting that those photos are bad. I'm suggesting that you can turn a record into a work of art without a whole lot of extra effort.

Try to capture images that go beyond the obvious or cliché. Keep an eye out for the unexpected or unusual. Get off the beaten path. Sometimes it isn't the destination or event that produces the great photo. It is the trip along the way. That great shot of Grandpa feeding his grandchild before his first birthday party may be the image that wins everyone's heart rather than the obvious "kid playing with cake" shot. Maybe the shots of the Mayan ruins in Mexico were nice, but it was the photo you took of a young boy and his even younger brother, selling Popsicles from a push cart on the way to the ruins, that sticks in your mind.

Even mundane or routine events that show the bonds between people or give insight into a culture can yield those truly special images. Sometimes finding the right shot is a matter of chance; sometimes you need to take the time to build a relationship with the people or with the place. Learn to trust your instinct for those just-right shots.

Chapter 20

Ten Great Digital Camera Accessories

*I*f you made the switch from a film camera to a digital camera, you may be interested in acquiring accessories to further enhance your photographing experience. Some of those accessories fall into the must-have category while others are nice to have. Acquire them as your budget allows, or drop subtle hints around gift-giving holidays and occasions.

Essential Accessories

There are a couple of accessories that are really more like necessities. It can be frustrating when you find yourself in the midst of a picture-perfect moment only to find that your batteries died, or your memory card is maxed out. So be the perfect Boy Scout and stay prepared with the following two accessories.

Extra batteries

You've got to have juice. Make sure and buy at least one if not a few spare batteries. The cost is really minimal in comparison to the agony you'll feel when (not *if,* but when) they run dry. Here are a few points to keep in mind about batteries:

✔ I recommend using rechargeable Nickel Metal Hydride (Ni-MH) cells along with a *trickle charger* (a low-current charger that continuously charges batteries without risk of damage) for the batteries. These batteries are more powerful than their counterparts, last the longest, and can even be repurposed for use in other devices in a pinch.

- ✔ If your camera uses custom-designed rechargeable Lithium-Ion batteries, shown in Figure 20-1, buy extras and keep the spares charged.
- ✔ Avoid alkaline batteries like the plague.
- ✔ To conserve battery life, use your AC adapter when you can. For example, bust out with the AC adapter when you're sharing your images with others by viewing them on the LCD or when you're transferring your photos onto your computer. These processes can quickly (and unnecessarily) eat up battery life.

Using a flash and the LCD when photographing tends to shorten your battery life even more. Don't stop using these functions (if you need a flash, you need a flash). Just be stocked with extra batteries, fully charged of course.

Extra memory cards

Digital cameras store their images in a few ways, in the camera's internal memory, on memory cards, or a combo of both. Whether your memory card is CompactFlash (shown in Figure 20-2), SmartMedia, Memory Stick, Secure Digital/MultiMedia, x-D-Picture, or some other flavor, having more cards means having more photos.

Figure 20-1: Having spare, fully charged batteries is a must for any photo excursion.

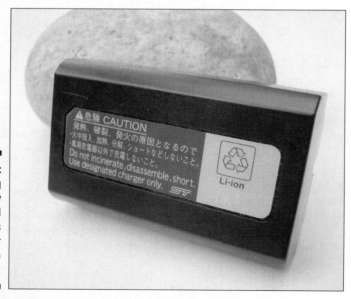

Figure 20-2:
Having extra memory cards means having the capability to take more photos without the worry of running out of storage space.

Card sizes currently range from 16 to 2GB (gigabytes), with a 4GB card just around the corner. The sizes available depend on your particular type of card. I recommend buying a card with the largest memory you can afford (or the largest memory that your camera can handle). Here are a few additional considerations:

✔ **For the budget conscious:** If budget is a concern and you're a casual photographer, you can get away with 32 to 64MB cards.

✔ **For photoholics:** If you're using a high-resolution camera, or shooting in high-resolution mode, you should really consider 256 to 512MB cards.

Although cards aren't as cheap as film, you can use them over and over, and they last for years.

Useful Extras

When you're fully equipped with spare batteries and memory cards, you can start to explore those accessories that aren't vital but can make your photo taking better, easier, and more fun. Here's a partial list. Look around on the

Web, and I'm sure you'll find lots more. Check out the Web site of your particular camera manufacturer for the latest gadgets for your model of camera. Or visit www.ritzcamera.com, a reputable dealer that offers lots of digital camera goodies.

Flashes

My biggest complaint when I bought my digital camera was the weakness of the built-in flash. It's no wonder — the built-in flash has the equivalent strength of about an ISO 100 film. After getting way too many dark images, I purchased an accessory flash for $150, shown in Figure 20-3. This particular flash is extremely easy to use, and I'm sure it's not an anomaly. I just slip it on the hot shoe of the camera. I don't even have to turn it on! And now even my interior shots look great.

If your digital camera doesn't allow for a dedicated accessory flash, you can always use a *slave flash*. These types of flashes do not require a mechanical or electronic connection to your camera. All you do is hold the flash toward your subject, and the flash does the rest; it automatically goes off at the same time that your built-in flash does. You also can buy a mounting bracket that allows you to fasten the slave flash to some camera models.

You don't have to use your flash just in low-light situations. You can use a *fill flash* to get rid of harsh shadows on your subject or to bring out details in a subject where the lighting is coming from the back.

Tripods or monopods

With the advent of image-editing programs, it is amazing how you can repair and enhance images. Unfortunately, no image-editing program can perform miracles. For example, you can't use Album (or even its heavy-duty cousins, Elements and Photoshop) to make blurry images, er, *unblurry*.

If you're tired of blurry images, and you're even more sick of using car roofs, tables, or ledges to steady your camera, add a tripod or monopod (like a tripod but with just one leg) to your camera bag. These accessories offer you several advantages:

- ✔ You can capture a sharp photo, especially in low-light conditions.
- ✔ You can shoot pictures at a slower shutter speed without the risk of getting a blurry image.
- ✔ You can use them for night shots. Simply set up your camera to a slower shutter speed to create streaks of lights or set it to a faster shutter speed to freeze the image.

Figure 20-3:
Getting an
accessory
flash will
make dark
interior
shots a
thing of
the past.

You also can purchase mini tripods for around $25 to $50. Mini tripods are compact and work great with digital cameras.

Lenses

Several manufacturers make lenses that can be used interchangeably with both digital and film cameras. For example, digital SLR (single lens reflex) cameras accept Nikon, Canon, or Contax lenses made for film cameras.

Manufacturers (like Nikon for example) also produce lenses intended specifically for digital cameras. Because they are designed for digital cameras, they are smaller and lighter than traditional lenses. So if you're a digital SLR owner, look into wide angle, telephoto, or fish eye lenses to add another dimension to your photo taking.

Filters

Improve the quality of your images with filters. Filters are like glass lens caps that you place over the end of your camera lens. Here are a few you may want to consider for your camera:

- **UV filter:** Helps to filter out UV rays and provide better contrast for your photos.

- **PL (polarized light) filter:** Great for shots involving reflections from non-metallic surfaces like water or glass.

- **FD filter:** Wonderful for shots under fluorescent lighting, giving a more natural-looking light rather than the dominant green tint often seen.

Lights, reflectors, scrims, action

Shooting in high midday sun isn't the greatest. It causes nasty, harsh shadows on people's faces, enhances flaws, and makes people squint. Here are a few accessories that combat these problems:

- **Reflector:** If you find that you do a lot of photographing in high, midday sun, you can purchase a reflector to block some of the sunlight or fill in the shadow areas. Here's how to use it:

  - To block the sun, hold the reflector between the subject and the sun.

  - To fill in shadows, hold the reflector next to the subject and bounce light onto the side opposite the sun.

- **Scrim:** Diffuses the harsh light. A scrim is white translucent fabric stretched across a frame. For smaller subjects or close-up shots, you can buy smaller diffuser panels. Position the scrim between the sun and your subject to soften the light.

You can purchase all these goodies at a photo supply store for a nominal cost.

Compact printers

Just as cameras are getting smaller while their quality is improving, so are other devices such as high-resolution printers. Manufacturers, like Olympus, Hewlett-Packard, and others are even making tiny printers. When I say tiny, I mean small enough to stuff in a camera bag! The quality is great, and they range in price from around $150 to $800.

These miniprinters connect directly to your camera and output 4 x 6 prints, which you can use as proofs or hand out to guests at gatherings. Canon recently came out with a postcard printer, which quickly prints out a coated postcard-size photo. On the back are spaces for the message, the address, and a placeholder for the stamp. Be sure and check the Web for sites like www.dpreview.com for the latest in digital camera accessories.

Paper and media

If you plan on printing your photos at home, invest in good quality paper. I recommend running tests with various brands of paper to see which works best with your printer. I have found that often the manufacturer's brand of paper just works the best with the manufacturer's printer. I have owned four Epson printers and have run tests with lots of brands of paper. I always come back to Epson paper because it gives me the best results. If you're a Costco member, you're in luck. You can get 100 sheets of photo quality paper for $20. If you find that a cheapie store brand is just as good, more power to you.

Digital prints tend to fade over time, especially if exposed to sunlight. Invest in archival paper if it is essential that your prints stay fresh and bright. Likewise, if you want to store your images on CD for eternity (or close to it), make sure and use an archival CD-ROM such as Verbatim DataLife. Archival CDs should last for up to a hundred years. Don't forget to stick a copy in your safety deposit box as a backup.

Just for fun

Although not an accessory, ultra-compact digital cameras are light, practical, affordable, and just plain fun. A few good ones are

- ✔ Minolta DiMAGE, which is the size of a deck of cards and costs around $400
- ✔ Sony DSC-U20 Cyber-Shot, which is 4.2 ounces and costs around $250
- ✔ SiPix StyleCam Blink, which is only 1.5 ounces and a measly $40

Although these cameras won't give you the highest quality large images, what you *do* get is convenience. Here are a few instances where they might come in handy:

- ✔ For photographing notes on a white board at a meeting or in a class.
- ✔ For quick on-site inventories of items.
- ✔ To photograph potential new cars you're considering buying.

✔ To photograph a car accident scene. You never know when you may get into a fender bender or witness someone else getting into an accident. Keep a camera in your car.

✔ For your kids to use. If you find your children begging to use your digital camera, buy them an inexpensive ultra-compact camera that they can take on field trips or outings with their friends. Then they can e-mail their photos to relatives and friends.

Don't leave home without it

If you are going on a photo adventure, remember that the best accessories to have are not necessarily camera-related. First and foremost, the best accessory to take is a cell phone — fully charged, with a spare battery if possible. If you are going to the great outdoors and the location is away from civilization, remember to take a flashlight, map, sunscreen, pen and pad of paper, water, snacks, a watch, and a jacket (even if it isn't cold when you leave).

I recommend leaving extra water, a blanket, a first aid kit and a change of clothes in the car. If you're trekking alone, let someone know where you are going and when you intend to return home.

Chapter 21

Ten Cures for Ten Problems

*F*ew events are more frustrating than when your computer or software applications don't do what they're supposed to. You're not asking the system to read your mind — just to perform the command that you ask it to perform. Right?

Unfortunately, I came to the realization long ago (and maybe you did too) that the computer and its buddies (the software applications) are just as human as the rest of us and have those moments where they just don't work at peak efficiency. Maybe they're a little overworked (need more RAM), or maybe they need a makeover (updated drivers), or maybe it's just — gasp — the infamous *operator error*. Whatever the problem, maybe you can find the cure here.

Another good resource is Adobe's Web site. Look at the Customer Support link where you can find a great user-to-user forum, knowledge base, and list of top support issues. Or you can always call your friendly tech support guy at Adobe. Don't be shy. I am sure he has heard it all and can lend you a hand. But be warned that this "live" advice may cost you some cash.

Update Now!

As I write this book, Adobe has just released a Version 1.01 patch for Album. Go to www.adobe.com and get the free download. If you have a slower Internet connection, you can request a free CD from Adobe Customer Service at (800) 492-3623.

As with most initial versions of new programs, the .01 patch fixes a host of bugs that users encountered in Version 1.0. Check the ReadMe file that accompanies the download to see what problems have been remedied. Who knows? Your problem may be fixed with the installation of the latest patch. The Web site also should have instructions on how to install your download in case you should need the help. Be sure and check Adobe's Web site periodically for updates.

You Can't Import Files

Problem: Short of gluing the photos on your monitor, you can't import any files into Album.

Possible cure: Make sure that the file formats of the files you are importing are one of the many formats Album can handle. Here are the file formats Album can import:

- ✔ **Graphics:** JPEG, TIFF, BMP, PNG, GIF, PSD, PDF, and PDD
- ✔ **Audio:** WAV and MP3
- ✔ **Video:** Motion JPEG, MPEG-1/MPG, QuickTime/MOV and Audio/Video Interleaved/AVI

For everything you need to know about file formats, see Chapter 3.

If you have All Files chosen in your Files of Type pop-up menu and you choose a file that Album can't import, an `Unsupported File Format` message appears in the Get Photos dialog box, as shown in Figure 21-1. If the format is one that Album cannot import, you may first have to bring your file into another application that *can* import that particular format and then re-save it in a format Album can deal with.

There are also graphic conversion programs such as Conversions Plus (about $60, `www.dataviz.com`), HiJaak (around $150, `www.imsisoft.com`), and Debabelizer ($450, `www.equilibrium.com`).

Some digital cameras use proprietary file formats that Album cannot import, such as Camera RAW or JPEG 2000. If yours is one of them, first try setting up your camera to use the JPEG format, if possible. If all you have are proprietary formats, you will have to use the software that came bundled with your camera to convert those files to a standard format, such as JPEG or TIFF.

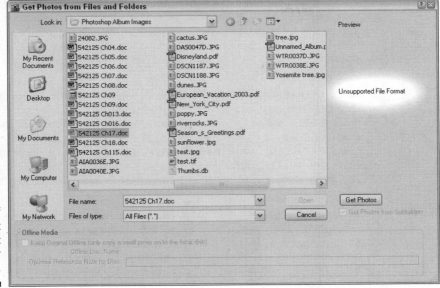

Figure 21-1:
Album
barks back
with an
"Unsup-
ported File
Format"
message if
it cannot
import that
particular
file format.

If you get an error message that the file is too large, Album is letting you
know that the file exceeds its 12-megapixel limit. This limitation has been
fixed in the Version 1.01 patch. In Version 1.01, the file size is limited only by
the amount of available RAM you have installed on your system. For example,
a 12-megapixel image requires 128MB of RAM, while a 20-megapixel image
requires 512MB of RAM. Insufficient RAM can cause a host of other problems
as well, such as problems in making creations, thumbnails that won't display,
and so on.

Your Devices Aren't Talking to Each Other

Problem: Your peripherals, such as your scanner, camera, printer, Zip drive,
or even your mouse, aren't talking to your computer.

Possible cure: There could be many reasons why this scenario is taking
place. Here are a few troubleshooting suggestions:

✓ **Check that everything is well connected and powered up.** Hey, I see you rolling your eyes! Don't be so sure your problem is a huge one until you rule out the possibility that the issue is a simple power supply problem. I have had a couple of instances where my printer and scanner cable connections weren't well seated, and my computer wasn't seeing the scanner or printer.

✓ **Make sure that you have the latest drivers for all your peripheral devices.** You also want to make sure that your drivers are compatible with your flavor and version of your operating system. This is an especially critical step whenever you upgrade your operating system. Just keep in mind that sometimes manufacturers are slow to provide updated drivers when OS upgrades are released, so you may experience a time lag. Make sure and check the manufacturer's Web site frequently for updates.

Occasionally, drivers get corrupted and need to be reinstalled. Just recently, a family member of mine had a dead mouse (luckily it didn't smell). After a little troubleshooting (like making sure the mouse was well connected), the culprit turned out to be a corrupted mouse driver. Reinstalling the driver brought it back to the land of the living.

✓ **If you purchased a new piece of hardware, and your operating system is on the outdated side, you may need to upgrade the OS before your new device can communicate with your computer.** Check the manufacturer's Web site for details.

✓ **Make sure your application software is up to date.** Check Adobe.com every now and then for patches and updates to Album. Do the same for your external image-editing program and your digital camera software.

If you've tried all the suggestions in the preceding list and still had no luck, here are a few possible workarounds:

✓ If your computer is communicating with your scanner, but Album itself just can't recognize the scanner, you can always scan your images using the software that came bundled with your scanner. Then, import your scanned images using the method of getting files from your hard drive, as described in Chapter 4.

✓ If your computer can see your camera, but Album doesn't recognize it, remove the memory card from the camera and insert it into your card reader. Then try and import the files from the card reader. If that doesn't work, get the images from your camera using the software bundled with the camera and copy them to your hard drive. Then import the files into Album from your hard drive, again as described in Chapter 4.

You Can't Print from Album

Problem: No matter how much you curse, perform voodoo, or kick the printer, no printed matter is coming out.

Possible cure: Because there are more reasons why you can't print than probably any other type of computer glitch, you may not find the cure here. The problem may require some serious troubleshooting and possibly the help of your local computer guru. But before you have to fork out some hefty per-hour consulting fee, try a few of these suggestions:

- ✔ **Try printing a small file, such as a one-word text file, to determine whether you can print at all.** Maybe the problem isn't isolated to Album. It could be the fact that you are short on RAM or hard drive space, and your file is too large to spool.

- ✔ **Make sure your cable connections are well seated.**

- ✔ **Make sure your printer is turned on and that the status says "Ready" or "Online."** Look for a nice, bright green light that says it's rarin' to print.

- ✔ **Make sure that there isn't a previous print job that is hung up or paused in the print queue.**

- ✔ **Make sure that the printer driver hasn't been corrupted.** (See "Your Devices Aren't Talking to Each Other" earlier in this chapter.)

- ✔ **If you're connected to multiple printers, either via a network or by cable, make sure that you have selected the correct printer in your print dialog box in Album.**

- ✔ **Reboot your system.** If you change the default printer in your Windows operating system while Album is running, Album may not detect the change until you close and restart the application.

- ✔ **Try disconnecting any peripherals you have attached to your computer that you are using.** Occasionally, conflicts can occur between peripheral devices and your computer.

- ✔ **If you are printing to a shared printer (one that isn't networkable), make sure that the computer that is physically connected, via cable, to the shared printer is turned on.** Otherwise you won't be able to access that shared printer.

- ✔ **Trash the Windows temp files that may be clogging your system.** If you're unsure how to do this, check your operating system documentation.

- ✔ **Check Adobe's online technical support documents.** They have some good, detailed troubleshooting guides.

Your Catalog Has Gone South

Problem: You attempt to open your catalog and get a message that there is a problem with your catalog or that your catalog is corrupted.

Possible cure: Best-case scenario, your catalog could have been partially damaged by a power outage or other kind of computer hiccup, but may still be recoverable. Worst-case scenario, your catalog is dead and unrecoverable.

- ✔ **First, try using the Recover command to see if it can repair the catalog.** Choose File➪Catalog, click the Recover button, shown in Figure 21-2, and then click OK. If the catalog was recovered and fixed successfully, Album will let you know.

- ✔ **If recovering fails, you need to restore your catalog.** That's assuming, however, that you made a backup of your catalog. If you were the ever-diligent Album user and you backed up your catalog, all you need to do is insert your backup media, choose File➪Restore, choose the media (or other storage volume) and select the backup copy of the catalog. Click the Restore button, and you're home free.

- ✔ **No backup copy, you say?** As painful as it may be, your only option is to create a new catalog and re-import your files:

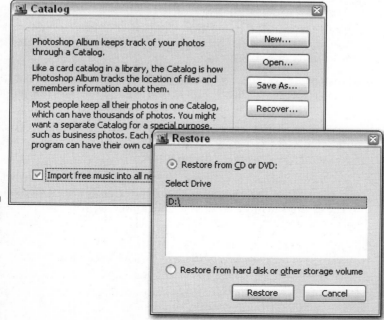

Figure 21-2:
Try to recover or restore your catalog if it is damaged.

For details on recovering, restoring, creating new catalogs and most importantly, making catalog backups, see Chapter 7.

Your Files Are "Broken"

Problem: You notice broken page icons on the thumbnails of your images in the Photo Well.

Possible cure: These icons, shown in Figure 21-3, indicate that your files are missing. Or at least Album *thinks* they are. Album works on the system of *linking*. Linking places a low-resolution, proxy image in your catalog with a link to the original, full-resolution image on your hard drive. If you move a photo, video clip, or audio clip from its original location to a new one, Album can't find the file and considers it missing. You just need to use the Reconnect Missing File command and show Album where the file now resides.

The Reconnect command doesn't work for files that have been renamed outside of Album or even worse, deleted from your hard drive. For details on reconnecting missing files, see Chapter 7.

Figure 21-3:
If you move the location of your file, Album thinks it's missing.

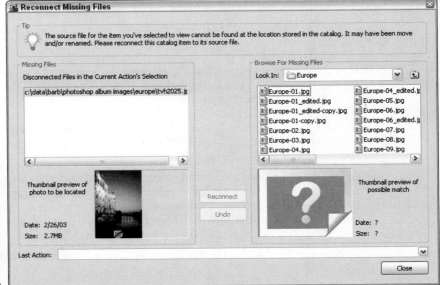

Your Images Are below the Optimum Resolution

Problem: When publishing your creation, you get the message that your image is "below the optimum resolution" for either printing or viewing at this size, as shown in Figure 21-4.

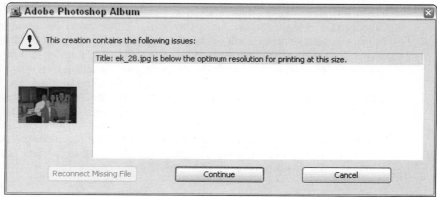

Figure 21-4: Album warns you if the resolution of your image is insufficient for your intended purpose.

Possible cure: You have several options, unfortunately none of which is a quick or easy fix.

- ✔ **If you took the photo with a digital camera, you need to reshoot the photo, if possible, using a higher resolution.** Of course, if the photo is of the Eiffel Tower and you're sitting in your office (which isn't in Paris), that option isn't very feasible. But if the photo is a portrait of a family member, and he or she is willing to give you another shot, then go for it. If necessary, check your camera's documentation to see how to increase the resolution of the camera.

- ✔ **If the image is from a scanned print, slide or negative, you need to rescan the image at a higher resolution.** Even though programs such as Photoshop Elements and Photoshop allow you to resize an image larger and at a higher resolution, you want to avoid resizing if at all possible. It is much better (if time consuming) to rescan the image.

  Check out Chapter 3, which tells you all about resolution and related topics.

- ✔ **If reshooting or rescanning isn't possible, you may have to live with using the image(s) in a different way.** For example, if you really wanted to create a photo book or print a greeting card and the resolution isn't sufficient, you may have to live with a slideshow or eCard instead. Viewing images on-screen requires a much lower resolution than printing them.

Finally, you could always try and find suitable substitutes for the images you initially wanted to use. I know that it's hard to find an equivalent replacement for the Eiffel Tower, but maybe in other instances it might be easier.

Your Files Are Marked with "?"

Problem: You see question mark icons on the thumbnails of your images in the Photo Well.

Possible cure: If there is no date embedded in the image, Album places a "???" icon on the thumbnail. If the clock on your camera or operating system is malfunctioning, the question mark may indicate an incorrect date and time stamp. Or you may have no date or time at all.

Dates are used extensively in Album as a way to identify, find, and organize your files, so it makes good sense to have a date and time assigned to every file. If you want to assign dates and times to all the files with unknown dates and times (see Figure 21-5), you can find all the vital details on making date and time adjustments in Chapter 5.

Figure 21-5:
Album
enables you
to adjust
the date
and time
embedded
in your files.

You Can't Edit Your Photo

Problem: You can't edit your image when you bring it into the Fix Photo dialog box.

Possible cure: Check the file size of your image. Album Version 1.0 can work with images with a resolution of up to 12 megapixels. If the resolution is any higher, Album won't touch it. If you have an external image editor, such as Photoshop Elements or Photoshop, you can downsize the image there. To fix the size limitation, make sure and download the free Version 1.01 patch from www.adobe.com. See the earlier section, "Update Now!"

You Can't Read Your PDF Creation

Problem: You, or your recipients, cannot open your creation in Adobe Acrobat.

Possible cure: First, check the version of Acrobat you (or your recipients) are using. Acrobat 4.0 and earlier versions are not compatible with certain types of Album creations. Make sure and use the latest version of Acrobat or Acrobat Reader. You can download Acrobat Reader for free from www.adobe.com. Make sure that you check the box to include the options with your Reader software, which includes the ability to view Album slideshow and eCards. Note that the file download size is 13.4MB, so make sure your Internet connection can handle that size.

If your recipient is a Macintosh OS X user, tell him or her not to double-click the PDF creation file itself. Instead, have the recipient launch Acrobat Reader and choose File⇨Open and choose the file from the Open dialog box.

To view your PDF creations with the best quality, especially with template styles such as "Casual" that have photos positioned at an angle, you should set your Acrobat preferences to enable "smoothing." Here's how:

1. **Choose Edit⇨Preferences⇨General in Acrobat and Edit⇨Preferences in Acrobat Reader.**

   The Preferences dialog box appears, as shown in Figure 21-6.

2. **Select Display from the left side of the Preferences dialog box.**

3. **Check the boxes for "Smooth Line Art" and "Smooth Images," shown in Figure 21-6. Then click OK.**

   Checking these boxes helps to prevent any jagged or raggedy-looking edges on your artwork.

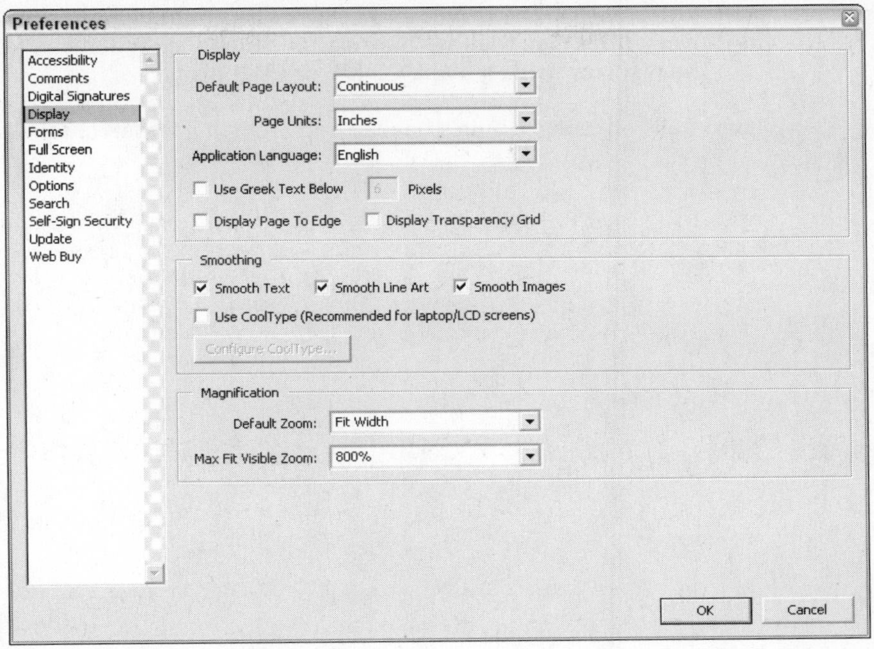

Figure 21-6:
Check the smoothing options in Acrobat to view your PDF creations with the optimum quality.

You Can't Burn Files onto Your CD or DVD Disc

Problem: You cannot burn creations, a backup catalog, or an image archive to your CD or DVD disc.

Possible cure: Here are a few troubleshooting tips:

✔ Be sure that you have the latest drivers available for your CD or DVD drive. And make sure the driver is compatible with your flavor of operating system. Although Album has been engineered to work with most CD and DVD drives, there may be some drives that it flat cannot work with.

✔ If you experience repeated problems burning your catalog or files to CDs or DVDs using Album's backup and archive commands, you may have to use a more manual method. If you have enough space, try backing up or archiving your catalog or files to your hard drive. Then use the software bundled with your drive, or an external burning program, to burn the files to the CD or DVD.

✔ With some CD-RW drives and CD-RW discs, Album may be unable to overwrite a disc that has information already on it. If it can't overwrite the disc, try using a blank CD-RW or CD-R disc.

For details on using Album's backup and archiving features, see Chapter 7.

Index